Gunkholing* in Desolation Sound and Princess Louisa

by
Al Cummings
and
Jo Bailey-Cummings

Photos by the authors
Drawings by Wm. Daniel
Charts by Kimberly Kincaid
Designed by Mary Kennedy Martin

Other books by Al Cummings and Jo Bailey-Cummings

Gunkholing in the San Juans (in its 5th printing)
Gunkholing in the Gulf Islands
San Juan: The Powder-Keg Island

**'Gunkholing', the boatman's term for cruising in sheltered waters and anchoring every night, may have originated among the shallow estuaries of Chesapeake Bay, where the anchor usually sinks into soft mud, or 'gunk'—thus gunkholing for those who engage in this low key, relaxed sort of cruising.*

Published by Nor'westing Inc.
Edmonds, Washington

Grace Stenlund "Nauti Grace" Kathy & Lee Hessler

Doris and Pete Wakeland Tan Bargeee

MICHAEL & VICKI & TRISTAN ZIEGLER

TOM KRIVANEK. Gerry & Jackie Carlstrom

Dennis Thomas and Pam Barber "Dulcinea"

WALTER C. Lockhart "ISHA"

Cork Foster - "Windhover" BILL & PAT KEELE

Gary P Green -

David & Nancy Plath (The Janie)

KEVIN & LAURIE PERKINS

BOB TAIT

FRANK JOHNSON

Karen Southern

KEVIN & PATTI Esping

Al & Kaye Lewin

AL & LOTTE WILDING

DEDICATION

This tome is gratefully dedicated to the hundreds of people from whom we cajoled information, and to the authors of books all of which we hope we have noted in our bibliography. Special thanks is due to the warm-hearted contributors whose names are lifted from the *Sea Witch* log and displayed on this page.

PETE HANNA

Thea & Ted Samson

LARRY & PAT GALLAWAY & SONS (SAM & MAC)

"HERBIE" - PAT, DALE, & CHRIS MALLOY

KATHY & ROSS KING

MICK & PAUL DECKHANDS

BARB & JIM ASHTON - THE JEB TUG

Horace & Audrey Becker

Roy and Nancy Cope

Joan and Hugh Lawrence

JERRY & Vi HERKES

Craig, Connie, Matthew, Martha Steenburg

Doug & J-Dy Day

GERRY LISTER, Ranger, Princess Louisa

Bill & Georgia Johnson "Leisure Li"

PREFACE

WE BET YOU WON'T READ THIS!

Hah! Gotcha! You are reading it, aren't you?

You said, "This is my book, I'm going to read what I want to and I don't want a couple of turkeys telling me what I am and ain't going to read!"

But we got you! Aren't we sneaky devils?

Not that we have any great, earth-moving things to tell you. Prefaces are like parsley...who needs them?

We do have a few things to say that are worthy of being chiseled in stone, but it's so hard to put stone tablets in a paperbound book.

For instance, we agonized about the fact that some of the stuff in the upcoming pages is going to change in the next year or two. The Canadian Government is probably going to upgrade some of the public docks, so there may be amenities there when you arrive that we couldn't know about. Some of the stores and marinas that we thought were hunky-dory may change hands and deteriorate. New businesses will probably spring up to serve you.

We know you are going to have a cat-fit when you read the 'Foreword' in a few minutes. We're sorry, but we don't want you to have rocks install through-hulls while you're sound asleep some night. You're precious to us because you're our one hope of getting out of debt by buying our books.

There are usually a few paragraphs in a Preface which are devoted to thanking everybody from your Aunt Minnie to the Pope for their help.

To start with, though, we need to give credit to some very valuable writers and their books. Bill Wolferstan's absolutely beautiful and informative book, *Desolation Sound and the Discovery Islands,* got thoroughly dog-eared by us thumbing through it. You should have a copy of it, and his Princess Louisa volume as well.

We got a lot of tips from another book you should have, an up-to-date copy of *Northwest Boat Travel.* It has a lot of material on ports and bays and commercial facilities from Olympia, Washington to Kingcome Inlet up in Canada.

What Northwest boater doesn't know about *Curve of Time,* by M. Wiley Blanchet? It's a must for Princess Louisa and Desolation Sound travelers.

We know you could find a list of other helpful books in the Bibliography, but that's too formal a place to show our appreciation of the following: *The Nelson Island Story,* by Karen Southern; *Upcoast Summers,* by Beth Hill; *Evergreen Islands,* by Doris Andersen.

In ways too numerous to mention, we are indebted to the Canadian Consulate in Seattle, and in particular our sidekick, Harold Tomsett, of their Tourism Department.

As you can see from the back cover, we have found a way to include those friendly Canadian and Yankee skippers and crews who came by and swapped notes and gave us fresh fish because they took pity on our inept fishing skills. You see, we may not have done well at trolling, but we made out like cat burglars when it came to 'mooching.'

Love,
Al & Jo

A FOREWORD

At the risk of being considered too forward, we would like to call your attention to a couple of navigation notes.

You will see that we hail you in the port of Nanaimo and lead you by the pinkies up to the glories of the nearby mainland B.C. Coast.

If your voyage begins down in Puget Sound, as far south as the Port of Olympia, let us recommend that you include in your on-board bookshelf a delightful and very helpful cruising guide: Walt Woodward's 'How to Cruise to Alaska (Olympia to Skagway) Without Rocking the Boat Too Much.' You might find that you want to consider continuing right on up to Skagway.

AND—if you want to dally around in the marine vacationlands of the San Juan Islands and the Canadian Gulf Islands, you might also pick up our two other guides: 'Gunkholing in the San Juans' and 'Gunkholing in the Gulf Islands.'

ANOTHER VERY IMPORTANT NOTE:

We have decided to run the risk of being called 'finks!' and 'traitors' and worse by using...METRIC in this book. Not only do we use it for one set of statistics, we don't even provide the comparable reading in 'feet.'

Here's the reason. When we first started navigating up in the Sunshine Coast area, we had some old charts and we bought all the new ones. The old ones had depths in 'fathoms', the new ones in 'metres.' Now we had no trouble breaking a fathom down into 6 feet. But it took us a long time to get used to making the conversion from metres to feet. Sometimes, we looked at depths on the new charts and decided when it said '0.6' it meant 'six-tenths of a foot'—even though the charts were clearly labelled, in big letters, 'METRIC.' We decided this was dangerous, and we don't want you to get into trouble. So, we are using the metric and only the metric in 'depths.' We also give berth-space figures in metres because the wharfingers figure the fee that way, and you have to learn how long your boat is in the metric system.

We also abbreviate 'metres' as m.

If you want a convenient rule-of-thumb for conversion remember this little slogan:

METRIC'S KEY IS 3.3

Metres are longer than feet—by a factor of 3.3. If you draw 4 feet, divide that by 3.3, for example: 4'/3.3 © 1.212121212 m. Now you can remember your draft, can't you? It's 1.2121212 metres. You might want to drop some of those 2's and 1's after the decimal point—unless you're picky-picky!

We still use feet **or** metres for heights and short distances. The rule here is: we use what the charts use. We use nautical miles for longer distances, because they don't use kilometres. No sense being accused of Emerson's 'foolish consistency.'

If it's any comfort to you fellow-Yanks, the Canadians are bugged by metrics too.

Cover Picture: *Al and 'Sea Witch' and 'Tan Barque' at Isabel Cove, Desolation Sound.*

TABLE OF CONTENTS

Portions of charts reproduced herein are illustrative only, and are not intended to be used for navigation. The authors suggest mariners navigating in the Desolation Sound and Princess Louisa Inlet make use of current editions of nautical charts produced by the Canadian Hydrographic Office, or the U.S. National Ocean and Atmospheric Administration.

Manufactured in the United States of America.

ISBN-0-931923-03-4

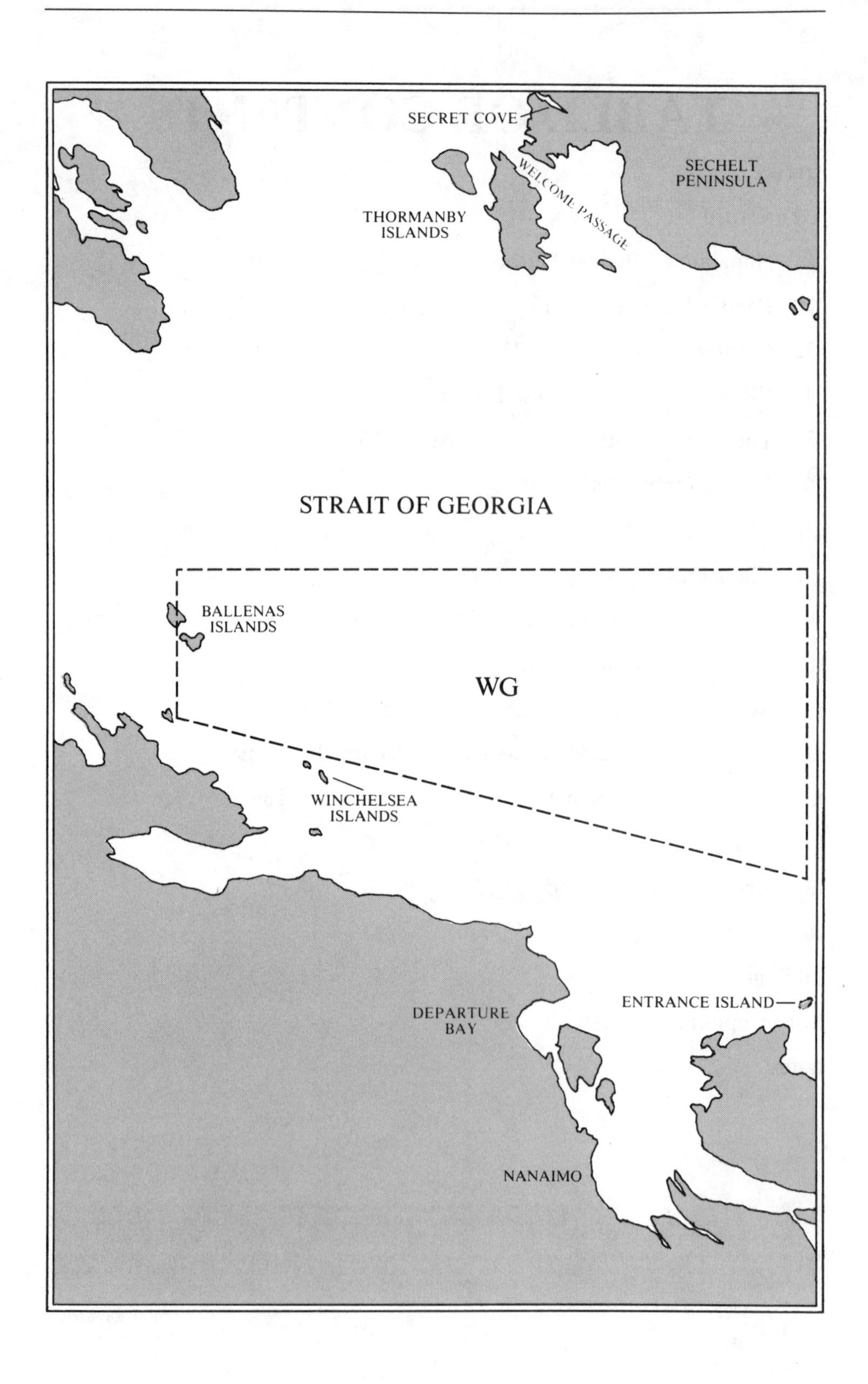
SECRET COVE
SECHELT PENINSULA
WELCOME PASSAGE
THORMANBY ISLANDS
STRAIT OF GEORGIA
BALLENAS ISLANDS
WG
WINCHELSEA ISLANDS
ENTRANCE ISLAND
DEPARTURE BAY
NANAIMO

Chapter 1

Entrance Island

Nanaimo to Pender Harbour

It's paranoia time—leaving **Nanaimo**. As you head out through **Departure Bay** you may have a towering ferry bearing down on you on the final leg of its trip across Georgia Strait from Vancouver. And rounding the light off **Horswell Rock**, you can look out and see what kind of seas you're about to encounter crossing **Georgia Strait**. If it's a weekday, you might see an old four-engine bomber making circles at low altitude. Welcome to the **Whiskey Golf** course!

Ah, yes, my seagoing friends, between Nanaimo and the entrance to Jervis Inlet, you have a little hazard blocking your path: a veritable school of finny metal monsters dropped by four-engine aircraft or shot from surface vessels. This is a primary testing range for new torpedoes manufactured for both the U.S. and Canadian Navies. Every single torpedo built is programmed to run a specific pattern, and then fired along a thoroughly instrumented course so its performance can be accurately monitored. At the end of its run, it is plucked out of the water by a specially equipped helicopter or a surface vessel, taken ashore and washed off, and either delivered to the appropriate Navy or returned to its builder for modifications, depending on how it ran its test.

We have been told that this area, right outside the busiest Vancouver Island port, is the only place in Pacific Northwest waters that has the ideal conditions needed for running these kinds of tests: deep, fairly protected and unobstructed water for 14 miles long by four miles wide.

They say, however, that it is very, very illegal to traverse the area when it is in use. On the one hand, the range safety officer brings all testing to a halt when a boat wanders onto the course, but on the other hand, anyone with even a quarter wit will also know that it is a very, very dangerous place to be with torpedoes flying around. Fortunately the course is very clearly marked on the charts. Unfortunately, it is not marked by buoys—not even at the corners. An economy measure, no doubt.

You can get permission by radio to traverse the field when it is not active—on Sunday (usually) and from 1730 to 0700 the rest of the time, although the chart warns against using the area during darkness. All well and good, but it might just be your luck to be out there in the middle of the area at daybreak some morning and have your engine go moribund, no appreciable current flowing and not even wind for sailing. Imagine your embarrassment when the big gray bombers swoop down over you like a scene from 'Tora! Tora! Tora!'

No, the prudent shot is to go around in what is called the 'Safe Corridor.' That's what we would like to discuss with you. First of all, make sure you have Chart L/C #3512. And to get out of Nanaimo, you should have strip chart #3310, #4.

You can get free printed information sheets about *Whiskey Golf* at just about any marine facility in Nanaimo Harbour. Notice that all the courses they give you are True courses, which is not what your compass reads. As a matter of fact, you might want to have one in your hot little hand before the crossing, along with #3512.

This chart tells you to check Notice to Mariners No. 35 each year for updates. You can never tell when the Navy might decide to change its rules.

Let's talk size, first of all. It's not a rectangle, it's a sort of irregular trapezoid or flattened-out pentagon, as you can see from the illustration. At the Departure Bay end it is 6 miles wide. At the Ballenas Islands end it is only 2 miles wide. The side nearest Vancouver Island goes from the southwest corner on a beeline 8.5 miles toward Grey Rock in Ballenas Channel. Before it gets to Winchelsea Island it goes veering off at an angle up Ballenas Channel—that is so the planes won't accidentally wipe out the pretty little Navy installation on Winchelsea where all those range instruments are housed. Just short of Ballenas Islands, 5.5 miles on this heading, it turns north and misses the land by about a half-mile—that's the 2 mile-long end. From this northwest corner it makes a straight line back down Georgia Strait to the northeast corner of the Departure Bay end. Did you REALLY follow all that?

Now, you may be saying, "Why the heck don't they just mark off the area with buoys. That would make a lot of sense."

But with Navy brass, Yankee or Canadian, 'good sense' is not always high on the

Straight Skinny On Whiskey Golf

Several years ago, the publisher and bottle-washer of **Nor'westing Magazine** got the opportunity to go up and watch the torpedo testing as part of a public information effort of the joint U.S.-Canadian Navies. He wrote an article which should be in the scrapbooks of all Desolation-bound skippers. It was published in May of 1985, in case you'd like to look it up.

Since this guy is our buddy and boss, we can steal from his article with impunity.

He said that the torpedoes are aimed at a target vessel several miles away. They scoot through the water at various depths and are tracked by a sophisticated monitoring grid system buried on the bottom of the Strait. The real danger is in the fact that when they finish their run, they shut down their propulsion and come up to the surface to be scooped up by a helicopter. He points out that it would be more than a little disconcerting to have a one-ton steel fish come up under your keel some fine day if you were trespassing.

There is a big plate glass window in the pretty white building on Winchelsea Island and...sitting behind

You'll pass fairly close to the Navy installation on Winchelsea if you go on the western side of WG.

list of priorities. There are uncharted unlighted buoys and lighted buoys randomly located within the area as well, some are moved from time to time, and none of them are of any use to the small boat skipper.

Just in case you are doing this caper in the fog and want to steer by the needle, don't forget to convert to compass! The first leg along Vancouver Island runs 300 degrees True, according to the sheet they give you. Ballenas Channel leg runs about

that window is a safety officer who keeps an eagle eye on the whole megillah.

He has radar and a telescope that is powerful enough to read the label on your underwear. And he takes umbrage at careless skippers who drift across the line into the danger area.

When someone does, he has to push a panic button and abort all activity on the course. The cost of operating this whole lashup is in the vicinity of $10,000 per hour. They don't threaten this, of course, but it might be legally possible to clock the amount of time wasted by shooing you out of the danger zone and send you a bill for it.

Something like:

TO: Captain Rodney Nerdville of the sloop **Cutesy Pie.**

FROM: The Canadian Navy.

BILL FOR SERVICES RENDERED: Intercepting your vessel and escorting it off the torpedo range—45 minutes at $10,000/hour. TOTAL DUE: $7,500.00

WE DO NOT TAKE 'VISA' OR 'MASTERCHARGE.'

000 degrees. The important thing is to keep your chart and compass handy and stay outside the 'pecked' lines.

The info sheet says you can contact Winchelsea Control on VHF Channel 16 or 11 and get information about activity in the area. You can try, but lots of luck! We've never been able to get them to answer. The alternative is to call Comox Coast Guard station on Channel 16. If the target practice winds up early, they may give you permission to cut across the range, it says.

Incidentally, we saw a seagoing turkey start to take a shortcut through the range when it was active. From out of nowhere came a very fast patrol boat which stopped the intruder. We saw lots of gesticulating on the part of both crews, and then the interloper high-tailed it back out to safety.

We met a skipper who claims that he heard that some of the unarmed torpedoes are 'heat-seeking,' and one day, he saw one of them come right up out of the water a few yards—aimed at a hovering helicopter! We don't know how true the story is, but it makes great scuttlebutt, doesn't it? In fact, what he probably saw was the range helicopter hoisting a spent 'fish' out of the water after its test run.

Before we leave this topic, one more comment. It may be all well and good to tell skippers to keep out of the target area. But we want to ask this: how do we know that some of those torpedoes won't take a notion to go over the invisible line?

Sobering thought, ain't it?

Malaspina Strait

Now that we've gotten you safely past the skeetshoot, let's discuss...(You *are* still there, aren't you?)...setting courses for Malaspina Strait.

It's time to consider some druthers. You can hole up in some of the neat spots in the Sechelt Peninsula and Nelson Island areas and recreate yourself and do some fishing in a few famous spots. Or you take off up Agamemnon Channel to the Reaches and make the long run up to beautiful Princess Louisa. Or you can run up Malaspina to the Desolation Sound area.

You can still use Chart #3512, but you will also need sheet #3 of the strip charts in #3311. They are invaluable.

If you get churned up a little too much on the trip across the Strait, you might want to get a breather by stopping in **Squitty Bay** on Lasqueti Island.

(Since we're primarily interested in getting you to the Jervis Inlet area, we skipped researching Texada and Lasqueti Islands. If you're planning on stopping at Lasqueti or the south end of Texada, we suggest the book of charts, #3312.) The course to the little peninsula outside this bay is about 320 degrees magnetic from the northwest corner of the bombing area. We haven't been in there recently, though, so we can only offer what the *Coast Pilot* says. There is a government dock of 30 m. that had garbage disposal at one time. The depth around the dock is 2.4 m. It also warns that there are several rocks in the entrance. It is so small on chart #3512 that there is no clue as to how to get in safely. You're on your own, we're afraid. If we ever meet up and you've been in there recently, how about sharing your expertise with us?

If you're Malaspina Strait bound, you want to head for **Upwood Point** on Texada Island which is about 340 degrees magnetic from that northwest corner.

Passing the tip of Lasqueti, you may see what our imaginations thought was an interesting sight. In our fantasies we could see the profile of a gargantuan ape. You can see his craggy forehead and his big pot belly. It looks like he is lying on his back and staring into the sky. Zozo remarked, after studying it for a bit, "I think it's a male ape." She's earthy at times.

Before the days of Whiskey Golf, we used to go straight across Georgia Strait from Nanaimo and into Welcome Passage between Merry Island and South Thormanby. Some people nowadays prefer to cross heading out from Porlier Pass or Gabriola Pass and the Flat Top Islands, staying east of Whiskey Golf. Either way is perfectly acceptable.

In any event, after what might have been an arduous crossing of Georgia Strait, you might like to stop for a breather in one of the coves just north of the Thormanby Islands.

Do you want to know how come the name 'Thormanby'? Would you guess that he was a member of Vancouver's hardy crew? A famous British General? A Lord High Somethingorother back in Merrie England?

None of the above.

He was a race horse! That's right—a fleet-footed equine who won the Derby in 1860.

Since there is a North and South Thormanby, one can only wonder which was his bum?

According to Captain John T. Walbran, who researched the origins of British Columbia place names, it was Captain George Henry Richards who commanded the survey ship *H.M.S. Plumper* who came up with this inspiration. The good captain also called the bay between the Thormanbys 'Buccaneer'—after an 'also-ran' nag he liked at Epsom Downs. Merry Island was named after J.C. Merry, Thormanby's owner. You will also recognize Epsom Point, Derby Point, and Surrey Island. Oaks Point was after a race for three year olds. Tattenham Ledge got its name from a turn in the course at Epsom Downs. Welcome Pass—get ready for this—was the body of water Richards was inspecting when he got the welcome news about the triumph of good old Thormanby.

It's quite possible that Richards had just about dried up for names when he got to this point. It is also possible he was totally wasted on Navy grog.

Whatever happened to Sir George? Did he succeed in his chosen profession: haphazardly naming points and islands? Did he get scalped by the wily Sechelts? Did he end his days as a bookie in Picadilly?

You may not applaud, but the good captain ended up as 'Admiral Sir George.'

Thormanby Islands

First, let's investigate the **Thormanby Islands.** From the end of Whiskey Golf the course is almost due north. That will take you to **Epsom Point** on **North Thormanby Island**. You'll see a white tower that stands 6.4 m. tall. North Thormanby has some of the most inviting beaches to be found on the Sunshine Coast. There is a drying spit that connects it to the larger **South Thormanby Island. Buccaneer Bay**, which lies between them, is a popular anchorage for local folks. They drop the hook at low tide, row ashore and hike the fabulous beaches on the western shore of North Thormanby, passing **Grassy Point**. There the eagles and the marine life are phenomenal, as well as the calm and the beauty.

The island is all private, but tide lands belong to 'the Crown' and they are open to the public to explore below the high tide line. But please don't dig the clams. That antagonizes the islanders, apparently for good reason: the major clam beds have been destroyed by commercial diggers.

There is a public wharf at **Oaks Point**, but it is only for loading and unloading for those folks lucky enough to live there.

The bay is not recommended for overnight moorage because of squirrely winds up Welcome Passage and wash from passing boats.

Up around **Tattenham Ledge,** which strings out from **Derby Point** off the northwest point of South Thormanby to the light buoy marked 'Q51', you can get down to a third of a meter at low water. This brings you to the entrance of one of the best known Marine Parks in the Sunshine Coast Area.

Where is the Sunshine Coast?

'Sunshine Coast' may seem a somewhat nebulous term, especially if it's pouring down rain. To clear up whatever confusion you may have, we have turned to a couple of sources.

Chart #3311, which contains five strip charts of the 'Sunshine Coast', defines it as the area from Vancouver Harbour to Desolation Sound on the Strait of Georgia.

Sailing Directions for the British Columbia Coast (which we refer to as the **'Coast Pilot')** gives the following definition:

"Between Point Atkinson and Sargeant Bay, 25 miles NW., the coast and islands in the entrance of Howe Sound are mountainous. This stretch of coast and the remainder of the NE. side of the Strait of Georgia as far as the north tip of Malaspina Peninsula is known as the Sunshine Coast."

Smuggler Cove Marine Park

For our money, this is overrated as a gunkhole. First of all, it has a lousy bottom for holding. Second, it has limited swinging room in practical depths. Third, it gets roily just out of apparent cussedness. Even so, it is beautiful in there.

It must be admitted, though, that there just *aren't* any other good anchorages in

Boats tuck into all the niches in Smuggler Cove Marine Park.

the area.

So, if we haven't dissuaded you, we'll visit it with you. The park comprises 400 acres, and it does have some interesting scenery. But even getting there can be hairy at times.

The sea in the general area of **Tattenham Ledge** can become very lumpy. The park has a hole-in-the-wall entrance which would be hard to find without its sign post at the entrance.

Approaching the narrow entrance to Smuggler Cove in breaking seas—especially if there are strong winds behind you— watching waves breaking over the reefs at the entrance, can intimidate a moderately-experienced skipper or a very prudent old one.

The best plan, as you will see—especially if you use the blowup of the cove on sheet 3 of strip chart #3311 which we feel is an absolute must—is to hug the northern (portside) shore of the picturesque **Isle Capri** *(That name had to be laid on it by a real estate developer!)* going in fairly slowly and hopefully not using the touch system. There are several reefs off to starboard which extend quite a way into the entrance, and a couple of rocky ledges off to port. There is one isolated rock which crops up a few yards beyond the visible edge of the inner reef. It is awash at two m. of tide.

The anatomy of the area consists of two roughly triangular bays, each about a hundred metres across, and a narrow finger extending to the southeast. The two triangles have depths of about five m. at low water.

If four medium-sized boats chose to ride free at anchor in the two major open areas, they would occupy most of the mooring space. So if you're in during peak occupancy, it would be considerate to stern-tie.

At the end of one walk you'll see Grant Island.

The inner finger is mostly shallow—low water of 1-1/2 to 2 m. It is entered through a very narrow channel—keep the marker to starboard—which can drop to about .5 m. at low tides. This passage is between two small islets, called **Kathleen Island** (the one to port on entering) and **France Island** (on the starboard.) At the head of the bay there are remnants of previous logging operations.

There is no public dock in the cove and no shoreside facilities except a pit-toilet at a campsite in the head of the inner cove. (*What's this: a 'head' in a 'head'?)* Several of the nice landing places are privately owned and you may not go ashore on them.

There are no inviting beaches in this park. The tidal pools are pretty much soft muck.

One more caveat about this area bears repeating: the bottom is not the best for holding. The layer of mud is quite thin in spots. This becomes a problem when westerly or southeasterly winds funnel through.

Lest this sound like a bum-rap for a very well-known gunkhole in the Sechelt area, we should point out the many pluses. There are large oysters to be found on the barnacle-laden rocks at low tide. There are some nice hiking trails which you can find at the end of the inner cove. One of them leads along the edge of the rocks and skirts the cove in a westerly direction. Another one, which we recommend, is found at the campsite. It leads past the pit-toilet and then across the peninsula to Welcome Passage.

You will come to a rocky beach overlooking Grant Island with South Thormanby in the distance. It's only a short walk—maybe a quarter mile at the most. If you go the other way, you'll wind up in about 20 minutes at a parking lot. A number of campers hike in from the main road there to enjoy a day or several days at the park.

The many tiny coves and bays, especially at high tide, are a treat for paddlers in kayaks, canoes or dinghies. Swimmers will love the water which gets into the seventies in the summer—just beware of too many boats that don't have holding tanks.

Lore has it that Smuggler Cove was, as the name implies, a favorite hidey-hole for contrabanders. It would be naive, however, to assume that the authorities were unaware of its existence as a shelter. Certainly, one drawback to using it for nefarious purposes is the fact that a police boat, parked in the entrance, would have the bad guys bottled and corked.

Good old Larry (Pig-Iron) Kelly, known throughout B.C. and Washington state for his smuggling operations, is supposed to have used Smuggler Cove to pick up Chinese workers with the intention of illegally transporting them into the states at $100 per head. He also used Smugglers Cove on San Juan Island as one of his drop-off spots. The story goes that if he felt he was about to be accosted by U.S. Customs agents, he would tie a chunk of pig iron to his human cargo and toss them over the side. A real sweetheart, wasn't he?

The alternative in this area to this marine park is a bay, just a short distance up the coast, that offers a lot of amenities but not much anchorage.

Secret Cove

Apparently the name of this cove does not come from its colorful history. As far as we can tell, there is no glorious or dire secret connected with it. Probably it's a descriptive term. Although we understand there were about 150 fishermen's shacks

Not the best beaches at low tide, but then smugglers weren't hunting for 'pretty' back in their heyday.

in the cove a couple of decades ago.

The entrance is a narrow gap, similar to many others on this Sechelt Peninsula shore, most of which do not open to large shelters. There is a shoal that sits in the middle of the entrance, but it is marked by a light on a mast set into a drying rock. It has a red and white triangular daymark and a quick-flashing red light. The most convenient course is that which keeps it to starboard. The island on your right hand is **Jack Tolmie Island.**

Secret Cove has three arms. The first arm to the left of the entrance is the largest and offers some moorage along the shore of **Turnagain Island**. The best ground is beyond a small tombolo, two thirds of the way to the northern end. The rocky shoreline across from the Secret Cove Marina has a narrow ledge with depths of about 3 m.

Two other bays open off to the right of the entrance, something like the thumb and forefinger of your left hand. The forefinger offers no swinging room for moorage and has a commercial marina and a number of private docks. The thumb bay is very shallow and would not be suitable for overnight moorage except at times when the low tides are not too low. The Royal Victoria Yacht Club has an outstation there.

We powered carefully around this bay at low tide in extremely shallow water, narrowly missing the shelf that a power boat—with much less keel than we—had grounded upon.

There is a government dock, visible upon entering the cove. It has limited space, 88 m., and electric power, but no water or garbage collection. There is a fee for overnight moorage, as in almost all government docks in B.C.

So—What's a 'Tombolo?'

Sounds like something you'd order at a Mexican Restaurant, doesn't it? "I'll have two enchiladas and a tombolo." If you got it, you wouldn't like it, though. It would taste like sand. That's because it's a hunk of shoreside real estate.

It's one of those 'sometimes islands,' the kind connected by a drying spit to the mainland. In the good old U.S. they are protected by law—the spits—not the owners. They aren't even allowed to dig them deeper or put a breakwater on them. 'Nature has to take its course,' says the government.

If that sounds like 'thicko bureaucracy' in action, it's not really true. Seems that down in Florida, real estate owners tried to build bulkheads on the beach to protect frontages of big luxury hotels and condos. The sea just made an end run and created a tidepool behind the buildings and wiped out any homeowners who didn't have enough dough to keep building concrete ramparts.

So, if you see one of those neat little islets that looks like you would have all the advantages of being an island and a hunk of the mainland—'tain't necessarily so. If you want to hear sad tales, just go ashore and talk to some people who own one.

Data on Datums

Want to have some fun? Get out your **Canadian Tide** and **Current Tables,** like Volume #5, which covers Juan de Fuca and Georgia Straits.

Now look up the tide in Seattle on, say, July 1, 1988. The low tide is a -1.0 m. Now that's pretty low, agreed?

Now check the low tide in Fulford Harbour—some 80 miles away. It reads, for the same day, -.1 m.

One more thing to notice. There's only one minus tide in Fulford all year long. There are dozens of minus tides in Seattle.

How come it gets so deep in Seattle and so shallow on Saltspring Island?

We puzzled about that and called the Hydrographic people in Victoria We asked them, how come they can hold their water so well?

"It's one of those strange things, old boy," he said.

"You Yanks are the only ones left in the world who don't go down to 'lowest **normal** tides' to establish datum."

We consulted good old Charles F. Chapman, who is the guru of things nautical. Chapman is very thorough. If you were to ask him the time, he would not just tell you how to build a watch, he'd also tell you how to operate the Bulova factory.

He says: "The principal feature of concern to boatmen and mariners regarding water area is the **depth.** For any system of depth information, there must be a reference plane, or **datum.** ... Each chart will have printed on it a statement of the datum from which depths, also called **soundings,** are measured.

"On the Pacific Coast it is the **mean lower low water.**"

That seems to mean, "as low as it gets **on the average** all year around, taking in both biggies and teenies."

So, a rock that usually pokes its ugly little snoot out at 0 tide, on your average low water in the U.S., can stick up like a 4-foot sore thumb at the minus tides.

Canadians, on the other hand, give you all the bad news up front. They say, if it's a 0 tide that rock will just touch the surface—except at a super-low tide it might be an inch or so above. 0 tide, in other words, is the bottom of the elevator—down there with the big spring and the cigarette butts.

It's what computer freaks call 'Wizzywig.' That comes from W.Y.S.I.W.Y.G., which stands for, 'What you see is what you get.'

So, mates, if your boat draws 1.2 m. and the chart says that a rock is down there at 1.2 m. and it's under your prop, when the tide gets down to 0, you're going to hear a little scraping, **in Canada**.

Of course, if you like to crunch numbers, you can always remember the handy little formula:

$$\mu = D + a1 \cos(\sigma 1t + \delta 1) + a2 \cos(\sigma 2t + \delta 2) + a3 \cos(\sigma 3t + \delta)$$

Which leads to:

$$\mu = D + \sum a \cos(\sigma t + \delta)$$

In which μ = height of tide and $\sum$ means you get egg rolls.

Secret Cove Marina has most everything you'll need.

Secret Cove Marina: This marina offers all boating facilities for its patrons. Besides permanent moorage, there is fuel, guest moorage with power, showers, toilet facilities, laundromat, water, and garbage dump. These amenities are available only to moorage customers. There is a reduced fee for three-hour tie-ups. The dockside general store sells groceries and fresh fruits and vegetables, hand-made hard ice cream cones, meat and ice. It also has a good selection of charts, tackle, live bait and fishing licences. Owners Hayden and Judy Killam, who live in a luxurious float house at the marina, pride themselves on the cleanliness of their marina. "People come here because they like the solitude," Hayden says. They stay open from 6 a.m. to 10 p.m. during the summer. Although they have no mechanics on duty, they'll call one for you if need be.

There is a restaurant with licensed premises close by.

Buccaneer Marina: This marina has been operated by the Mercer family since 1967. It offers fuel, propane, CNG, ice, groceries and fishing gear, including live bait. The marina stocks a large supply of marine parts and hardware. It has haul-out facilities for boats up to 35 feet, providing hull repairs, steam cleaning and bottom painting. A staff of mechanics handles engine repairs, and the marina is an authorized dealer and service facility for Merc, Volvo and OMC engines. Although most of the moorage is on an annual basis, there is always space available for boats with problems.

Jolly Roger Inn: Transient moorage is also available at the Jolly Roger Inn, where there is also a motel, restaurant and lounge. It lies at the entrance to the forefinger, in between Secret Cove Marina and Buccaneer Marina.

Lord Jim's Resort Hotel: This luxurious resort which offers dining, fishing charters and sumptuous accommodations, is just a quick phone call away from Secret Cove, but you won't find a spot to moor your boat.

To sum up for Secret Cove: it's a haven for social boaters. It's the pits for folks who like seclusion.

Secret Cove to Pender Harbour

Wood Bay: North of Secret Cove about 1.5 miles, there is a small indentation of about 150 m. It is noted in some cruising guides as a possible moorage to escape northwesterly and southeasterly winds. It didn't look too hopeful when we passed it, especially as there was a fish farm in there. The *B.C. Coast Pilot* ignored it. So did we.

McNaughton Point: It isn't very much of a point. Its name has a nice familiar ring to it. Good place for A.A. meetings.

Bjerre Shoal: About 1.2 miles northwest of the above mentioned point is this shoal, which probably won't cause you any problems as it has 6 m. over it at low water.

Harness Island: This name might have been another of Capt. Richards' horseracing inspirations. It has been described as 'fair' in terms of shelter from Malaspina Strait winds. There is a marina and an oyster culture farm in there. Go in carefully between the tallest islet and Harness and look out for kelp-covered rocks off Harness. If we're this close, we'd prefer to go on in to Pender Harbour.

So—let's start another chapter. Okay?

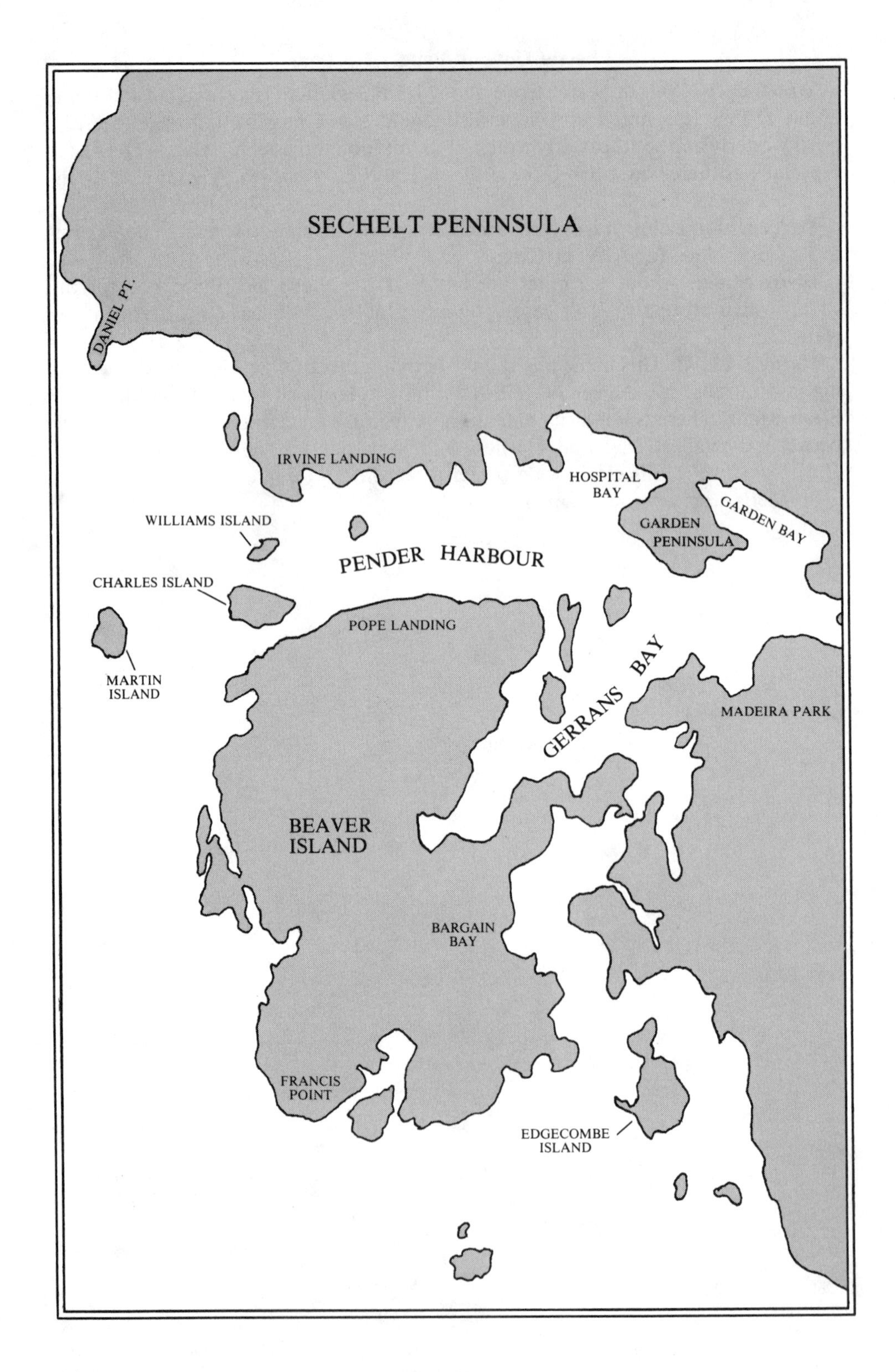
SECHELT PENINSULA
DANIEL PT.
IRVINE LANDING
HOSPITAL
BAY
GARDEN BAY
GARDEN
PENINSULA
WILLIAMS ISLAND
PENDER HARBOUR
CHARLES ISLAND
POPE LANDING
MARTIN
ISLAND
GERRANS BAY
MADEIRA PARK
BEAVER
ISLAND
BARGAIN
BAY
FRANCIS
POINT
EDGECOMBE
ISLAND

Chapter 2

Garden Bay, Pender Harbour

Pender Harbour

Before we explore the Pender Harbour area, let's take a look at the surroundings. There are some moorages and hazards. The best chart is strip chart #3311, sheet #4; it has a 1:12.000 scale.

Bjerre Shoals is not a hazard unless you're in a boat that draws more than 18 feet—in which case we are amazed you're even looking at this book!

(Also, the shoal is on sheet #3 of #3311.)

Whitestone Islands: If you don't choose to make any stops before you enter Pender Harbour, just keep Whitestone Islands to starboard and keep going. The complex consists of three dry areas surrounded by some nasty shoals. There should be some good bottom fishing in the area, though.

Edgecombe Island: Don't try to go east of Edgecombe as it's foul in there and there is a submarine cable. The island marks the southeasterly edge of Pender Harbour harbour limits.

If you don't like the hustle-bustle of Pender Harbour, you might find some protection around behind Edgecombe in about 7.7 m. of water.

Best to scout the place out at low tide and find the shoal in the entrance just off the northern tip of the island. It's got 1.4 m. of water over it at lowest tides, but it might make you nervous.

Bargain Bay: This provides sheltered anchorage but southeasterlies trend into the bay. To enter, stay west of Edgecombe Island, then as you enter stay to right of center, watching for shoals to both right and left. There is a fairway of over 300 feet between them. Then head on up into the bay where you can anchor in between 6 to 8 m. at low tide. There are several old fishermen's shacks along the shores. Bargain Bay was also known as 'Bargain Harbour' by some of the early settlers who arrived there around the turn of the century.

Francis Peninsula: This peninsula, which was formerly known as 'Beaver Island', is still an island at high tide, joined to the mainland by a bridge at Bargain Narrows. It was called 'Canoe Pass' in the early days. There are many homes on the peninsula with roads circling much of the area.

Francis Point: At the southwest tip of the island there is a light at 34 feet in a white circular tower. It flashes three white quickies. The point also marks the southwest

There are old fishermen's shacks along the shores in Bargain Bay.

point of the harbour limits.

Francis Bay: There are high cliffs and shallow fingers offering no protection from the Strait.

Moore Point: Keep going past Moore Point, which is the western extremity of Francis Peninsula. It could have been named for either Lewis James Moore, 2nd lieutenant on the paddle sloop *H.M.S Virago*, or after George Moore, master of *H.M.S. Thetis,* or perhaps after neither one of those.

You might want to do your master's thesis on the subject. We don't.

Martin Island: If you're coming up from the southeast, keep Martin island to port.

Charles Island: Keep this to starboard. Frankly, we wouldn't want to run *The Gap* between Charles and Francis with all those reefs except in the kayak. If you insist, we'd advise hugging the right shore at the south entrance until you pass the dry rock then go over and hug the island. The depth at the entrance can get as low as .2 m. Do it on a rising tide—pack a picnic lunch in case you get hung up.

Nares Rock: This little rock with a daybeacon can be passed on either side as the junction signal indicates although if you're coming from the southeast you might as well leave it to port. It goes dry at .6 m.

Fisher Island: A pretty-much no-count hunk of real estate. It's relatively flat, jellybean-shaped and has boo-boos off both ends. It's exposed to winds, too. There is a small, private moorage between it and the mainland.

And now let's do our homework on sheet #4 of strip chart #3311 if you want to find your way into busy Pender Harbour.

Williams Island: Keeping this mark and island to your starboard, you are now entering the favored approach to Pender Harbour. While it's clear between Williams and Charles, there is a drying reef at the eastern end marked by a daybeacon and not the best way to go.

Henry Point: This is the point of land to port. As you pass by, notice the lovely home with a statue right at the top of the rocks—it's very conspicuous and charming.

Pender Harbour

Pender Harbour is a large, wonderfully sheltered harbour, and a mighty center for sports fishing, as well as a favorite harbour for visiting cruising boats. The many fjord-like bays extend deep into Sechelt Peninsula. The waters are ruffled with wakes of constantly passing boats, adding a feeling of hurry-up to this essentially benign area.

Just about every cove and bay has a marina where you might be able to tie up, or at least rent a boat to head out to the fishing grounds. Since we do some fishing and practically no catching, we can't give you much accurate information about where the action is, but we can quote the local experts. According to them, the hot spots for trollers are along south Texada Island, south Lasqueti Island, Bjerre Shoal and Quarry Shoal. Moochers should have good luck if they know where the holes are near the 'A-Frame' on Texada, up Agamemnon Channel, Fearney Point, Daniel Point, Quarry Bay, Bargain Bay, Green Bay, Bargain Harbour and the 'Pilings' on Texada Island.

We saw fishermen bringing in everything from 8 pounders to 34 pounders while we were in Pender Harbour—and we hated all of them!

Irvine's Landing at Joe Bay was the home of one of the first settlements in Pender Harbour.

Garbage In, But No Garbage Out

Time was, we can remember, when boaters in an anchorage would get together and swap sea stories. We'd recall 'the time when...' and we were hit by a 'sudden Nor'easter', which came up 'out of nowhere.' We'd describe the howling in the rigging, the enveloping whitecaps, the buried bows and submerged rails—possibly stretching the truth a little in the interest of a good yarn.

Nowadays, we talk about a more serious menace—the blasted garbage that is piling up in plastic bags with no place to dispose of it.

When the weather is not dangerously dry, it's possible to go ashore and burn some of the paper trash. Leftover food can be donated to the gulls and crabs. But that still leaves a cargo of bottles and cans and accumulated trash that has to be toted from place to place, looking for disposal sites.

We think it's a wonder that the beaches and bays are not strewn with trash like a Mexican roadside. Boaters are a remarkably ecology-conscious group!

Sure, there are wonderful garbage barges in Prideaux Haven and Tenedos Bay in Desolation Sound. But they are the exceptions. Most of the public docks do not provide garbage disposal. They collect overnight moorage fees, but they do not provide dumpsters.

At one of the public docks there are dumpsters, but there is a sign up saying that trash can be dumped only by paying customers. We talked to the wharfinger about it. He said that he now has a mandate to operate his dock at a break-even point. Before he put up that sign, big boats would stop at the dock and offload as many as a dozen 30 gallon sized bags of trash. The cost of disposal service at this place was very high. In order to adjust the rates for providing this service, he would have to go above the established limit on berthage rates.

We suggested that he make the service available on a 'fee per bag' basis. We said we would be glad to pay four bits per bag. At some private marinas, the price is as much as $3.00 per bag—and those operators say they are still losing money on the service. Our friend said that he would have to have someone available at all times to collect the dump fee. Also, he would have to make out official receipts in triplicate and account for the funds. He pointed out that he does not have money for more staff and he has a full-time job just meeting and assigning berths to newcomers in the peak seasons. He admitted he hated to be such a hard-nose about the matter.

In some ports with public docks, there are stores and malls which survive on the tourist trade. But they do not provide disposal service either. We didn't discuss the matter with store owners, but we can guess what they would say. They would tell us that visitors are often shocked at the cost of food and merchandise in these outlying stores. If they had to add for the considerable cost of garbage disposal, the prices would go up even further.

So, go fight Parliament. And you know how that drill goes!

There are four government docks in Pender Harbour. They primarily serve the fishing fleet, so two of them are reserved for that purpose. The two open to boaters are at Madeira Park and Hospital Bay. The wharf at Gerrans Bay (Whiskey Slough) and the one at Irvine's Landing are not for pleasure boaters, but the Gerrans Bay one can be used for overflow from Madeira Park when the fleet is out. Rates are set by the Department of Fisheries and Oceans. The established rate in 1988 was $1.10 per metre, maximum. It used to be $.35 per metre until 1987. The few Transport Canada docks are $.60 per meter.

In Pender Harbour they allow a transient tie-up of only 45 minutes. To stay longer requires paid berthage. Non-paid moorage does not permit garbage disposal.

Irvine's Landing in **Joe Bay**: This is the first of numerous fishing resorts and marinas you will encounter when you enter the harbour. Turn left just as you pass Henry Pt. There is a dock with fuel, power, water, ice, live bait and tackle, and moorage. Also offered is a boat launch, restaurant, and R.V. parking. But of particular interest to boaters are the good shower facilities. They are very clean and coin operated—25 cents for 1-1/2 minutes. The people were friendly. We asked the lady on the dock if she minded if transients offloaded garbage.

She said, "I tell them to take it up behind the house and put it in the dumpster. I tell them they have to carry it themselves, though." We couldn't believe it! As we have pointed out, ridding your boat of garbage is a major problem, and here was someone who was willing to make the facility available! However, by the time you get there, it's possible that a number of inconsiderate turkeys will have abused the privilege and she might say "stick it in your ear!"

There is a government wharf in Joe Bay which has been leased to a fish buyer, and despite the familiar red-painted hand rails, it is not for public use.

Skardon Islands: These two small islands are off to the right as you enter the harbour. The outer island has scrub on it. There are old shacks which have fallen down. They may have been squatters' cabins or fishing huts. The innermost islet has a dozen or so trees on it. The shores are barnacle-crusted rocks. The marker between Skardon Islands and Donnely Landing is a red spar buoy and the one near the islands is green. They both indicate rocks that are marked '+' and that means they are a nuisance.

Bill Bay: The next bay along the left side as you head in has privately owned floats. Anchorage would be exposed to southerly winds anyway.

Dingman Bay has a concrete bulkhead, a long ramp and a little dock. It apparently belongs to the private residence above it.

Farrington Cove: Next along the way is this cove with an attractive sign outside which announces its name. There is a dock in the cove but it is private.

Duncan Cove: This cove has a resort with moorage for boats up to 80 feet. It has cottages and sites for RVs. For the boaters there is propane, clean showers, washrooms, laundry facilities, a launch ramp, bait and tackle, and they will quick-freeze your catch.

Hospital Bay is the next cove and considerably larger than the others along this shore. While anchoring is not too good, unless there isn't much wind, it does have other facilities and a bit of interesting history. On the hill in the eastern corner of the bay is a building you would swear is a hospital, especially if you think of the name of

Once St. Mary's Hospital serving many north coast communities, this is now the Sundowner Inn.

St. Mary's Hospital

On a bluff overlooking Hospital Bay is a large white building that you are certain must be a hospital. Well, you're partially right.

What is now the Sundowner Inn was originally built as St. Mary's Hospital in 1929-30 on land donated by a man named R. Brynildsen. Senior Lieutenant R.R. Bruce formally opened the hospital on Aug. 16, 1930. At that time there were 12 beds, 2 solariums, a maternity ward, nursery and operating room. It was run in cooperation with the Anglican Church to serve miners, loggers and fishermen and their families all along the coast. The small chapel next door was St. Mary's Garden Bay Church. The Union Steamship Line served the area and ships docked at a government wharf just below the hospital where it could unload hospital supplies and patients.

There is still a government wharf there today, but much smaller than the one used by the steamers.

The hospital closed down on November 30, 1964, and the patients were transferred to Sechelt. The little chapel, which still looks like a chapel, is now a smokers' dining room.

the bay. Well, it was, but now it's not. It is now the Sundowner Inn—a hotel and bed and breakfast. There are 16 units, a dining room and licensed premises, or if you're Canadian, it has 'licensed' premises.

John Henry's Marina, Inc., just below the hospital/hotel in Hospital Bay, was formerly Taylor's Garden Bay Marina. The marina has fuel, propane, charts, a post office, groceries and fresh meats, liquor, fishing equipment and licences, marine hardware, paperbacks, and hot coffee. The owners said they plan a laundromat, showers and washrooms in 1989. Most of the moorage is permanent. Just above the dock is Harbor Electronics.

To the left of the marina is the government wharf which is open to the public. There is garbage disposal for overnight boaters, power and lights on the dock. Berthage space is 305 m.

Up the road is a fast-food restaurant called Captain Flounders.

Just before you get to John Henry's, on **Garden Peninsula,** is Fisherman's Resort. It has moorage, boat rentals and launching, showers, ice, bait, laundry, lodging, trailer and campsites.

A.B. Haddock Marine Ltd. is also in Hospital Bay on the northern shore. There is a marine ways for boats up to 45 feet, plus complete mechanical repairs, sales and service and boat moving.

Garden Bay

Not as good a moorage as one might think. The wind can whistle in there. A few boats drop the hook along the north shore which is undeveloped Indian Reserve property. There is room for several boats with short scope in the western part of the bay.

Garden Bay Marine Park: Do you like mysteries? Here's one for you. **Find** this park! The pamphlet put out by the B.C. Ministry of Environment and Parks lists it. There is also a little chartlet which purports to show where it is. Apparently it includes a one hundred acre area around Mt. Daniel and a sort of dogleg access from the waterfront. This shore area is about 700 feet wide. But where it starts and ends is a matter of conjecture—we couldn't find any markers. It is probably the shoreline shared by the westernmost of two Indian Reserves. Peter Chettleburgh, who wrote *An Explorer's Guide: Marine Parks of British Columbia,* writes, "Indeed, the steep, rocky shore makes beaching a small boat so difficult that the park is almost unusable for any but those who hike in from the road behind." He is referring to Clayton Road which runs far inshore on Garden Bay. He says that if you are lucky and plucky enough to find it, you "will come across a small clearing and the scattered remains of a small house that was razed by the Parks Branch in 1978 in a successful bid to thwart vandalism." We wonder about that rationale: "Tear it down so people won't wreck it!" Reputedly, there is a small clearing for camping, but fires are forbidden. After reading this, you're all fired up to go see it, aren't you?

Well, in his book, Chettleburgh also writes about Mt. Daniel's being the site of puberty rites of Sechelt Indian maidens. Did that pique your interest?

Gunboat Bay

This is the most northeastern of all the bays in Pender Harbour, and the least populated. We've heard all sorts of good and bad things about Gunboat Bay, so decided to investigate it by kayaking in. We immediately met a woman who lives there full time and she gave us the skinny on the whole place. She said not too many boats anchor there in the summer, probably because of the narrow entrance with rocks in it. She told us there is a rock on the left as you enter, so stay to right of

The Pender Harbour Story

Pender Harbour was known for years by the romantic name, 'the Venice of the North'. It was accessible only by water from its beginning in the mid-1800s until the 1950s. Small boats and steamers were the one way in and out of the fjord-like harbor. The vessels of the Union Steamship Line stopped regularly at Irvine's Landing and later in Hospital Bay when the Columbia Coast Mission Hospital, St. Mary's, opened in 1930. The steamer landing was the center for the economic and social life of the community, and 'steamer day' was the day for visiting, gossiping and games.

Then a dirt road—the Sunshine Coast Highway—was punched through the forest from Gibsons to Pender Harbour in 1936. With the coming of the road—which wasn't paved until the 1950s—the close-knit, water-dependent community slowly changed. As land travel became easier and faster, the Union Steamboats were no longer needed to tie the many coastal communities together.

Steamers, with the friendly whistle announcing their arrival, no longer stopped in Pender Harbour after 1959. The end of an era.

Many of the first settlers in Pender Harbour were fishermen and loggers. There were gillnetters and seiners, even a herring saltery barge. An old timer tells that there were so many herring the harbour was 'polluted' with them. They would be killed by oars as a boat was rowed along, so the story goes. It is estimated that at one time in the early part of the century more than 800 fishermen's shacks dotted the harbour's shores.

A store was built by an enterprising Englishman named Charlie Irvine in the bay just inside Henry Point about 1880. Before that there are rumors that a Chinese ran a cannery there. Soon loggers and fishermen started calling the place Irvine's Landing. After the establishment of a post office, settlers with their families started arriving.

By the early 1900s Pender Harbour was termed the 'land of Portuguese Joe'. Joe Gonsalves and his wife—an Indian princess from the Squamish tribe and a relative of Chief Dan George—with a friend, Theodore (Steve) Dames, bought the store at the landing where they built a hotel and post office. Joe didn't have enough money for lumber, and when a log scow was wrecked off Pearson Island in a storm, Joe salvaged the timber and built the hotel, store and cabins. Other homes were also built from the logs.

Dames married one of Joe's daughters and all were well-known and loved in the community. There were often impromptu dances in the hotel, sing-alongs and parties. Madeira Park in the harbour was named for the islands where Joe was born.

The Rev. George Pringle, a traveling Presbyterian minister, arrived at the landing occasionally in his boat **The Sky Pilot.** He was warmly welcomed. He would deliver a sermon to those at the landing and they would listen and sing before they saw him off down at the wharf.

As the population increased, more stores were opened at Pope's Landing and Donnely Landing on Francis Peninsula.

The Klein brothers, Bill, Fred and Charles, built a logging camp at the head of Pender Harbour, in the area now called Kleindale. They cut the original trees of Lumberman's Arch monument in Vancouver's Stanley Park.

Scottish fishermen and their families settled around Whiskey Slough (Gerrans Bay) in the area known as 'Hardscratch.' They weren't too well liked by other early settlers because seiners and handliners thought they caught more of the fish than they should.

The first school in the harbour was built in the 1920s at Donnely Landing on Francis Peninsula. According to Martha Warnock's recollections published in the **Raincoast Chronicles** logs for the school were beachcombed by her husband. He then towed them to Vananda sawmill on Texada where they were cut into lumber which he towed back to the Landing. She said a building bee was formed and all the people of Hardscratch and the Klein families carried the lumber up the hill. Within a short time the school was built. It burned down a short time later and she said they repeated the whole process and built another school.

With a burgeoning population, three more schools were soon built at Kleindale, Irvine's Landing and Silver Sands.

Pender Harbour is no longer the isolated community it once was, but its 2,500 residents are still dependent on the water for their livelihood in many ways. It is the center of a large sport fishing business and marinas and fishing resorts now line the shores instead of fishing shacks. Small fishing boats dart in and out of the many bays constantly, on their way to and from the rich fishing grounds nearby. Visiting boaters tie up at the marinas, stock up at the stores, dine at the restaurants.

Modern homes and docks share the shoreline with resorts. Retirees are finding the harbour a good place to live. Tourists have discovered Pender Harbour. The hospital is now an Inn. The slow-paced living of the community changed when the steamers stopped and the highway was paved.

center—"almost mid-channel is safe." But watch for kelp and keep away from that—it covers the rocks. You do have to watch the tides too, for the current can run pretty fast through the entrance, particularly at very low or very high tides. She suggested trying to enter about high slack.

She said she didn't think there were any more mosquitoes in Gunboat Bay than anywhere else in Pender Harbour—which was one of the bad things we'd heard. Of course there are so many mosquitoes everywhere in the Sunshine Coast, it's hard to find any one area that has an exclusive franchise on them. And she said the water is wonderfully warm for swimming in the summer. The power lines that cross the entrance are 32 meters or nearly 100 feet high, which shouldn't pose a problem to the average sailboat.

The first cove, which has the best anchorage, is off to the left with a mud bottom. A little hook protects boaters from the flukey winds which come down from the mountains. The bay opens up into two other fingers, both of which go dry at low tide. If you want to investigate those bays, keep **Goat Island** to starboard, passing homes with docks. The finger to the right goes to Kleindale, a community named after the Klein family who still live in the area. The finger to the left is simply a large bay that becomes a mud flat.

The point of land on the eastern shore of the entrance to Gunboat Bay has a house with a big gun in the yard. We suspect it's used to intimidate water-skiers—a legitimate effort, agreed?

Headwater Marina is located in a little cove to the right before the entrance to Gunboat Bay. There is transient and permanent moorage, marine ways for boats up to 40 feet, power, water, repairs, launch ramp, ice, showers and campsites.

There is a telephone booth on the **Madeira Park Public Dock,** which is in **Welbourne Cove.** There is water, power, parking and a crane. Garbage disposal is allowed only for moorage customers. There is a public launching ramp next to the dock. It is sort of the hub of the area. The only public rest rooms are at the Information Offices near the shopping center, and they are closed until July and after September.

Madeira Park Shopping Center. It's a couple of blocks from the public dock there. You hike across a school playground and duck through the fence. There is an IGA supermarket and another somewhat smaller grocery, the Oak Tree Market. If you promise to return it, you can maybe borrow a grocery cart from the IGA to take your purchases back to the dock. Oak Tree Market will deliver for you. There is a government liquor store, a well-stocked and modern drug store, and a hardware store. You will find two beauty parlors, a branch of the Bank of Montreal, a Chinese-Canadian restaurant, and a Sears agency cum boutique in the same store. There is a wonderful second-hand store with just about everything in it, all neat and nice. (We bought a tennis ball for a dime to put on the bow of the kayak so it would quit gouging out the *Sea Witch* hull every time it got too close.) There are marvelous hamburgers at the Legion, and an art gallery in a house just up from the wharf. There is a Post Office, a fire department and ambulance service, Pentecostal church, and you can do Xeroxing at the real estate office. There is a lumber supply store just out of town about a half-mile. Go up the spur road to the highway and turn right. It has a lot of hardware items for boaters.

Madeira Marina, next to the public moorage, has launching, repairs, water taxi

Madeira Park Public Wharf gives access to the nearby shopping center.

service, a ramp, hardware, motel, campsites, laundry and fishing licenses.

Lowe's Resort is a short hike from the government dock. (Actually it's in a small lobe of Gerrans Bay). You can take a small boat in there very carefully, wending your way between the reefs and islets and following the buoyage. We found the people there warm and friendly. They welcome anchor-outs (not many do) to use their coin-op facilities: showers and laundromat which are scrupulously clean. They have some transient moorage for small boats (probably less than 25'). There is a dock store offering divers' air, bait, pop, ice, fishing equipment and licences, and if you don't want to bring your own boat, you can rent one of theirs. They will even freeze fish for you. There are cabins, RV spaces and a sandy swimming beach, something you don't find in too many places.

Coho Marina Resort is also a short walk from the government wharf. There is moorage for small boats with water and power on the docks, showers, a book exchange, ice, tackle, marine hardware, campsites, space for mobile homes and a boat launch ramp.

Continuing around the harbour the next large bay and anchorage is Gerrans Bay, known locally as 'Whiskey Slough'.

Gerrans Bay. We understand it was named this for the Scottish fishermen who used to drink a wee bit there on weekends after arduous fishing.

There is good anchorage near the head of the bay before the public wharf, which is reserved for the fishing fleet. Services at the wharf include a grid, derrick, garbage and power. As far as we're concerned, Whiskey Slough is our favorite anchorage in

Pender Harbour.

If you wish to enter Gerrans Bay as you come into the harbor, keep **Mary Islet** to port and **Calder Island** and **Dusenbury Island** to starboard, watching out of course for the daybeacons which dot the harbor. There is a passage between Calder and Dusenbury Islands and Francis Peninsula, but it is shallow, dotted with rocks, and there is an overhead power cable of 16 metres or about 50 feet. Small boats can go through there, but it's iffy for larger ones, except at high tides. The controlling depth is 1 m. at datum. Mary Islet can be passed on both sides.

Anchor Flag

Once you get that good old hook down and you've set it by backing up hard on the line, you're ready to relax. If you're free-anchored, your boat will wander all around in a circle as the tide and winds change. Sometimes you will be right over it. Most often, you are out at the end of the scope. After making a few revolutions, you may not be able to remember exactly where, on the bottom, that old pick is.

If somebody comes in and starts to anchor near you, he may think he is going to lie at a good distance away, but is in reality centered very close to you. And it often doesn't help to look at the angle the line makes going down. It can be doubled back or turned in a wide loop on the bottom.

What you need to know is: just where is the danged thing?

Another problem can come up. You might just get it dug in with its flukes tucked nicely under a one ton flat rock on the bottom. Or particularly up in coves that have been logged, there can be a virtual net of 2" steel cables across the bottom. If you catch one of those, you are going to put a lot of elbow grease in getting your precious anchor back on board.

In that case, you need to lift it out like getting a fish-hook out of your sleeve—turning it out. So, you need to pull up on the flukes. But anchors get their holding power by making the shank always pull against the flukes.

One trick is to make a tag-line that goes from the surface to the center of the flukes, which is called the 'crown.' It should be long enough to reach the surface, it should float and it should be stout enough to unhook an anchor which is lodged. We use 1/4' polypro. On the surface end, we tie a plastic oil bottle or Clorox container. In order to spot it easily, we put a small dowel with a flag on it. Then we always know exactly where that hook is. And if we get it stuck, we stop yanking on the anchor line and pull it up by the tag line.

Keep the tag line as short as possible. Ours is about 30 feet long. We seldom anchor in deeper water. That way we can pinpoint its position more accurately. We try to make sightings of it against points on shore so we can tell if it has dragged.

It also tells other boaters where **not** to drop the hook.

We advise against taking a large boat through Bargain Narrows. It got so shallow at low tide we had to carry the kayak over the rocks.

Griffin Ledge shouldn't cause you much concern—it's 2.2 m. at lowest.

Over in the southeast corner, before you get to the head of Gerrans Bay, is a smaller bay with lots of drying reefs on the way to Bargain Narrows. Three marinas are in there, mostly for fishermen. This is not a very good spot for a deep keel boat.

Coho Resort is first on the left. The third resort is Liddle Bay Marina which is just past Lowe's Resort, which we discussed above in connection with Madeira Park. Liddle's rent cabins and boats and will take you charter fishing if you wish.

Bargain Narrows: This is a narrow pass that offers passage at high tides to Bargain Bay. Note on the chart that the area is colored green and is marked '2.1.' The underlining the number means that the bottom goes dry at that height above datum. Now, remember, in Canadian Charts, 'datum' is 0 tide.

So, mudflat-fans, when the good old tide stands at 2.1 m. water is just starting to cover the muck. If your boat draws, say, 1.3 m. you could begin to negotiate it at a tide of 3.4 m.

The bridge over the Narrows is 4 m. above water at high tides—so this is not advisable for sailboats. It would seem that this stretch might merit the investment of some dredging so boaters could have a shortcut from the outside, through Bargain Bay and into Pender Harbour. The folks who have mooring buoys and docks in Bargain Bay might howl at the idea, however.

Actually, the pass was widened nearly one hundred years ago. John Wray was an early settler in Pender Harbour, arriving in 1894. He worked as the government road foreman and was responsible for the widening of narrow 'Canoe Pass'. Until that time the pass between the two harbours could be navigated only with small boats no larger than Indian canoes—hence the name.

Donnely Landing, on the tip of Francis Peninsula, had a dock with a large building. It had been an ESSO gas dock, but was closed when we were there. It's a spot with some interesting history. A tiny general store was built there in the 20s by a man named Bob Donnely. He became concerned about the fact that the fishing and logging families who were moving into the area had children who needed a school. He provided space for a schoolroom and kids rowed in from all points nearby to 'get educated.' Later, the tiny store became a school. In a few years more school space was needed so the residents got together and built a larger building just above the old store.

Near the old store building you will find a fish-processing plant and, we are told, you can buy fresh-caught fish there.

Pope's Landing. It may have been a popular landing spot in the early 1900s, but it doesn't offer any moorage to transient boaters. It is used as a fuel storage dock by PetroCanada.

Although there are good depths for anchorage in front of the dock, there is little shelter from Charles Island, and wind and wash can come through The Gap.

In addition to all the public resorts and marinas, the islands and coves in Pender Harbour are covered with private homes and docks. Still the place is incredible—and when you consider at one time there were over 800 fishermen's shacks in the harbor, it is obviously just living up to its history.

A not uncommon sight in Pender Harbour is a seaplane in the front yard.

If you pay overnight moorage at the government wharf you are allowed to dump your garbage.

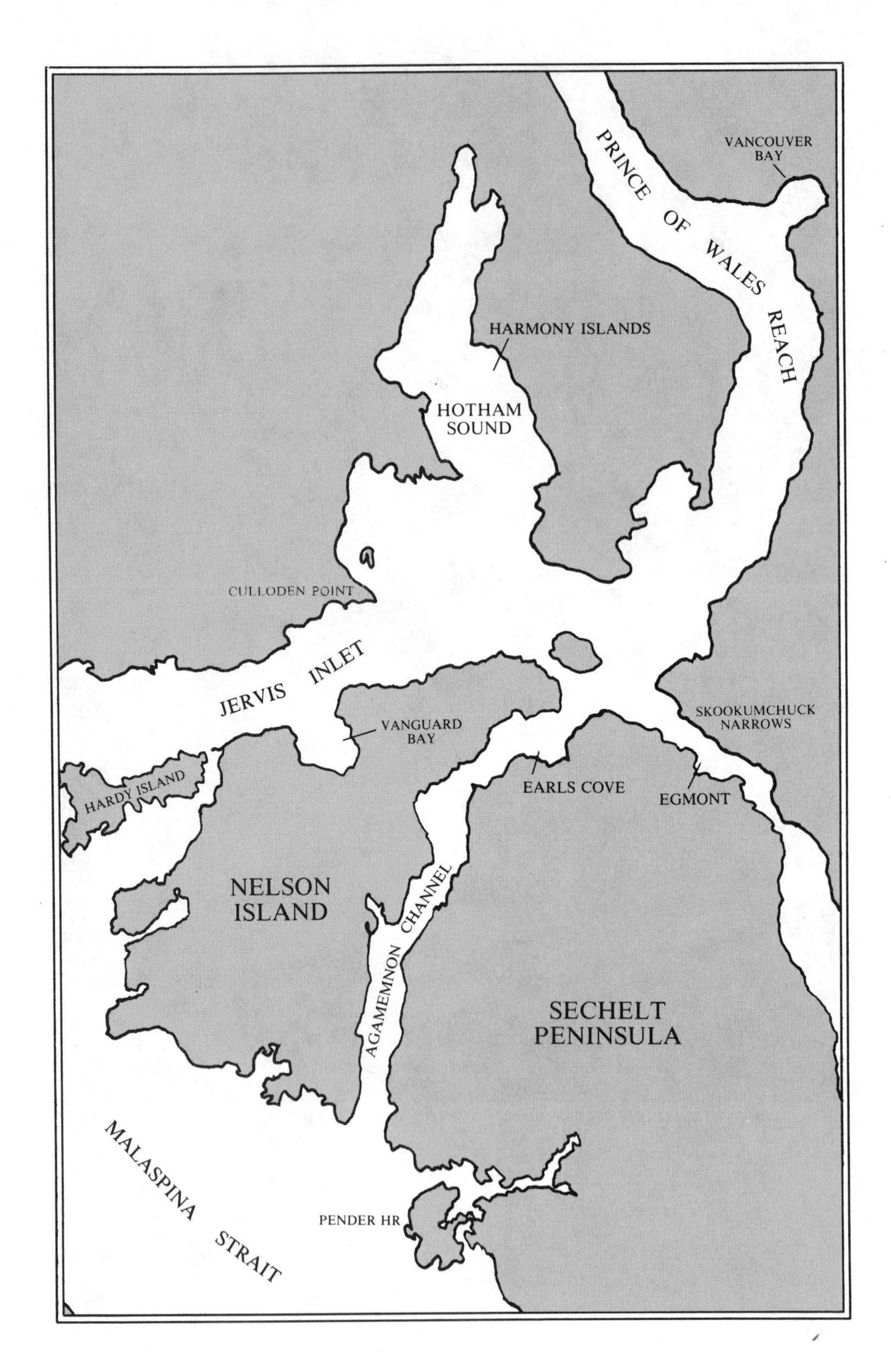
PRINCE OF WALES REACH
VANCOUVER BAY
HARMONY ISLANDS
HOTHAM SOUND
CULLODEN POINT
JERVIS INLET
SKOOKUMCHUCK NARROWS
VANGUARD BAY
HARDY ISLAND
EARLS COVE
EGMONT
NELSON ISLAND
AGAMEMNON CHANNEL
SECHELT PENINSULA
MALASPINA STRAIT
PENDER HR

Chapter 3

Gibsons Landing

Jervis Inlet

First of all—let's get the pronunciation of the name right. It's '**jar**vuss'. None of that 'jer' business, if you please! Just as the local Canadians insist on pronouncing Genoa Bay in the Gulf Islands 'Jen**O**ah'— never mind that town in Italy.

At this point, we're going to take the 'Bound For Princess Louisa' bunch on up the Reaches to Chatterbox Falls. If you're not going to make this run, you might want to skip over to page 97 in Chapter 8 and meet us at Scotch Fir Point for the run up Malaspina Inlet.

Incidentally, we're going to include some spots on Nelson Island and Hotham Sound as part of the trip to Princess Louisa. There are plenty of worthwhile gunkholes in the Jervis Inlet area and you might like to spend a few days getting acquainted with them.

Jervis Inlet was named, if you care to know, for Rear Admiral Sir John Jervis by Captain George Vancouver in 1792, because of his celebrated victory over the Spanish fleet that year. Now, open up your big chart book #3312 to page 2 and let's head north toward:

Agamemnon Channel: Round Henry Point once again and past wide open **Lee Bay**, which would not make a good moorage. There is a private dock in behind **Fisher Island** and not much room for anything else.

Agamemnon Channel was known as 'Leal-Ko-Main,' meaning 'little channel,' by the Sechelt Indians. It was named by Captain Richards for the *H.M.S. Agamemnon*, the 64-gun first line battleship commanded by Lord Horatio Nelson, the hero of the British Navy. The channel separates Nelson Island and the Sechelt Peninsula.

Daniel Point: The cove just beyond Daniel Point that contains the rock shown on the chart and mentioned in the *Coast Pilot* has an aquaculture installation. No room for anchorage.

Seaward from Daniel Point is **Pearson Island**, a good place to avoid. And just northwest of that island are the **Hodgson Islands**, another group of islands to avoid.

There is a little niche at the bottom of Sakinaw Lake creek with an old rusting donkey engine on skids. It is an Indian Reserve. A submerged power line extends from the point north of the creek to the foot of the cliffs on **Nelson Island.** It travels up a ravine to the top and then runs across the island to Blind Bay. It goes underwater again from there to Scotch Fir Point. This is a shortcut for the power lines northwest along the coast instead of following the shoreline.

Nelson Island was named, naturally, for Lord Nelson by Capt. Richards, who named many of the spots in this area.

But how well can they paddle?

Agamemnon Channel

Agamemnon Channel, Jervis Inlet, was named after the immortal Lord Nelson's ship, the **H.M.S. Agamemnon,** by the surveyor Capt. Richards in 1860. Lord Nelson was appointed to the 64 gun vessel on Jan. 30, 1793, after it was launched at Buckler's Hard, a hamlet near Beaulieu river, Western Hampshire. The two-decker ship had a keel length of 132 ft., gun deck 160 feet, and weighed 1,384 tons. She was at the battle of Trafalgar, then commanded by Captain Sir Edward Berry, and was one of the weather division led by Nelson in the Victory. "She was totally lost in the Rio de La Plata on June 20, 1809, having run aground, and then settled on one of her anchors, which, upon the sudden shoaling of the water, had been let go to bring her up," according to our good source, Walbran.

Admiral Sir George Henry Richards

By now you may be wondering who on earth was this Captain Richards who named so many of the places in British Columbia before he became an admiral. (If you aren't wondering, bypass this section.)

Well, he was born in 1820 and entered the British Navy at the age of 13 and while still very young proceeded to distinguish himself in surveying in all parts of the world, according to Walbran. In 1856 he commissioned the steam sloop **Plumper** for a survey in British Columbia waters, arriving at Esquimalt Nov. 9, 1857.

The vessel was replaced by the paddle sloop **Hecate** in 1860. Richards continued surveying until 1863 when he was sent back to England, appointed hydrographer and eventually was knighted, became an Admiral and was appointed a Fellow of the Royal Society. He died in 1900.

A little beyond the Indian reserve on the peninsula side there is a house with a long aluminum ramp leading to the water. A sign on it reads 'Thursday's Bluff'. Could it belong to a doctor who has Thursdays off?

Shallow bights all along Agamemnon Channel have aquaculture installations. One on the peninsula side has a log booming area associated with it.

There are giant marker boards on both sides of the channel marking the overhead cable about 2-1/2 miles north of the creek. They are not shown on the charts. They are probably there to call attention to the cables in the dark or the fog when they would be invisible. They do not represent a hazard to any normal boat. The cables are about a hundred feet above the water in the middle. Our old chart #3589, dated 1977, did not even show the power cables to Nelson Island, leading us to believe they represent a recent improvement. While the power cables cross Nelson Island, there is no power to the island itself. The 1986 charts show the 24 cables.

On the Sechelt Peninsula side of Agamemnon Channel you will see on the face of a rock a circle with an arrow drawn it pointing to the cable drop. A yellow fishing boundary triangle is across from it. There is a log skid just south of the power lines.

On the Nelson Island side there is a big log skid and dump just south of the power line.

Look out for drift logs in Agamemnon Channel—they are everywhere, including those the towboaters call 'propeller inspectors'—lurking below the surface.

Green Bay

It's a harbour on Nelson Island. There is a fairly wide entrance curving off to the left with a small finger off to the right as you enter this quiet little cove. You sense immediately that some romantic named this bay because of the placid green waters reflecting the deeply forested shores. However, it was not named by a romantic, but for the original owner, W. E. Green. The area around the bay has been logged over several times since the white man found it, and it was several times the site of 'gyp-po' or independent logging operations over the years.

The preferred anchorage is tucked back into the left where there is a concrete bulkhead and a ramp—possibly the start of a development. Stern- tying would make room for a fair number of boats in this protected inner area. Strong southeast winds tend to curl into here, however. Waters in the middle of these coves are quite deep; they vary from 12.8 m. to 31 m.

In the angled bight to the left, you will find a waterfall that is very handy as a shower in the early summer. There is an old dock there and some logging equipment. From this dock you can walk up a stream bed to a little unnamed lake. It's about one quarter mile from the dock. The pond is overgrown and muddy around the edges and is not an inviting place to swim. On the Green Bay shore, near the dock, there is the remains of an old boat: only the keel and a few ribs are left. In the marsh there is a two-story building and some fish-farming gear. A nice green sign on the entrance to Green Bay says: "Please help us to preserve the natural beauty of Green Bay. No hunting, no littering, no smoking in the area." A realty company has its name on the bottom.

Beyond this bay is a shallow finger with a reef part way across the opening. This cove is often used as a booming ground.

As you continue north in Agamemnon Channel you will see piles that are shown on the chart. They are made of concrete and are used to hold log booms.

On the Nelson Island side of the Channel, near the second booming ground, there are two old snags on a low hill. One of them contains a clearly visible eagle's nest.

One of the fish farms on the Sechelt Peninsula side has been named 'Skookum-chuck.'

There is an unnamed prominent rock about 100 feet offshore just south of Caldwell Island across the channel on the peninsula side. It should be visible at all times as there is grass growing on top of it. The chart says it is 2 m. above high water. It is indicated on the chart by a tiny yellow dot which you could overlook easily.

This must be a good fishing spot; we saw a lot of boats fishing the point just south of Caldwell Island.

Caldwell Island, which has a house with a satellite dish, is connected to Nelson Island by some fish pens. The island was nicknamed 'Alcatraz' as a joke by George Read, who grew up on the island in the 1950s. George never learned to swim, even though he could run a boat or yard logs. In the 1970s he apparently lost his balance in his 14-foot runabout, and went overboard and drowned in the choppy waters of Agamemnon Channel.

The power lines just beyond Caldwell are 125 feet above high water. Seems like the guy who has the house on Caldwell could get some free electric power. He could go out and do a Benjamin Franklin with a kite and some wire. He'd want to wear gloves, incidentally. There are six cables.

Earls Cove

This is the location of the ferry dock. The ferry takes cars and passengers around the northeastern end of Nelson Island to Saltery Bay where Highway 101 continues as far north as Lund.

For us the exciting thing at Earls Cove were the pictographs. They are in a niche a couple of hundred yards south of the cove. Look about 15 or 20 feet above high tide line. There is a small ledge beneath the painting where an Indian must have stood to paint the red lines. It's in light gray rock—the kind of surface on which kids like to write graffiti. The shape is that of a target, with concentric circles. The circle represents a rainbow which Sechelt Indians believed was a promise by their Divine Spirit that the land would never be flooded again. The concentric circle design is a common rock art motif along this coast, according to Doris Lundy of the Canadian Rock Art Research Associates.

"It is also a very old design, as it is widely distributed from the eastern Soviet Union to California. It is variously interpreted as a sun symbol among the Tlingits where it is also associated with a magical whirlpool and a famous shaman. It may be a shamanistic symbol on the central B.C. coast as well. The designs at this and many other sites are most likely the result of a guardian spirit or vision quest. That is, they are the work of adolescents commemorating a successful spirit quest. They may also also be territorial markers delineating a family or clan resource area such as a fishing station," Mrs. Lundy has written.

Now move onto page #3 of Chart #3312.

Agamemnon Bay. There is not a marina in the bay, as indicated on the chart. It has been converted to a fish farm.

Annis Bay: there is another big fish farm installation in this bay on Nelson Island. At the head is a small logging operation with a very pretty log cabin.

Nile Point: just off **Agnew Pass** between Nelson and Captain Islands, boasts only a fishing triangle. Booms are held just inside the point in a shallow cove.

Heading down **Sechelt Inlet** to Egmont, the **Sutton Islets** divide the inlet. The islands have strings of kelp, particularly down near the southern end where there is a flashing green light on a drying rock. The tower, with a green band at the top is 6 m.

The first pictograph—just around the corner from the ferry landing.

The bright pink of Bathgates' Store just above the public wharf in Egmont is a landmark. Bathgates' marina is next to the public dock.

high. Across from the islands there is an old fish cannery or bunkhouse and a ways. There is also a tombolo with a house and a power line tower.

There are two fish processing plants on shore just before Egmont. One is Egmont Fish Co. and the other is Aquarius Fish Co., both of which process fish from the local aquaculture farms.

The Egmont Marina and Backeddy Pub are in a cove just before Egmont. There is plenty of inexpensive moorage for both transient and permanent boats, fuel, a boat launch, dive shop and air, fishing tackle, pub, restaurant, convenience store, showers, laundry and camp space. The trick to landing at the marina is to come in **against** the current which can run up to 13 knots there. You can go in between the marker and the docks—it's deep everywhere.

Secret Bay — Egmont

This community may be best known for the bright pink paint on Bathgates' Store. It's been pink for years, and the new owners, who took over in 1988, promise they won't change the color. The Bathgates finally retired and are off doing whatever retired folks get to do.

The pink store is just above the public wharf and the marina. Moorage at both places is the same price. But Bathgates has showers and a laundromat, propane, and marine fuel. The public wharf has 295 m. of berth space, garbage disposal, a derrick and a seaplane float.

The store, open from 7 a.m. to 5:30 p.m., has a little bit of everything you need. In fact, you can find articles here you couldn't get other places. It has food, including some fresh stuff, meats, baked and dairy goods, fishing tackle, pots, pans, clothing, etc., etc. For, in addition to supplying visiting boaters, Bathgates is a center for many of the workers at the fish farms and others who live on nearby waters. The store was built in the 1940s as a coop. (That may be misleading—the word 'coop'—it was built as a co-op, not a place for chickens. Got it?)

The only public phone in town is inside the store, so time your arrival so you can use it.

There is a post office in Egmont, no liquor store, a tennis court and a playground at the school which is no longer in use. Kids now are bussed to Pender Harbour. You'll also find Egmont Community Hall and a thrift store that's open on Wednesdays.

If you hanker for a bit of culture, you might like to know that Egmont was not named after a piece by Beethoven, but by Capt. Richards after the *H.M.S. Egmont* which had 74 guns and was flashing them about 1860. And all along you thought we were making overtures to you, didn't you?

Incidentally, **Skookumchuck Narrows** is that stretch of water from Egmont Point to the **Sechelt Rapids** which are just a little over a nautical mile south of Egmont. The *Coast Pilot* says that vessels longer than 131 feet and drawing 11 feet of water should not enter the area because of the rapids which can get up to 16 knots and have an overfall of 6 feet.

We're not going any farther down Sechelt Inlet. If you want to go messing around down there where currents go bonkers—it's your skin. We don't want to lure you down there with information. Besides, we were scared of the whole shebang. (See page #4, Chart #3312.)

This creek is no place to be at high current—even with a paddle.

Vera, the Wharfinger-ess

Before 1946, Egmont was actually across the Skookumchuck Narrows in a little nook at a spot then called 'Codville', just this side of the large gravel pit, according to Egmont Wharfinger Vera Grafton. There was a post office, two stores and a fishing camp at the 'original' Egmont.

"When the fellow running the post office on the other side moved, the post office was moved here to Egmont in 1946," she said.

She said three different Indian bands used to camp at 'old Egmont', and that she had found lots of arrowheads there.

Vera has lived at Egmont since 1927 when she was eight years old. Her father was a timber cruiser. At that time there were only three houses on the present Egmont side. "School was down in the bush. Our teacher was Miss Chatney who had 60 kids in grades 1 to 10. Now there's no school here and the building is used by the nurse."

She's worked as a commercial fisherman and also as a logging camp cook in the Jervis Inlet area: Deserted Bay, Brittain River, inside Malibu when there was a golf course, Slade Creek, Skwawka River and others.

She told us that there are a few anchorages in the reaches between Egmont and Princess Louisa — they are mostly hidey-holes the fishermen use. She calls them 'safety coves'. She said you can tie up in McMurray Bay, also this side of Seshal Creek, and take refuge from a southeasterly in Deserted Bay. We checked these out and they do look like possibilities, but we weren't sure we'd want to stay there unless we had to. She also said that if you get to Princess Louisa before the slack current at Malibu, you can wait at Potato Creek.

A visit with Vera is a 'must' in Egmont.

In her job as wharfinger she enjoys talking with visiting boaters and remembers who you are from year to year. She figures about 17,000 boats annually head to Chatterbox Falls at Princess Louisa.

One last thing, Vera said when the ring around the sun is reflected in the water, prepare for bad weather.

When you go to Egmont, be sure and meet Vera — tell her we sent you.

We hiked the couple of miles through the woods to the rapids. After seeing them in full force we decided that was a trip we didn't want to make in the *Sea Witch*, although we know there are interesting spots to visit farther along into **Narrows Inlet**, through **Tzoonie Narrows**, and into **Salmon Inlet**. Besides, we made a point of limiting this exploration to 'no rapids.'

Off to the Harmonies

So, let's head up to the Harmony Islands which is one of our favorite spots. (Page #3, #3312 again.) It's about 7-1/2 miles from Egmont. Backtrack out of Sechelt Inlet and head northwest. You can go on either side of **Captain Island**. If you go between it and Nelson Island, you will be in **Agnew Passage** and perfectly safe. If you want to go north of Captain I. you will see rather unremarkable **Foley Head**, with **Mt. Foley** in the distance off to your right. There is aquaculture in the bight at the western end of Captain Island, named by Capt. Richards for the *H.M.S. Captain.*

Hotham Sound: This is a six-mile long sound ringed by high mountains and offers precious little anchorage. The Indian name for it was 'Smait', meaning, according to one translator: "This was not an easy place to come upon marine foods." Either the Indian language was very abbreviated or the translator was very verbose! He could have said it meant something like 'Fishin's lousy!'

Hotham Sound was named after Admiral William Hotham who, according to a quote in Walbran, was "a good officer and a man of undaunted courage...but he was wanting in the energy, force of character and decision requisite in a commander-in-chief." *(Want to re-think the 'good officer' tag, Admiral?)*

Local folks, like commercial fishermen, say you can drop the anchor in the nook behind Junction Island near Elephant Point. They also say that they have spent the night comfortably in a cranny between Sykes Island and its tiny satellite to the north. But then, Jervis Inlet fisherfolks are famous for their seamanship and their propensity to pull the legs of 'furriners.'

St. Vincent Bay

It has a big active log camp. There are booms all along the southern shore. A couple of small indents at the northern end are guarded by rocks in their entries. The Indians originally called the bay 'Tahk-Whoh'-Tsain', which meant 'from land to water.' The bay was named in 1860 by Capt. Richards for Rear Admiral John Jervis when he was named Earl St. Vincent after his victory over the Spanish fleet in St. Vincent's Bay in February of 1797.

Sykes Island in the south end of St. Vincent Bay has a small nook in its southern face that is filled with oyster culture lines. There is an old log skid in this nook. Log booms extend from the west end of Sykes Island. Very marginal moorage might be found in the small triangular cove between Sykes Island and a small islet to its north. This island was named after John Sykes, an able seaman in the British Navy and a faithful follower of Lord Nelson.

Furthermore, **Elephant Point** looks nothing like any elephants we've seen. Actually, there is a spot up in Desolation Sound that **does** look like a pachyderm. You'll read about it later.

Granville Bay: This is a large bay off to the right with a couple of homes along

Why 'Sykes' Island?

Sykes Island is a rather pretty little island in St. Vincent Bay in Jervis Inlet. It is practically useless to boaters as the one available bay is filled with aquaculture, and the shores surrounding it are often used as booming grounds. So why are we telling you about it now?

The simple fact is that the island was named by Captain Richards in 1860 for John Sykes, an able seaman in the British Navy, and for many years an old and faithful follower of the famous Lord Nelson. According to Walbran, in Lord Nelson's account of the capture of the Spanish ships **San Nicolas** and **San Josef** at the battle of St. Vincent, 14 February, 1797, he states that when standing on the quarterdeck of the **San Josef,** "I was surrounded by Captain Berry, Lieutenant Pierson, John Sykes, John Thompson, Francis Cook and William Fearney, all old Agamemnons, and several other brave men, soldiers and sailors—thus fell these ships."

Walbran quotes an Annual Register: "Deaths, 31 May, 1841. Lately. Suddenly, at his little fishmonger's shop, in Church-passage, Greenwich, that venerable tar, Nelson's coxswain, Sykes. He was upwards of eighty years of age, and was with Lord Nelson during the whole of the time of his glorious deeds. He saved the life of that illustrious hero in the bay of Cadiz, when his barge containing twelve men was attacked by a Spanish gun-boat manned by twenty-six, by twice parrying the blows that were aimed at him, and at last actually interposed his own head to receive a sabre-cut which he could not avert by any other means, from which he received a dangerous wound. The gun-boat was captured and eighteen of her men killed and the rest wounded. He also greatly distinguished himself at the battle of Trafalgar."

The waterfall in Hotham Sound is visible for miles around.

shore. In calm weather you could probably anchor off the shallows of **Lapan Creek**, but you might not sleep soundly.

You've probably been seeing here in Hotham Sound the beautiful waterfall that comes down from **Freil Lake** far up the mountainside. There is one main drop and then a small one off to the side. They are magnificent as they roar down the straight cliff. We always find ourselves paddling back to them after we've anchored at Harmony Islands to take a refreshing (cold) shower. It's about a half mile row. There are no beaches to land your boat on at the exits of the creek. You'll have to pull it up on the rocks. You may have to scramble under some overhanging limbs to find the pools. On a hot day, the water seems heaven-sent. But, on the way back, don't be surprised if you work up a swea....er...perspiration and get all mungy again!

And another tidbit: the Indians called the falls 'Tay'-Eh-Khain,' meaning 'height', both literally and figuratively, according to Lester Peterson as quoted in *The Nelson Island Story.*

Harmony Islands

These four small delightful islands are close to the east side of the sound, about two-thirds of the way between Granville Bay and **Syren Point**. Most boats anchor in the pass and then stern-tie to shore. When it is really crowded there, as it can be, some boats stern-tie to the mainland shore. There is also a basin, called Kipling Cove, formed by the three north islands where several boats can anchor, also with stern-ties. It might be possible to squeeze a boat larger than a shore-boat through some of the openings between the islands at high tide—sort of a 'Rudder Russian Roulette'!

We have seen boats anchored farther up behind the small islet just southeast of Syren Point. We haven't explored that area, so you are on your own.

The coves are delightful to explore by shore boat or by foot, and there are oysters to be picked, just don't take more than your limit, please. Water is warm for swimming, in the 70s, making it an ideal spot to take the kids to play.

The Indian name for these charming islands is 'Kohk-Soh-Whe-Ahm,' which means 'surprisingly broken up.' We know some couples who are 'Kohk-soh-whe-ahm.'

A small caveat is in order...(Anybody like a little caveat?). When you are stern-tying, whether here or anywhere else, it is important to have a clear picture of the bottom in a circular area of maybe 50 yards in all directions, including the space between your rudder and the shore. We have seen boats tie up in what looked like plenty of water at high tides find themselves sitting on an isolated rock or reef when the tides go out.

The northern reaches of **Hotham Sound** have very little to recommend a trip. We went part way up and looked at it with binoculars and made the determination: 'Zip!' There's a small marsh at the end of **Baker Bay** and some aquaculture in a tiny niche on a point just south of it.

As a matter-of-fact, Harmony Islands are about the only places you'd be interested in in Hotham Sound. And, you may get there at the height of the cruising season and find the whole place chock-a-block with established boats. So, our advice is: plan to get there early enough so you can go to an alternative anchorage if the place is full.

The Arduous Art of Stern-tying

We have gone blithely on through the first chapters of this book talking about 'Stern-tying' as if everybody knew what it meant. As a matter of fact, in most of the U.S. anchorages, you don't often see it.

So, for the uninitiated, let's get initiated.

It means fastening the non-pointy end of your barque to something solid, like a rock or tree on the shore. It is part of a two-point system: you have a hook on the sharp end, too—the anchor.

Whuffo? To keep the boat from swinging, taking up a lot of room, or dislodging the anchor—that's whuffo. This technique is mostly used when the depths near the shore are too great to set an anchor without a country mile of scope. ('Scope' is the amount of line or chain from the anchor to the boat). It's like staking out a cow in a pasture.

Some sagacious old mariners prescribe that skippers ride on a 'rode' (another name for scope) of 5:1. What that means is: if you are anchored in 60 feet of water, you would let out 300 feet of anchor line. It also means that you will be making big...and we mean BIG..circles around the center. In many bays, you will be taking up more than your fair share of the available space. And, in the middle of the night, you might have to come out on deck in your skivvies and pull in the line because you are playing bumpsy-daisy with a neighbor.

Up in the Desolation Sound Area, you will often find nice bays that are quite deep. In these places, you drop the hook to...say...15 metres and continue toward the shore until it catches in an underwater bank. Now, you won't be able to dig it in well enough to be sure it won't dislodge. So you take a long line ashore and tie it off to something stable. Then you take a slight strain on the line and make it fast to a stern-bitt. Now, if the current or the wind tries to move you out into deep water, the boat stays put.

It is considered good form to use polypro line (which floats) or put bottles or fenders on the shore line. This warns passing skippers not to go behind your boat.

How does tide change affect this lashup? Not much. If it falls a lot, you might roam back and forth a little along the shore. If it rises a lot, you might find the line getting a skoshie taut. If it starts to get tight enough for you to play 'Melancholy Baby' on it, slack off a bit.

One more tip: carry **lots** of sternline; and not too heavy. You're going to have to row ashore in your dinghy tugging it. All the while you are paddling manfully (or womanfully), the darned boat is going to be wandering downstream and you will have to tugboat it back in a line with the shore if it's too short.

Another tip: tie it off on shore to something that you can get at if the tide is far out or far in. We suggest making a loose loop around your tether and tying it off 15 or 20 feet

The fine art of stern-tying—Al makes it look simple.

from the moorage point.

A final tip: don't yell pet names at your wife, like 'dingbat!' or 'dimwit!' if she says she can't help you by swinging the boat while you're rowing. Starting up the engine with those lines trailing can produce rolls of cordage around your prop-shaft. Try to anticipate which way it's going to drift and stop the engine up-current a ways.

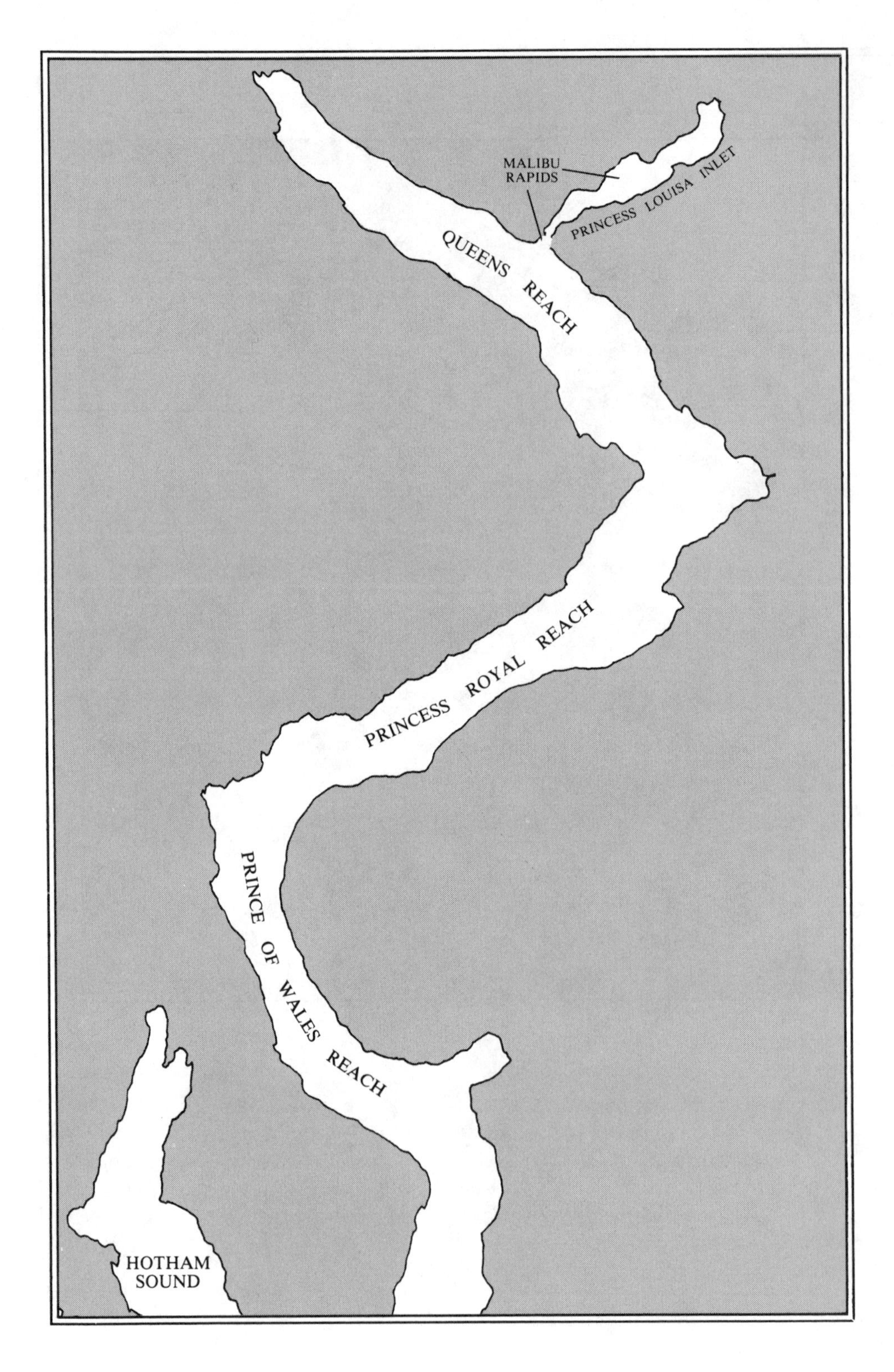
MALIBU
RAPIDS
PRINCESS LOUISA INLET
QUEENS REACH
PRINCESS ROYAL REACH
PRINCE OF WALES REACH
HOTHAM
SOUND

Chapter 4

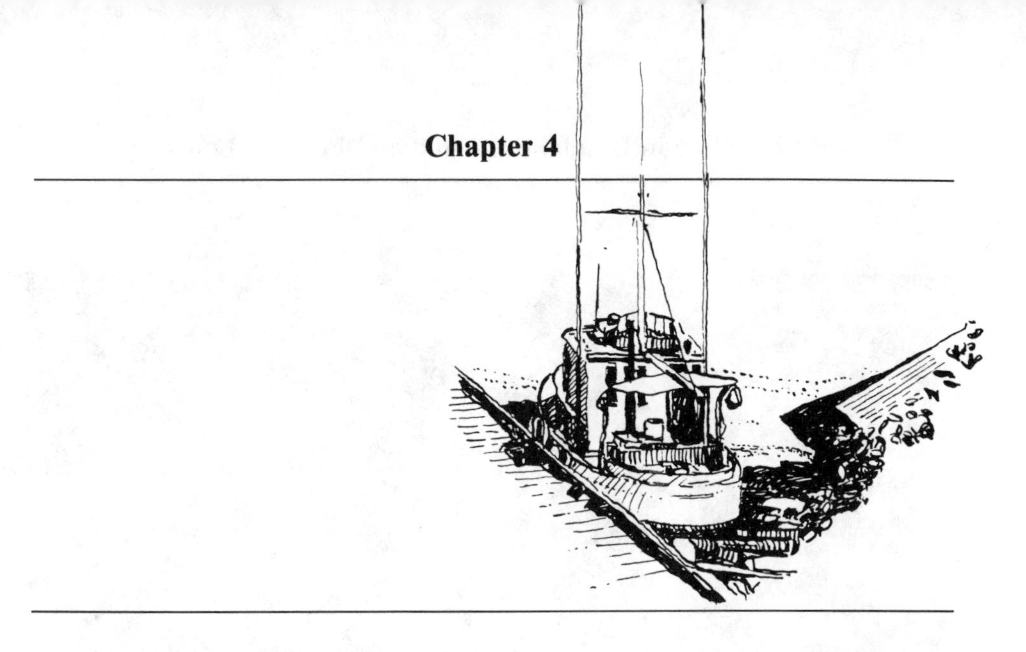

"Reaching" for Princess Louisa

Let's go up and listen to Chatterbox Falls. If you have a 5-knot boat like the good old sloop *Sea Witch*, you're going to want to roust your crew early in the morning because you've got quite a few hours of cruising ahead of you.

And—a little timing is in order. You're going to want to get to Malibu Rapids at slack current. And if you miss the slack by much, you'll find yourself dawdling around in some not-too-inviting anchorages waiting for the next open house.

Another tip: you won't find a lot of good stopping spots once you start up the reaches. So, drain your pooch, find toys to occupy the ankle-biters and prepare to do some maintenance and marlinspiking during the long wheel watches. We **do** have some more Indian pictographs for you to find, if you're interested in such artifacts. Fishing is not particularly good on this run, but you might want to haul a hoochie off the fantail—just in case you encounter a salmon with a strong death-wish.

Make sure you have your big chart book, #3312, handy, (pages 3, 6, and 7, scale 1:40,000, with 1:12,000 at Malibu) or at least #3514, which is a scale of 1:50,000 for the reaches, and also 1:12,000 at Malibu.

We're going to start you off from that Jervis Inlet crossroads: the intersection of Agamemnon Channel, Sechelt Inlet, Jervis Inlet and Prince of Wales Reach. This Prince was the son of Queen Victoria and he was 18 years old when Captain Richards of the survey vessel *H.M.S. Plumper* decided to christen the area. (You did make a note of this, didn't you? It may appear in a quiz at the end of the chapter and if you flunk we may take your boat away from you.)

Foley Head, on your left at the entrance to the reach, was named after the mountain that towers over it and the mountain was named for Sir Thomas Foley, G.C.B., Admiral of the White and Rear Admiral of Great Britain in 1808. We toss this in because it's all that Foley Head has going for it. (We're on Page 3 of #3312 right now.)

Dark Cove. The locals say there is some moorage inside **Sydney Island**—probably with stern-tie—in Dark Cove. We looked at the shoreline of the island and were skeptical. Not only that, there is aquaculture around it. Maybe you'd be more daring than we were, though. The head of the cove has a fish-farming installation. There is some anchorage available behind the fish-pens and near shore on the north side. If

The fish flop in the pens at feeding time.

you hail one of the workers, they will escort you safely past the mooring lines and help you get anchored.

Goliath Bay. The eastern end of Goliath Bay has a very extensive log booming area. Onshore is a towering orange derrick and a small stiff-leg crane. We saw several boats stern-tied on the western shore. It seems very exposed to winds up Jervis Inlet.

If you're a steam train buff you will be interested to know that there was a standard gauge logging railway which delivered logs to the head of an incline in the southern part of Goliath Bay in the 1920s. The 50-ton Climax locomotive pulled the 22 log cars over about 4.5 miles of tracks near Freil Lake.

The southeast portal to Prince of Wales Reach is **Egmont Point**. Due north of it is an islet, **Miller Islet** and a rock just south of that dries at a 1.2 m. tide.

Killam Bay is a very shallow bight with a breakwater. This is the site of the Pacific Logging Camp.

A Jackpot, Vintage 1762

Dacres Point was named after Vice Admiral James Richard Dacres. In the year 1762 he was skipper of the **Active.** On May 21 of that year, he nailed the Spanish ship **Hermoine** which was described in Walbran as 'A very rich register ship from Lima.' The galleon was the richest prize of the war. When the cargo had been sold, there was the sum of about 520,000 pounds to split. Dacres' crew was entitled to the whole bounty, but he split it with the Captain of the sloop-of-war **Favorite,** a Captain Pownell.

Dacres got 65,000 pounds, his three subordinate officers got 13,000 pounds each and each seaman collected 500 pounds.

Not bad for a day's work, eh?

Farther north on this shore, roughly east of **Dacres Point.** you will find a large, ugly swath cut through the valley. It is a gravel pit. Above the gravel pit is a complex of switchback roads that is impressive. The operation has a loading dock and conveyor belt for loading gravel into barges.

As you go up Prince of Wales Reach those rugged snow-dappled peaks that you can see to the northeast are called Marlborough Heights. They rise to about 6,000 feet.

Waterfalls cascade down the cliffs all along the reaches on the way to Princess Louisa. In June there are far more to be seen than later in the summer when the snow has retreated or disappeared.

So we're following the route of Captain Vancouver and his botanist, Archibald Menzies on this trip up to Princess Louisa; (you know, of course, that they didn't enter the inlet.) Later, M. Wylie Blanchet did so. We feel compelled to use some of the wonderful descriptions we found written by them. Vancouver was not very happy with the sights he saw, while Menzies was overtly enthusiastic, and Blanchet added her own ideas.

Captain Vancouver was still searching for the elusive Northwest Passage opening to the east which would link the Atlantic and Pacific Oceans without going around the dreaded southern tip of South America. With this goal in mind he viewed the Jervis Inlet area as something less than fulfilling:

The shores we passed this day are of a moderate height ...and are principally composed of craggy rocks, in the chasms of which a soil of decayed vegetables has been formed by the hand of time; from which pine trees of an inferior dwarf growth are produced, with a considerable quantity of bushes and underwood...sounding with the hand line could not be gained; nor had we any where in mid-channel been able to reach the bottom with 100 fathoms of line, although the shores are not a mile asunder. The width of this channel still continuing, again flattered us with discovering a breach in the eastern range of snowy mountains... We seemed to have penetrated considerable into this formidable obstacle; and as the more lofty mountains were now behind us, and no very distant ones were seen beyond the valleys caused by the depressed parts of the snowy barrier in the northerly quarters, we had great reason to believe we had passed the center of this impediment to our wishes.

I was induced to hope we should yet find this inlet winding beyond the mountains, by the channel through which we had thus advanced upwards of 11 leagues, though for the most part it was not more than half a mile wide. The surrounding country presented an equally dreary aspect...and the serenity of the weather not adding at present to the natural gloominess of the prospect, was counterbalanced by the rugged surface of the mountains...a tremendous snowy barrier, thin wooded and rising abruptly from the sea to the clouds; from whose frigid summit the dissolving snow in foaming torrents rushed down the sides and chasms of its rugged surface, exhibiting altogether a sublime but gloomy spectacle which animated nature seemed to have deserted. Not a bird nor a living creature was to be seen, and the roaring of the falling cataracts in every direction precluded their being heard had any been in the neighbourhood.

On the other hand, as we sailed and powered up the reaches we were fascinated with the wildlife. There were seals, salmon jumping, gulls and 'guard eagles' on nearly every high snag who watched our slow progress through the channels. There was most certainly NOT a 'gloomy spectacle which nature had deserted.' But then we weren't hunting for a strait to the East. Thanks to Vancouver, we knew the reach would end.

And Menzies, the botanist, apparently more concerned with observations of natural phenomenon than with the opening to the east, wrote in his journal as the

Captain George Vancouver

Captain Vancouver is renowned for his many explorations and discoveries on the West Coast of North America in the **Discovery**.

Vancouver was born at King's Lynn, Norfolk, 22 June, 1757. He joined the Royal Navy in 1771 and sailed with Captain Cook on his second voyage of discovery from 1772-1775 in the **Resolution** as a junior officer. He sailed on Cook's third voyage from 1776 to 1780 as a midshipman on the **Discovery**, according to Walbran.

After various promotions on various ships, he was promoted to commander on 15 December, 1790, and given charge of the expedition to **survey the west coast of America** from 30 degrees northward. He arrived on the coast on Tuesday, April 17, 1792, by way of Cape of Good Hope, Australia, New Zealand and the Sandwich Islands, eight months after his departure from England. His surveying explorations went as far north as Cook Inlet on the Alaskan coast, and included Washington and British Columbia as well.

We are interested in him because he explored and described in his journal much of the area which we are covering. He named many of the bays and coves, points and islands. Early in June, 1792, he left his ship, the **Discovery**, and the armed tender, **Chatham**, at anchor in Birch Bay, near the international boundary. With Archibald Menzies, the botanist, and four others in the small yawl, and Peter Puget in the launch, Vancouver explored the coast to the north, including Jervis Inlet, but did not discover Princess Louisa. Later that month and in July, he led the entire expedition into the Desolation Sound area, again naming many of the geographical points.

Although he was reputed to be a stern disciplinarian, he was also apparently fair to his men. For when the expedition returned to England 24 September, 1795, it was noted that "the **Discovery** sailed from England with 150 men on board, and such was the attention of the officers to their health that only one died in the course of a very fatiguing voyage of four years."

Vancouver died at the old Star and Garter Inn, Richmond Hill, Surrey, 10 May, 1798, only 41 years old.

two boats entered the reaches on June 17, 1792:

About noon on the 17th they entered another narrow Arm which carried them northward in a winding direction about 40 miles between two ridges of high steep snowy mountains—they did not reach the head of it till the afternoon of the following day when they found it terminated in low marshy land about the Latitude of 50 52' & Longitude 235 18' East, where they saw two Huts & some Indians curing Fish, some of which they easily procured for small Trinkets—In this branch they also met with whitish water but no Soundings with a hundred fathoms of Line, nor no regular Tides towards the head of it but a constant drain down.

In going up this Arm they here and there passed immense Cascades rushing headlong down Chasms against projecting Rocks & Cliffs with a furious wildness that beggared all description. Curiosity led them to approach one of the largest where it poured its foaming pondrous stream over high rugged Cliffs & precipices into the fretted Sea with such stunning noise & rapidity of motion that they could not look up to its source with being affected with giddiness nor contemplate its romantic wildness without a mixture of awe & admiration.

But Vancouver was concerned that they had only carried provisions for seven days and by now they had been out for six days so they hurried up a bit before everyone died of malnutrition or scurvy or something. Strange to think that Vancouver would be off hunting for the elusive route through North America and take only one week's provisions.

On your charts you can see many of the rivers leading to the falls romanticized by Menzies. Some are named, some are not. But on the right, **Treat Creek** is one of those with a name. It is used as a log sorting and booming area and has a pier. There is a bare gravel hillside near the creek entrance.

Guess who **Saumarez Bluff** was named for? Right! Admiral James, Lord de Saumarez. How did you guess? If you're terribly bored with the trip past his nothing bluff to your left, across from Perketts Creek, you could get out your copy of Walbran's *History of B.C. Coast Names* and read about his battles—like the time his ship wasted a French frigate in 1793, killing and wounding 120 Frenchmen while none of his boys even got a Tylenol headache. If your crew is bored, read it to them, start a mutiny.

Also, if you're unsure of how to pronounce Saumarez, just think of those goodies you make for the kids using marshmallows, chocolate bars and graham crackers: 'S'mores!'

Fishermen sometimes stern-tie in the tiny nook just south of Saumarez Bluff.

South of Perketts Creek there is a very badly burned area. Most of the charred logs seem to have been cut before they burned.

Perketts Creek enters the reach with a small, pretty pebbled beach.

The creek comes down to a mouth with a logging road leading down to it. The logging road comes through a badly scarred area of clear-cutting.

If you're interested in pictographs, it's time to start getting familiar with Page 6, Chart #3312. Bear in mind that the scale of this chart is 1 mile 1-7/8 inches.

Notice that there are two unnamed creeks north of Perketts. A pictograph is located half way between the second and third creeks. You will find the picture of a

Archibald Menzies

Archibald Menzies was a valuable member of Captain Vancouver's expedition when they surveyed the west coast. Menzies, born in Scotland in 1754, joined the crew as a surgeon and botanist in 1791. He made a large collection of plants during the voyage and among his discoveries was a species of arbutus that grows on this coast and was named after him: **Arbutus menziesii.** He also went in the two small boats with Vancouver when they went up Jervis Inlet. He was much more enthusiastic about the trip up the inlet and what he observed than was his skipper.

The Perketts Creek pictograph.

man with kind of halo over his head. The drawings are somewhat higher than usual, about 30 feet up. There is a ledge leading up to the spot where the artist stood.

Pictograph expert Doris Lundy terms this, "A lovely site containing human figures with power symbols above their heads. These signs, often rayed arcs or rayed sun-like symbols, suggest that the human figure is a shaman or visionary in contact with the spirit world." She said the site may also have served as a resource marker for good fishing. Resources and visionary experiences were often associated phenomenon.

If you want to double-check the location of the second creek, look for some rock rubble and a pebbled beach at the northern end of a long shallow bight.

There is an old abandoned log skid just a few hundred yards beyond the third creek.

Vancouver Bay. There is a rock at the entrance to Vancouver Bay that is somewhat farther out from the shoreline than it would appear from the chart. It is awash only at about 3 m.

The northern side of the entrance to Vancouver Bay has some massive high sheer cliffs. There are yellow triangular markers on both sides. The chart says the dock is in ruins but it appears very serviceable. It is on the eastern side of the bay. There is a big oil tank nearby. A sign says it is a 'private aircraft dock—surface vessels stay clear at all times.' You will see a beautiful big house in the meadow at the head of the bay. The Indian Reserve off to the left side of the bay has a fish farm. A very pleasant river—the **Vancouver River**—flows through the reserve. There is a small bridge over it. The river mouth has some floating sheds on it. The roof to the big building on the fish farm has the words 'Bay Fresh' lettered on it.

There is some graffiti on a rock face near the entrance to Vancouver Bay. What is 'Regulas'—a boat?

Vancouver Bay was named by Capt. Richards after Captain Vancouver who anchored and spent the night there on his way up the reaches. Mrs. Blanchet and her children also anchored in the bay while she went trout fishing in a stream. As she put it, "Vancouver Bay...only makes a very temporary anchorage good for a couple of hours on a perfectly calm day. It is a deep bay between very high mountains, with a valley and three trout-streams. You can drop your hook on a narrow mud bank, but under your stern it falls away to nothing."

About the turn of the century logging was big in Vancouver Bay, and there were 2.5 miles of narrow gauge (three feet) railway in the river valley in 1905. By 1929 there were three engines, a 50-ton Climax locomotive and two Davenport rod engines, 24 log cars and 8.5 miles of track. The company operated until 1940.

If there has been enough rain, you will find a very picturesque waterfall on the north shore of Prince of Wales Reach just beyond Vancouver Bay.

We found a pictograph about four miles south of McMurray Bay across from Moorsam Bluff. It's on the west shore of Prince of Wales Reach. It's very difficult to locate. It took us a couple of hours of scanning the rocks with binoculars before we finally found it. Here are some admittedly sketchy directions.

You have to locate a series of creeks north of Saumarez Bluff. The best way to find the first of them is to draw a line across the northern shore of Vancouver Bay extending across the channel. It will bring you to a fairly substantial creek which flows down from a tiny unnamed lake high above. Now find three more creeks north

Vancouver Took Some Latitude With Longitudes

You are hip to longitudes, aren't you? You know the lines that run from the top navel to the bottom navel of the orange?

And you know that they begin at a town called Greenwich in Merrie Old England and they go in both directions until they collide in the Pacific. And that is the 180th Longitude. Agreed?

Okay, now how about this quotation from Captain Vancouver's log:

"...(we) passed through a very narrow, though navigable channel, amongst a cluster of rocks and rocky islets, lying just in front of its entrance, which is situated in latitude 49 degrees 35 1/2', longitude 236 degrees 26'."

Did you catch that '236 degrees longitude?' You may ask, where **was** that dude—on the moon? Well, it turns out that sailors in those days had their own system of longitudes.

What the good Captain was talking about was a spot on the entrance to Jervis Inlet, which is on about 124 degrees W. longitude. Apparently, they both stopped and started at Greenwich. And it went around through Europe and Asia and across the Pacific. He was 56 degrees east of the present international date line. So he had just discovered something tomorrow!

Little wonder he didn't discover Princess Louisa!

He didn't even know what day it was!

of this one. The fourth one comes down into a very shallow cove with a reef. On the chart it looks like a set of green false teeth. Half way between this creek and the next one you will see some high rock faces. You are looking for one cliff that has a few trees with a slanting rocky ledge and a squarish white area. Near the bottom of this square and in the center you will see a faint red drawing. It is supposed to represent a man in a canoe. It is pretty badly faded and it looks more like a sausage than a canoe. Remember, we're not talking great art here!

The last creek this side of McMurray Bay has a dried-up soda bed.

Moorsam Bluff on the east shore of the Reach does not look much different than other bluffs here. Apparently it was not named by the early English surveyors because there is no reference to it in Walbran's book.

There is a nice waterfall in **McMurray Bay.** The water is very deep right up the mouth of the creek, we thought. We didn't find the 0.9 m. shallow that is shown on the chart. There is a small shell beach. We didn't go ashore, but it looks like the kind of place where you might find Indian artifacts. The creek that comes down from Barren Lake should provide fresh water the year around and it would be typical of the small coves where natives could set up camp.

McMurray Bay is one of the places that Vera from Egmont named as a 'safety cove.'

For some strange reason, the charts do not show a name for the bay that is formed by Treth Creek and Brittain River. Let's call it 'Brittain Bay' if nobody objects.

There are two Indian enclaves here, consisting of several modular housing units at the end of Brittain River and a couple of nice permanent houses. There is an old truck and an old school bus up in one of the yards. A logging road and a creek lead into the community. There is apparently a shake mill there; we saw a number of bundles of shakes stacked along the shoreline.

Where Treth Creek flows into the bay, there is a marshland with a number of old pilings and breakwaters.

In *Curve of Time,* Mrs. Blanchet described the winds in this area just as we found them:

The wind hit us as we came opposite Brittain River, just as it usually does. It blows out of the deep valley of the Brittain River, and then escapes out through Vancouver Bay. After we had slopped ahead out of that, we met the wind that blows out of Deserted Bay and down the full length of Princess Royal Reach. So for the next ten miles or so we battled wind. It is not a nice wind in among the mountains. It picks you up in its teeth and shakes you. It hits you first on one side and then on the other. There is nowhere to go, you just have to take it. But finally, everybody tired and hungry, we rounded Patrick Point into the gentle Queens Reach—and there, there was no wind at all.

Princess Royal Reach

Shazam! (Remember 'shazam?') We are now in Princess Royal Reach. This royal personage was Empress Frederick of Germany a.k.a. the Princess Royal of England.

We thought of this lovely boat as possibly a close cousin to M. Wylie Blanchet's cruiser, 'Caprice.'

She was married to the German Emperor Frederick. We wonder what **her** name really was?

On this leg of the trip to Princess Louisa, we will encounter, mates, some abandoned log camps, oyster farms and another pictograph. Exciting, eh?

As the reach turns northeast, you will find on the north shore, south of **Seshal Creek**, some modular houses and trucks and old gear of an abandoned logging camp. There seemed to be a caretaker there, because we saw a couple of small boats tied up to a float.

Fishermen tie up in a shallow bight about 1-½ miles south of Seshal Creek, another 'safety cove.'

Across the reach on the south shore, Glacial Creek has some permanent buildings—probably involved in aquaculture. Big switchback trails behind it lead up into the mountains—probably logging roads.

Seshal Creek has some distinctive orange colored buildings and some oyster buoys.

This must be a good area for shrimping—there are buoys all along these reaches, and occasionally you see a shrimp boat checking the pots.

The next pictograph is a lot clearer than the previous one and a lot easier to find. It is a little more than half way between Seshal Creek and Osgood Creek headed upstream. On the chart, you will see a reef offshore just north of Seshal Creek. The land bulges out into the reach at one point about a half mile south of Osgood Creek. You will find the picture in a triangular section of white rock in a niche about 20 feet above the waterline. It is a stick figure with a crude headdress.

The Reaches

With M. Wylie Blanchet's **Curve of Time** as our Bible, we read her description of Jervis Inlet—one that is so perfect, we decided to share it with you here, rather than try and describe it ourselves:

"Originally perhaps a fault in the earth's crust, and later scoured out by a glacier, since retreated, it is roughly a mile wide, and completely hemmed in on all sides by stupendous mountains, rising from almost perpendicular shores to heights of from five to eight thousand feet. All the soundings on the chart are marked one hundred fathoms with no-bottom mark (this was about 1928)...right up to the cliffs. Stunted pines struggle up some of the ravines, but their hold on life is short. Sooner or later, a winter storm or spring avalanche sweeps them out and away; and next summer there will be a new cascade in their place.

"...You just have to keep going—there is no shelter, no place to anchor. In summer-time the wind blows up the inlet in the morning, down the inlet from five o'clock on. In winter...the wind blows down the inlet most of the time—so strong and with such heavy williwaws that no boat can make headway against it."

The Sechelt Indian village at Deserted Bay welcomes visitors to 'Tosh-Nye.'

Princess Royal Reach widens on the southeast side before it joins Queens Reach at **Patrick Point**.

The creek bed just above Stakawus Creek, once called 'Slate Creek', has the remains of an old dock. The creek itself is the site of a log camp. It is on an Indian Reserve that extends up to Deserted Bay. The 'ruins' noted on the chart at the end of the tideflat is that of an old dock. Way back about 1917 the Vancouver Lumber Company had a logging camp here. They had three miles of railroad tracks, one locomotive and seven log cars. Before it closed down in 1937 there were more than 15 miles of track, including two switchbacks.

The cove just outside **Deserted Bay** has a house and an old partially sunken barge. The house has a big flagpole and several small boats tied to a float. This bay has an unusually nice sandy beach north of the exit of the Deserted River. The water, just off the beach, is ten fathoms. Above the river entrance is a little Sechelt Village with modular houses and a power plant. The sign says 'Private Property, Sechelt Bands Land.' There is a dock with two floats. Near the dock there are fuel tanks labeled 'diesel' and 'gas.' There was a fishboat tied up at the dock when we visited.

A frozen creek comes down the mountainsides across from Deserted Bay. You can see where the ice ends and the water begins.

Patrick Point was named after Prince Arthur William Patrick Albert (*Four first names! Wonder what his mother, Queen Victoria, used to yell when she called him for lunch?*) Patrick Point has some flatland and just beyond it is a tiny cove for stern-tie moorage if you feel you must tie up here.

The scenery in the reaches is fantastic—and just inside the niche at the upper left is yet another pictograph.

Queens Reach

We are now in Queens Reach. Walbran doesn't discuss it, but you can make book that old Capt. Richards, in his flurry of naming places, dubbed it after Victoria.

Northwest of Deserted Bay there is a small cove where a couple of folks live. They have a a cabin and a dock, but weren't around when we went by.

The cove just south of **Crabapple Creek** on the left shore is very wide and at the northwestern part there is a house with a dock and a very nice beach.

Potato Creek shows up in a niche right below a beautiful glacier covered mountain. There is a pebbly beach off to the north of the creek. This is a good place to anchor if you have to spend a few hours waiting for the current to change at Malibu. It has a small Indian Reserve.

Hill Rock is a threat only to boats that draw more than 3.2 m. If you're interested in jigging for cod while waiting for a slack at Malibu, try here.

Let's bypass the entrance to Princess Louisa, figuratively speaking, to take a look at the top of Queens Reach.

There's a very interesting bunch of pictographs beyond the entrance to Malibu on the right side. You go along shore 2-1/8 miles until you come to a rocky point that is aimed at you. This is the first occurrence of such a point. There are trees on it, and it looks like the prow of a boat. This is the site of the pictographs.

If you overshoot this point, you will find several logs tied together with cable which are fitted neatly in a notch between two rocks. They are a log skid for a former floating logging camp. Interestingly enough, we tied to the logs at the logging camp a few years back and visited with the caretaker. He never mentioned the pictographs.

The shore rises at about a 45 degree angle eastward from the logs. It ends in the rock faces which comprise the 'boat prow.' If you stand fifty yards or so offshore, you will be able to spot an abandoned blue station wagon on the logging road above. It was apparently left there by the loggers. About 15 feet above high tide you will see the picture of a man and some fish and what looks like arrows. This is a very distinct group of paintings.

Slane Creek has a log skid and some old derelict boats.

On the tideflat created by the **Skwawka River** there is an Indian Reserve encampment. It has quite a lot of logging gear on it. We could see a log hoist, barge and some houses.

Where **Lausmann Creek** empties into the Reach, you will see some rotted pilings, an old dock and a house.

It's rather strange to come to the end of the reach. Off ahead are the lowlands with snowcapped mountains behind. But it's all over as far as cruising any farther. Vancouver didn't like it either:

Having dined, we pursued our examination. The inlet now took a N.W. by W. direction without any contraction in its width, until about five o'clock in the evening, when all our hopes vanished, by finding it terminate, as others had done, in a swampy low land producing a few maples and pines. Through a small space of low land, which extended from the head of the inlet to the base of the mountains that surrounded us, flowed three small streams of fresh water, apparently originating from one source in the left hand corner of the bay...in which point was seen an extensive valley.

On our approach to the low land we gained soundings at 70 fathoms, which soon decreased as we advanced, to 30, 14, and 3 fathoms on a bank that stretches across the head of the inlet, similar to all the others we had before examined.

At noon I considered that we had advanced some miles within the western boundaries of the snowy barrier, as some of its rugged mountains were now behind and to the south of us. This filled my mind with the pleasing hopes of finding our way to its eastern side...where all our expectations vanished in finding it to terminate in a round basin encompassed on every side by the dreary country already described.

Not a little mortified that our progress should be so soon stopped, it became highly expedient to direct our way towards the ships..at least 114 miles away.

We've now come to the end of all the Reaches. Let's go back and take a look at the wonderland of Chatterbox Falls, which brought us all the way up here.

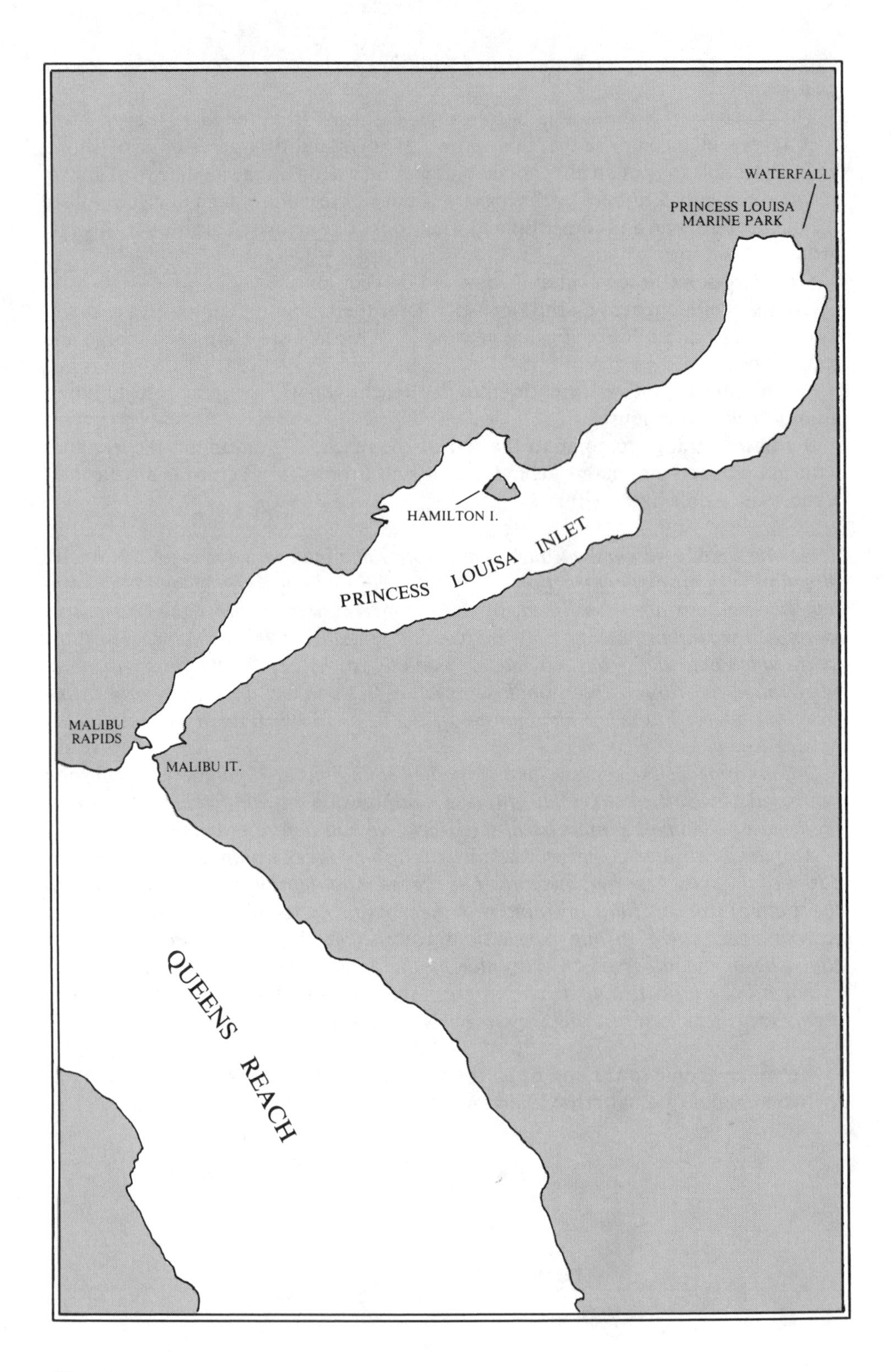
WATERFALL
PRINCESS LOUISA MARINE PARK
HAMILTON I.
PRINCESS LOUISA INLET
MALIBU RAPIDS
MALIBU IT.
QUEENS REACH

Chapter 5

Chatterbox Falls

The Princess and the Chatterbox

Here's how we feel about **Princess Louisa Inlet**. We've been there twice. The first time, we were awed by its grandeur. No question about it: it's one of the most beautiful spots this side of Alaska. The second time we went, it was to get research for this book. Would we go again? Possibly, if we wanted to take somebody we cared about to see it. But, then, we travel in a 5-knot boat and it's a big push. We know people who have fast power-boats who wouldn't think of missing their yearly visits to the Inlet. Some of these good folks belong to the Princess Louisa International Society which helps support the Provincial Marine Park.

If you're trying to make up your mind about going up there, let us give you a dash of nitty-gritty. First of all, in late July and early August, you may find the place packed—unless the weather has been lousy. In which case, the weather there is not likely to be that much better. And the joy of the area depends somewhat on clear skies to see the glaciers and waterfalls and peaks. And, speaking of weather, sometimes 'The Princess' gets into a snit and goes on a rampage all by herself!

There may be mountains all around, but it's not impossible to have 50 knot winds whistle up the Inlet and bounce you around. If you like thunder and lightning, you'll love one of those ad hoc tempests.

Actually, it's a place everyone should see at least once—and possibly twice—because it really is as fantastic as you thought it was after you saw it the first time! Realize you can only reach Princess Louisa by boat or float plane, the nearest public road is about 40 miles away.

So we've warned you newcomers. You will need Chart book #3312, Page 7, or chart #3514. You're familiar with these since you had to use them to get here.

Now to business.

Let's begin with basics. Who was 'er 'ighness, anyhow? The history books are strangely silent on this matter. Was she a noblewoman with a shady past? Not bloody likely. The late Bruce Calhoun, in his book *Mac and the Princess,* says it was named after Queen Victoria's mother, Princess Victoria Maria Louisa of Saxe-Coburg and Duchess of Kent.

Long before the white men arrived, however, the Indians knew of the inlet and

The camp for teenagers at Malibu Rapids—the entrance to Princess Louisa Inlet.

called it 'Suiuoolot' or 'sway-we-lat', which means 'sunny and warm', or 'where the sun shines'.

It's time to tell you what you'll find when you get there.

Unless you've got a lot of horses hooked up to that prop, you'd better wait for slack water. The current can run 9 knots. Not only that, but you could encounter an 'overfall,' a sort of wall of water. Another complexity you might encounter is the fact that on large tide changes 'slack' as predicted in the *Canadian Tide and Current Tables*, green edition, may be several minutes later than predicted. Sometimes the water gets backed up in there and is still fighting its way through when the deeper currents are nil. The rule we learned from reading about it in *Northwest Boat Travel* is not to enter while you can see a line of white water across the opening.

We've been through the rapids four times at slack in the *Sea Witch* with a chicken skipper and we've never had any problems—however, we do breathe easier after we've gotten past.

You should have no problems figuring out how to enter **Malibu Rapids**. There is a light tower on a rock with a green band on top on the west side. It flashes green at night. Keep it to port, naturally.

The little islet to the right is **Malibu Islet**. There is a rock which lies in front of it so swing wide. Unless you are sure there's a high tide, don't try to go behind this Islet, there are reefs, and it's best not to go behind it anyway.

You make a dogleg through the narrowest part of the rapids and suddenly you are inside.

The big lashup to your left with literally hundreds of teenie-boppers milling about and doing all those noisy things that they do, is called Malibu Club. It is a summer nondenominational religious camp for young people, run by the Young Life Campaign. There is a float, and you may tie up temporarily to go for a tour of the facilities. We didn't take advantage of the opportunity. We did see the kids careening down a high wire from a cliff and dropping into the water shrieking. We naturally wondered if their mothers knew what those little turkeys were doing?

Captain Vancouver did not find the entrance to Princess Louisa Inlet—he skated right past it. But he did see the entrance and describe it:

About two leagues from the head of the inlet we had observed, as we passed upwards on the northern shore, a small creek with some rocky islets before it, where I intended to take up our abode for the night. On our return, it was found to be full of salt water, just deep enough to admit our boats against a very rapid stream where at low tide they would have grounded some feet above the level of the water in the inlet. From the rapidity of the stream, and the quantity of water it discharged, it was reasonable to suppose, by its taking a winding direction up a valley to the N.E. that its source was at some distance.

Mrs. Blanchet's kids were delighted that the famous explorer had missed it, and scornful that he thought the entrance shallow. But she agrees that it would be hard to see inside the inlet as the mountains do obscure the inlet itself:

From water level, the points on one side and the coves on the other fold into each other, hiding the narrow passage. It is not until you are rushed through the gap on a rising tide that the full surprise of the existence and beauty of this little hidden inlet suddenly bursts on you...the inlet is about five miles long, a third of a mile wide and the mountains that flank it on either side are over a mile high. From inside the entrance you can see right down to the far end where it takes the short L-turn to the left. At that distance you can see over the crest to where all the upper snowfields lie exposed, with their black peaks breaking through the snow...three miles farther down the inlet the high snowfields become obscured—the mountains are closing in. You turn the corner of the great precipice that slightly overhangs—which the Indians used to scale with rocks tied to their backs: the one who reached the top first was the bravest of the brave and was made the chief...

Then suddenly, dramatically, in a couple of boat-lengths, the whole abrupt end of the inlet comes into sight—heavily wooded, green, but rising steeply. Your eye is caught first by a long white scar, up about two thousand feet, that slashes across...and disappears into the dark-green background. Again, another splash of white, but farther down. Now you can see that it has movement. It is moving down and down, in steep rapids. Disappearing...reappearing...and then in one magnificent leap plunging off the cliff and into the sea a hundred feet below. As your boat draws in closer, the roar and the mist come out to meet you.

In other words, Princess Louisa is absolutely spectacular and something you shouldn't miss. It's been called a 'Yosemite at sea level'.

There is an interesting history about the place which you might want to discover

The legendary 'Chatterbox Falls.'

by reading Calhoun's book, *Mac and the Princess.* There is also a pamphlet which you can get from a kiosk on shore at the head of the Inlet that gives a bit of the history of the place.

The renowned mystery writer Erle Stanley Gardner was a devotee of Princess Louisa, and the pamphlet quotes what he wrote about it:

There is no use describing that inlet. Perhaps an atheist could view it and remain an atheist, but I doubt it.

There is a calm tranquillity which stretches from the smooth surface of the reflecting water straight up into infinity. The deep calm of eternal silence is only disturbed by the muffled roar of throbbing waterfalls as they plunge down from sheer cliffs.

There is no scenery in the world that can beat it. Not that I've seen the rest of the world. I don't need to, I've seen Princess Louisa Inlet.

Every day showed some new glimpse of nature. Constantly changing clouds clung to the sheer cliffs for companionship, drifting lightly from crag to crag, lazily floating along above their swimming reflections giving ever new light combinations, new contours. Clouds, water, trees, mountains, snow and sky all seem to be perpetually the same through the countless ages of eternal time, and yet to be changing hourly. One views the scenery with bared head and choking feeling of the throat. It is more than beautiful. It is sacred.

The Inlet is about 4 miles long, from the entrance to the foot of Chatterbox Falls. Anchorage is skimpy in the entire area, but you're not thinking about that when you first enter the inlet. The magnificence of hundreds of waterfalls cascading down from the mile high cliffs is overwhelming in the early part of the summer. By late summer, those falls have dwindled to a countable number as the glaciers retreat.

There is one wide bay which has some acceptable depths behind **Macdonald Island.** (In some old charts, it is called **Hamilton Island**). Since the area is a Marine Park, the government has installed some mooring buoys in the shallows just north of the island. They get snapped up pretty quickly in peak seasons. There are some houses on shore near the Island, which are occupied by the staff of Malibu Club.

The rock just off McDonald Island has a warning marker, a stick with a rough triangle tied to it. It will be visible at high tides.

Because the walls of the Inlet are steep, finding the combination of a proper depth for the hook and an accessible rock or tree for the stern line is not easy. There is a government dock at the head of the Inlet, near the falls. It has 273 m. of berthage and it is free. There is fresh mountain water at several taps on the dock, but there is no electricity. Garbage disposal facilities are ample, but they do attract bears.

The favorite anchorage is in the shallows at the foot of the falls. The current from the creek is so fast that it keeps boats at the end of their rodes just as if they had been double-anchored. The sound of the rushing water is very soothing. The shallows are very tricky, however. They are in a narrow band along the shore and the scouring effect has made the water quite deep close in, about 20 m., unless you anchor like we did in about 10 feet. Another factor: the bottom does not have the best holding quality and if one of the sudden squalls makes up in the area, you may have to hoist anchor and beat a retreat to the dock or up behind Macdonald Island.

We have both anchored and tied at the dock and, same as everywhere, there are advantages and disadvantages to both.

A flotilla of Nordic Tugs at the dock in Princess Louisa—everyone on board had a copy of "Curve of Time."

Anchoring in front of the falls was sort of exciting, because at low tide with the *Witch* almost on the ledge, we could wander around her in our bathing suits and check out her bottom. The waterfall, of course, held us off the shore and there was no need to stern-tie. It was noisy, of course, with Chatterbox Falls only a few hundred feet away. As Blanchet wrote, "That waterfall can laugh and talk, sing and lull you to sleep. But it can also moan and sob, fill you with awful apprehensions of you don't know what—all depending on your mood."

Tying to the dock in Princess Louisa is a much friendlier experience than in other places. Perhaps it's because everyone is in awe of the majesty of the park. It becomes somewhat overwhelming, looking all around you at all this beauty which changes constantly, depending on the angle of sun or clouds. And there are always boaters who have never been in the inlet before and they are even more impressed with the scenery. People seem more willing to visit and help each other tie up, have dockside potlucks, go hiking together, whatever. It's as though we're all inspired to be at our best.

Once when we were there in June a group of Nordic Tug owners pulled up to the dock. Those of us already secure helped them tie up. We visited for quite a long time before we learned one of the neophyte skippers, on his first trip to the area, was a well-known TV actor who appears as a judge.

Another thing. When you're at the dock you'll find that practically everyone has a copy of *Curve of Time* on board, and you'll get into some pretty good discussions with other boaters about which is 'Trapper's Rock', and which of the pools are 'Big Wash, Big Rinse and Little Rinse', names which the Blanchets used. Then the conversation turns to 'where is the Trapper's Cabin?'

Where Are The Sherpas?

(The following is a transcription of a tape made by that somewhat-trepid mountain climber, Al Cummings. It was taken from a cassette recorder he carried while climbing up to 'The Trapper's Cabin' at Princess Louisa. The audio was very indistinct at times because of puffing, wheezing and gasping. At other times, it was very clear but totally unusable because it contains phrases that would redden the cheeks of a Lascar Pirate.)

HERE we go up the hill to the Famous 'Trapper's Cabin'. We have heard that the view is sensational from up there. It is near the top of the creek that pours into the harbor next to the mooring floats.

You start out by going to the garbage dump. This is a "must visit place" for masochists or people with bad sinuses. It has one big plus, compared to the climb so far, it is on level ground! And that's a blessing. We have been climbing for ten minutes and I am trying to decide whether to weasel out and go back down or wait until I get a coronary and the medics carry me down in a comfortable stretcher.

Once you leave it, you start up...and up...and up. Maybe as much as 2,000 feet, someone said. To put this in perspective, the altitude is 2,000 feet. The path to that height is probably three miles almost perp-biGod-endicular. At this point there should be a sign like the one in the 'Wizard of Oz' that says, 'DANGER. I'D TURN BACK IF I WERE YOU!' If there were, I tell you what I'd do—I'd do a 'cowardly lion' turn and go back down to the boat and put my feet up!

Maybe I should stop here for a moment and dictate some information—in case I take the easy way out and jump off a cliff somewhere.

Pass the garbage dump. Go up the path until you come to a sign that says the water source is just beyond and you are not supposed to go further in that direction. Then you turn left and continue. You will now leave the Provincial Park and you are on your own.

We asked the warden about the hike. He said, "If you get lost up there, we're not going to come and hunt for you—it's not our territory." It is clear that he has the correct instincts for self-preservation and does not approve of such meandering and he doesn't want to be wakened in the middle of the night to go hunt for some nerd who has wandered off the path. And who can blame him?

Not me!

How could anyone get off the path, you might ask. And I can tell you. You might have someone in your party like good old Yours Truly, who has the notion he is a latter-day Mohican and can follow paths by looking at overturned blades of grass. In our case, the guide, ME, led the party up along the rocks that flanked the rushing waterfalls. We came to spots where there was nothing but solid rock and no overturned blades of grass. I made guesses inspired by some primitive instinct that probably led certain prehistoric tribes to become extinct. I led our party to a rock face that defied crossing without extra long fingernails. At that point, I admitted that somehow I might have missed the trail.

Someone in the group suggested that maybe we should look for some kind of signs—like blazes on trees or footprints. Those somewhat less skilled in woodcraft but nonetheless having good common sense, agreed. The party retraced its steps and came back to the main path at the sign about the watershed, having wasted a half hour.

Strange...there was a path that seemed to branch off away from the creek that looked like humans had put foot on it in recent weeks.

"Humph" I humphed, "When we get up there we'll probably find it has Golden Arches!"

Okay, break's over. We're climbing again. At this point, a warning. If after a few minutes you do not come to an old log skid, you are on the wrong path and you are trailing a mountain goat.

We are following the log skid. A log skid is a bunch of logs about ten feet long that are placed across the path to make a kind of bumpy roadway. They are put there to facilitate getting cut timber down the hill.

At this point, we guess we have about two hours ahead of us.

We are continuing on the log trail. It will sort of peter out at places and then pick up again. It follows an old stream bed.

We are now finding blazes—chopped scars in the sides of trees. I suppose I am telling you to go to blazes, har! har!

We are now at a rock face that is not too steep but will require us to impersonate a slug if we want to climb it. The alternative is along a fallen log that you can shinny up. It is slower but safer, and that's the way I'm going to go. To hell with dignity!

We have stopped to catch our breath. I am of the opinion that this supposed house was built by a 'trapper' who was only 16 years old.

And when he was 18 years old, he probably said, "to Hell with it...it's too big a drag getting up there!"

A little farther on now, and we have come to the first of a number of old fallen trees that cross the path. You can wriggle under them or you can try to belly up over them. Either way, you're going to get muddy.

Now we've come to a lot of fallen logs that seem to have some sort of order and you think—"Hallelujiah—the log cabin!" It ain't. It's just fallen logs. Cruel mirage!

Now we've come to a lightning-shattered tree. It's very dramatic.

We just got to a moss covered rock which splits the trail. Both sides look equally logical. We took the left-hand trail. It brought us to a blaze on a downed log on the path.

Now under an overpass created by one giant log, high over the trail—you can almost stand under it. We figure we are about 45 minutes away from the cabin. 45 minutes!

Now more fallen trees—worm your way under or clamber up over. This is an obstacle of about a half dozen trees. We have been climbing about a quarter hour since my last report.

You now skirt along under the face of sheer rocks. They are moss covered—about 50 feet high.

You come to a level stretch of path, nicely defined, which heads toward the sound of the falls.

Hey! Suddenly we see it! The cabin!

I am now flaked out on the floor of the porch. This cabin is a wreck! Boy is this ever a 'fixer- upper!'

To tell you the truth, I wish it did have Golden Arches. I could use a Big Mac and a shake right now!

Jo and Al (without sherpas) at the Trapper's Cabin.

We are up near the first giant fall from the top of the mountain. The cabin has a small porch that faces down the hill. It is a one room affair. It had a big front window in it at one time. The frame is still there, stored under the porch, but most of the panes of glass are gone. You can't help but wonder how the guy who built the cabin ever got all of those supplies up there. There are two bare bedsprings along the back wall. Did they have helicopters back in those days?

The following report is almost drowned out by the sound of rushing water:

The falls at this point are savage. You think of waterfalls as having some kind of order. But this particular one is totally mad. Great gouts of water will come flying off the top of the cliff and sail through the air smash into a rock ledge and turn to foam in a giant explosion. Another wave will hit every bench and turn cartwheels. Some thousand-gallon bolts of water will carom off rocks from side to side as they rocket down the face of the mountain. The noise is almost painful, as you can probably hear. There is no discernible rhythm. Sunlight creates rainbows and halos that flicker from one patch of foam to another.

The view is...so-so; hardly worth the trip up the mountain.

What is exciting is the sense of being present at the creation of gargantuan natural

The waterfall at the top.

The view from the top.

forces—like burrowing down into a mountain and watching the rock turn to lava and rocket upward.

Just below the cabin is—you are not going to believe this—an open-air privy!

Now how in Hell did that get there?

It's inconceivable that the guy who carried all the food and building supplies up that mountain, who lived in the constant roar and moisture of an unceasing battleground of cannonading water without even the comfort of a stove or fireplace—was so cultured that he couldn't bring himself to go potty without sitting on a comfortable throne!

Gotta admit though, he would have a great view!

We are ready to head back down.

Wish I had two husky sherpas who knew the 'fireman's carry.'

END OF TAPE

There are several shoreside facilities, including an information board and guest book where you can pick up a brochure, barbecue pit, toilets, tables and a 12-sided picnic shelter especially designed for the site. There is also a pylon with the names of some of the original members of the Princess Louisa Society inscribed.

There are several hikes in the area, and you can take your pick of short and easy or long and difficult. The short hike is a loop trail to the last drop-off of Chatterbox Falls. It is an absolute must-see. The trail is well defined and off to the left as you leave the dock area. There is a grim warning not to get off the trails and get too close to the rapid water near or above the falls. A sign shows that at least 13 persons have lost their lives when they have slipped on the wet rocks and been swept to their deaths over the falls.

Now the other hike is much longer and more difficult and the 'blazed' trail often trails off into nothingness. This will take a sack lunch, grubby clothes and hours of work. Is it worth it? We did it once. Say no more.

A sidelight. The Park has a ranger, of course. And one of his jobs is to dispose of waste. There is a big dump at the end of a path and out of sight of the park visitors. Biodegradable stuff is reduced in a big kiln which is powered by propane. When we were there, the vegetable matter and waste paper were piled in a big heap because the burner was malfunctioning—and this was only June. The poor warden was trying valiantly to keep a fire going inside the kiln by pouring kerosene and lighting matches. The weather was hot. The odor was numbing. The bees and flies made clouds. Recent rains had made the whole area a mud-bog. Standing there in front of the

The picnic shelter with the pylon and the names of the original members of the Princess Louisa Society.

The defunct incinerator and a frustrated Warden Gerry Lister.

door to the kiln, stripped to the waist, sweating and brushing off insects all the while wearing his 'Smokey the Bear' hat, we found the poor Ranger. He was a handsome young man who would have been considered a 'hunk' by the girls in a social situation. Despite the fact that he was involved in a hopeless and thankless task, he still managed to keep his sense of humor and joked with us.

One of the fascinating sights you may find is a group of mountain goats in tiny grassy spots on the side of the mountain. They will appear as small whitish spots if you spot them with your binoculars from the dock. You will wonder how they managed to get to the locations; sometimes there are no visible paths leading there. We kept an eye on them all day long, waiting for them to exit. When darkness fell, they were still there. The next morning, they were gone.

Showers are a problem here, as usual, if your boat doesn't have an indoor one. There are no public freshwater bathing facilities at the falls. It would be very dangerous to try to get into the frigid pools at the bottom of the falls. There are signs on the paths which lead up to overlooks, warning about going into forbidden areas. If you have a sunshower and are at the dock, be prepared to have an audience.

All is not hopeless, though. There **is** one spot where you can bathe in fresh water. It is at the foot of a creek and waterfall that is not shown on the chart. You will find it on the curving shore on the northwest side of the head of the Inlet. Look for a break in the sheer cliffs, with a creek disappearing into it a few hundred feet above. Many of the frequent visitors to the area know about it. They refer to it as the 'Bathtub.' If it is being used, you will see tenders pulled up onto the narrow rocky ledge nearby, with a large rock just beside the bathing area. You would be advised to wait your turn because there probably are skinny-dippers just out of sight in the small pool. As you might suspect, the water is clear and pure and sweet and **COLD**. The adjacent saltwater is usually warmer. In June it was only in the low 60s, but it does better than that in July and August.

Princess Louisa Inlet History

Now we've told you all the present-day pertinent facts. It's time for a little history lesson. It would be presumptuous to think only boaters in the 20th century know about Princess Louisa.

Sechelt Indian lore has it that somewhere long ago there was an Indian village near Chatterbox Falls called 'Qua-Ma-Meen' or 'Qualmamine,' according to Calhoun. Above the falls, the cliffs were called 'Tuktakamin' which meant a 'fence' or 'barrier'. There was also a Sechelt village at the entrance to the inlet where Malibu Lodge is now located.

Between the time Vancouver missed the inlet in 1792 and Capt. Richards surveyed and charted the area in 1860, there is no written record of inhabitants, but Calhoun is certain there were Indians, white trappers, voyageurs, fishermen or loggers in that time.

He writes of a young Sergeant Major in the Kaiser's German Army named Herman Casper who deserted the Army after he knocked out an officer, an offense that would have cost him his life. "He got to Switzerland took passage to Canada, and ended up on Jervis Inlet at the entrance to Princess Louisa. After he received his Canadian citizenship, he took up a homestead and built a cabin on the other side of the rapids from where the Malibu Lodge now stands.

"Herman Casper was a fine tool maker and all around mechanic. He made his living by hand logging and repairing implements for other loggers. He was a jolly, friendly man who welcomed everyone to his cabin. He played the zither and made his own guitar. Casper sold his property to Thomas F. Hamilton, the founder of Malibu Lodge, for $500."

Rumor has it that there is a pictograph on the rocks near the entrance to the Inlet. About three quarters of a mile from the Malibu float, on the northern walls, there are smudges of what looked like ochre paint on the face of a sheer rock which don't look like they were there naturally. They may be the remains of a pictograph.

Steef cliffs and deep waters make even stern-tying difficult.

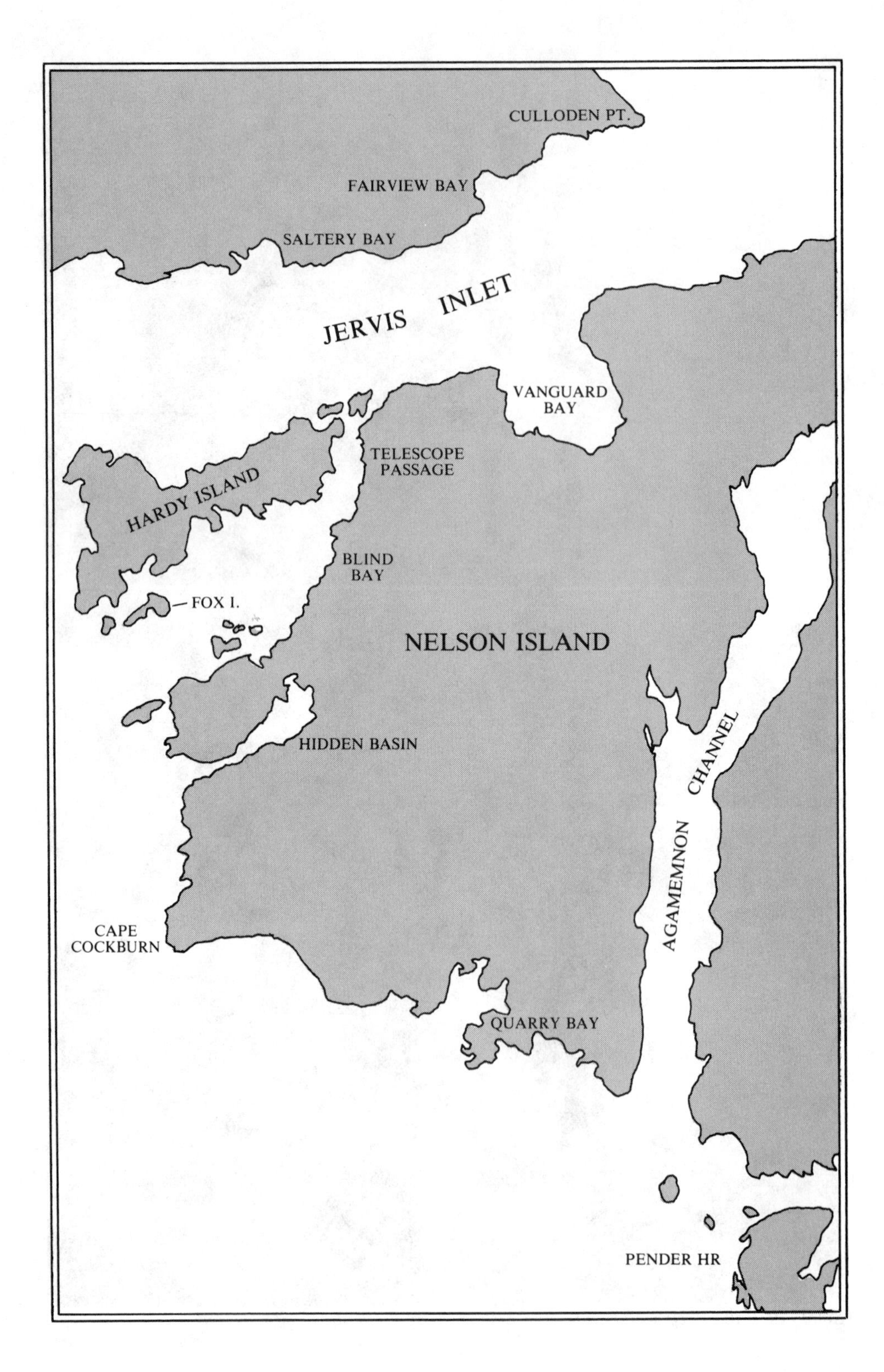
CULLODEN PT.
FAIRVIEW BAY
SALTERY BAY
JERVIS INLET
VANGUARD BAY
TELESCOPE PASSAGE
HARDY ISLAND
BLIND BAY
FOX I.
NELSON ISLAND
HIDDEN BASIN
AGAMEMNON CHANNEL
CAPE COCKBURN
QUARRY BAY
PENDER HR

Chapter 6

Michael's Bay

Bound for the Sound

The Jervis Inlet Run

Well, mates, have we got Princess Louisa out of our blood for this year? For this century? Is it about time to take off for the big Boaters' Playground?

We read several Elmore Leonard books on the tedious trip back down the Reaches. Most of the time we motored, so we could flake out in the cockpit and steer with our bare toes and read. One of our crew, who is of the power-boat persuasion, grumbled at the fact that the Skipper-person does not believe in automatic pilots. The trip was so uneventful that we looked forward to seeing drift logs.

When we got to Foley Head, we had to stir our bones and start taking pictures and notes again. We were on a new leg of our journey.

We went over and nosed around the entrance to Jervis Inlet.

Culloden Point, at the northeastern corner of the Inlet and Hotham Sound has nothing going for it but some history. It was named after the *H.M.S Culloden,* which had 74 guns, weighed in at 1,638 tons and was built on the Thames in 1783. There! Did that make your day?

Well, actually the ship was put under the command of Sir John Jervis and fought at the Battle of St. Vincent in 1797, hence some of the names hereabouts.

The *B.C. Coast Pilot* says that the area in Jervis Inlet where it intersects with Hotham Sound is a torpedo firing ground, called 'Whiskey November.' Nobody we talked to remembered ever seeing it used, however. You can check its boundaries on page #3 of #3312 which we have been using.

There are power cables that cross Jervis Inlet just west of Culloden Point. They are 170 feet in the air. There are six cables, three each in two bundles. They would be almost invisible in cloudy conditions.

Vanguard Bay

Chart book #3312 (still on page #3) leaves some shoreside areas unmarked for depths. The two islets on the northeastern side of the bay do have some shallows behind them, and we saw a couple of boats anchored there. Cruising guides, including the *Coast Pilot,* talk about logging operations dominating the bay. There appears to be no active logging in the area now. There are several large mooring

Frank Johnson, skipper of the tug 'Happy Warrior' helps boaters in the Jervis Inlet area.

Culloden Point

We have a secret yearning to tell all we know about British Naval history apparently, for we keep coming up with all these fabulous facts about naval heroes and ships.

You undoubtedly sailed past Culloden Point as you left St. Vincent Bay. And of course you asked yourself where the name came from. We turned yet again to Walbran to give you the following information: "The **Culloden**, Captain Thomas Troubridge, 74 guns, 1,638 tons, built on the Thames, 1783, was one of the fleet under the command of Sir John Jervis, and was hotly engaged at the battle of St. Vincent, 14 February, 1797.

"The Spaniards were caught in confusion because they had never expected ...that Jervis would venture an attack, but now to their dismay they saw the fifteen British ships approaching with intimidating order and resolution. The British steered silently for the gap in the Spanish line, and as the **Culloden** approached, a huge three-decker was on the verge of crossing. The **Culloden's** course would certainly bring the two vessels into collision, and the first lieutenant of the **Culloden** called out anxiously to Troubridge of the impending crash. 'Can't help it, Grif-

buoys and booms are probably still tied off there. There are a half-dozen aquaculture farms in the bay now. The floats are not noted on the chart. The fish farm on the northern shore is called Royal Pacific Sea Farms, Ltd.

There are some attractive beaches on the southern shores of Vanguard Bay. One is the site of a wreck, as you can see from the chart. In fact, there are *two* abandoned boats on the beach that you can see before you come to the remains of the *Sandy Cape*.

One is a yard-tug, rusting away. The other is the remains of the *Vanguard* which belonged to Lew and Joan Milligan. It was wrecked during an icy northeaster in January 1950. During the storm—termed the worst in 50 years by locals—giant waves tossed logs onto the float, smashed the freight shed and shoved the *Vanguard* onto the beach, piling boomsticks over her. The old white hull is all that is left.

Vanguard Bay was often a stop by skippers of power boats after the annual International Power Boat Race from Puget Sound to Alaska.

Fairview Bay in Jervis Inlet southwest of Culloden Point is not mentioned in the *B.C. Coast Pilot* for some strange reason. It appears to be filled with fish-pens. Logs can be boomed along the mainland shore.

Ahlstrom Point, under the second run of power cables, has some fish farming on shore. The rails on the pens are painted a bright orange-red.

Jervis Inlet has a lot of traffic: the ferry, tugs with large log tows, fishboats and a lot of recreational boats heading toward Sechelt Inlet, Agamemnon Channel, Hotham Sound and the Prince of Wales Reach up to Princess Louisa.

Now, flip the page of Chart #3312 over and we're back on page 2.

fiths,' replied Captain Troubridge, 'let the weakest fend off,' and the ship held her way.

"In silence he approached the three-decker, till through all her ports the crew could be seen at their quarters; then in quick succession two double shotted broadsides rang out from the **Culloden**, fired with terrible precision and regularity 'as if by a second's watch and in the presence of a port admiral's inspection.' As the cloud of dust cleared away, which this fearful 'fire of hell' had sent up from the Spaniard's bow and side, she gave way, her crew falling into such dire confusion that they did not even discharge their guns. The Spanish line was broken.

"The **Culloden** was also one of Nelson's fleet at the battle of the Nile, 1 and 2 August, 1798, but was not able to participate in the action because of unfortunately grounding on the shoal, the extent of which was unknown, off the western point of Aboukir Bay, while entering the anchorage where the French fleet were lying on that eventful night. The vessel was, however, useful in her distress, by acting as a danger mark to the ships following her. She was floated from her dangerous position on the succeeding day."

Remains of the 'Sandy Cape' in Vanguard Bay.

Sandy Cape

The **Sandy Cape** is only vestigial. Its remains on the beach are a part of recent Vanguard Bay history. Originally a fish packer, it must have been about 65 or 70 feet long. A venturesome soul bought it in sad condition and labored mightily to refurbish it, according to a Nelson Islander we met. It was anchored just offshore. In 1982, a 90-knot storm drove it up on the beach and it caught fire. The story goes that the insurance on the boat was due to expire the day after the storm, so it was not a total loss to the owner. All that remains are some sections of frames and a keel, some of the wood is blackened from flames.

Saltery Bay

The government dock is to the right of the two ferry slips about a hundred feet. It has two floats with 270 m. of moorage space. There is garbage, parking and power, but no water. The dock is used each morning and afternoon by the folks who commute by boat to the Hardy Island Sea Farms, a large employer of local workers across the channel. Besides the ferry dock at Saltery Bay there is a telephone booth a block or so up the road, and a fast food place. There are no other facilities. The ferry shuttles between Earls Cove and Saltery Bay, and is actually part of the Highway system that continues north to Lund. It's about a 15-mile drive from Saltery Bay to Westview.

To the right of the dock is a log skid and a booming ground. The area has several nice pebbly beaches. If it were not for the fact that the area is open to winds from Malaspina Inlet, there would be good anchorage in the cove to the west. A small drying reef lies south of the ferry docks, behind it is a tideflat. A small stream leads down into the beach and tideflat.

Highway 101 runs along the shoreline here, ending at the ferry dock. There is a

The Saltery Bay public boat wharf is adjacent to the ferry landing.

small strip of public land south of Saltery Bay, **Saltery Bay Provincial Park.** It is primarily for visitors who come by car. Another strip of land forms a second part of the Park where it leads to a boat launching ramp. There are nice beaches to the east of the ramp. Some summer homes line the beach.

Thunder Bay

It's next, on the mainland shore. The area along the peninsula and along the south head of the bay has many summer homes, but the shoreline between the two heads is forested and there are no houses. The preferred area for overnighting is in the small cove on the south shore because, as you can see from the chart on page 2, the bottom is a 'fur piece' down in the main body. You can find depths of 9.4 m. just off the tideflats. There is a rock which bares at a 2.4 m. tide close to shore on the western side of this cove, known as Maud Cove.

Now, let's apply some logic to the anatomy of Thunder Bay. If the water in the center of the area is from 60 to 30 m. what does that mean? Right! The wind drives the seas into the bay from Jervis Inlet. So...if northeasterlies are forecast you are going to be looking into the face of some brisk breezes. Now...it's not so apparent, but nevertheless true, that winds from the Southwest can kick spray in your face. This is because there is a saddle in the peninsula that invites winds from Malaspina Strait to whistle through it. The bottom is good for holding, so you may have a rough night, but probably be pretty safe. If you are on one of those rag-driven boats, you may want to put up some kind of steadying sail to keep the snout into the wind. All in all, Thunder Bay is aptly named.

Backtracking a Little

Notice that we are temporarily ignoring one of the most inviting of all the anchorages on the Sunshine Coast; Blind Bay. That's because we're going to skip back to our starting place at Fearney Point and continue northwesterly along the shores of Nelson Island.

This is for you folks who opted not to go up and expose yourselves to the glories of Chatterbox Falls and decided to beeline it for Desolation Sound.

There is a white rectangle on **Fearney Point** saying 'sport fishing boundary'.

The long shallow bight west of Fearney Point has a number of little coves with shallow water, but even though it has some attractive coves, would not offer anchorage except on a short-term basis. It is too open to winds from the southwest up Malaspina Strait.

Quarry Bay

There are no names on the points at the entrance to Quarry Bay. Names would be very valuable. They are definite navigation points. We have seen so many points that have no real navigation value but have been named by surveyors, that this seems a serious oversight. It makes you want to create handy names for them, like maybe: 'Amos Point' and 'Andy Point.' These shorelines have been marked off in subdivided areas by developers and you can see the parcel- numbers. The granite rock faces along this shore are spectacular. Rock stratas angle up and down along the face and in places are parallel to the water line in terraces. At places it looks like the shoreline has been paved with pink marble.

Quarry Bay has some intimidating features. The entrance to it is quite fair, however. One of the problems is the fact that there are submarine telephone cables in the inlet and you cannot anchor over them.

There are three coves in Quarry Bay, one west, one center and one east. The eastern bay is the largest but it has the greatest number of hazards. The right side on entering is loaded with rocks and you need to exercise great care in finding an anchorage. Rocks which flank the entrance have been marked with private signals. The one to the right is a rod about 6 feet tall and it has a streamer on it. The quarry from which this bay derives its name is in this lobe. The granite faces which provided the rock have been covered with trees and shrubs. The center cove looks quite attractive until you get close and discover that it is quite narrow and is studded with rocks in the widest part. At the entrance, the house has a yellow road sign with a picture of a man holding a flag. The western cove offers no particular problems. The depths are not unusual. The house on the point has a very commanding view out over Malaspina Strait. It also has a small dock for kicker boats.

Sadly, one realizes that Quarry Bay will shortly be almost lost as a stopping point for transient boaters. The shoreline will all be private and since all land above the high tide mark can be signed 'No Trespassing', boaters will have to free-anchor because they cannot go shore to secure stern lines. They will swing on the hook, looking into the residents' rock-strewn front yards.

Anchoring in Quarry Bay has another problem. The bottom is rock and shale. If your hook gets caught in an underwater crevice, it may not be easy to recover. We suggest that boaters put a trip line on their anchors so they can be lifted straight upwards, freeing their flukes.

The western cove is the best bet for moorage. There is a pebbled beach near a house in this area. The rocks on the western side of Quarry Bay are close to shore and should cause no problems. They should be visible at all tide levels except unusually high ones.

Quarry Bay

Jo says: Quarry Bay in 1988 was a **deja vu** trip for me. But I won't go back again—the lovely spot we first visited in 1965 is not the same.

Back then—'in the good old days'— Quarry Bay was everything we wanted in a moorage: it was isolated, it was beautiful, it offered protection from weather, and the many rocks shown on the charts scared off most other boaters.

If you look closely at a chart, you will see a tiny dot representing an islet way back in the far eastern cove. We anchored by that dot and looked with awe at the gigantic, closed down granite quarry on the northeastern shore of the bay. In fact, we climbed through the bush and trees and over the granite and the old abandoned machines. The kids made up fantastic stories about the quarry itself. And we wondered about the quarry's early history.

We found one small, apparently abandoned, cabin back in another finger off 'our' bay. Other than that we were alone. We hiked up overgrown logging trails to the lake above the bay.

But now there are homes and cabins and signs showing subdivisions and the ambiance is no longer there. There are other people around. And I guess that's progress. It probably wouldn't have bothered me if I hadn't seen it in its pristine beauty nearly 25 years ago.

Now, a little more about that islet back in there. It was really just a very large rock outcropping, with a small tree or two and a sparse blade of grass or two embedded in a tiny bit of dirt. But it was a wonderful islet. We dived from its high rocks, swam around it, lay in the sun on it to dry off, ate on it, read books on it—it became our outdoor living room.

We even brought our boat cat over so he could stretch his legs and prowl. Possibly then he would stop tearing the sail cover to bits with his claws. But he really didn't like it. He wanted no part of the sailboat or the rock—he wanted to be HOME. A boat cat he wasn't. And he proved it one day when he disappeared from the islet. He was gone, and the only way he could have left us was by swimming. We had a family 'emergency alert' and we all swam ashore to find the cat. The younger, more agile family members climbed a steep cliff and we could hear them hollering and calling to each other as they beat through the brush for the cat. And finally the triumphant shout: "I've got him!"

Then despair. "He clawed me and he's gone!"

More searching, more shouting. In about five minutes two small boys appeared at the top of a cliff. They were both trying to hold onto a snarling, struggling, wild-looking wet cat. Even from a distance we could see bloody scratches, torn clothes and dirty knees. They helped each other carry the miserable cat down the cliff and we rowed him right back out to the **Sea Witch,** dumped him unceremoniously into the cockpit and began repairing hurt flesh on the boys. The cat sat on the cabin top glaring at all of us in his imperious way, washing his fur, daring us to scold him for his attempt to run away.

"Next time he swims ashore, he lives on Nelson Island forever," I said. The statement went unchallenged.

Granite cliffs abound on the western shore of Nelson Island.

The big cove west of Quarry Bay is dominated by the gravel pit and its giant conveyor structure. The beaches here are pebbled and very attractive. It would be nice to drop the hook in this area and comb the driftwood beaches in nice weather. This area is named **Fleetwood Gravel** on the charts. There is a small unnamed islet and some reefs off this shoreline.

Don't worry about **Acland Rock.** It never gets shallower than 7.9 m. Might be a good place to jig for cod, though.

Cape Cockburn Light is on the shore 15.2 m. above high tide; it's a circular white tower banded red at the top. It flashes white three times. There is another light a few hundred yards N. of this one which flashes yellow and marks the entry of the underwater B.C. Hydro cables.

Cape Cockburn was called 'Skwalt' by the Indians. In *The Nelson Island Story*, Karen Southern quotes Sechelt legend: "A renegade band somewhere up the coast where native peoples had come into contact with liquor and guns, raided this spot and killed many villagers."

Cape Cockburn was named after Admiral Sir George Cockburn, who entered the service of Her Majesty in 1781 when he was 9—yes 9! He was famous for trashing Washington D.C. in the Revolutionary War and for ferrying Napoleon to St. Helena. He would not be particularly flattered by having this point named after him. It's just a granite cliff with a few scruffy trees.

Just outside Cockburn Bay, there are a number of rocky islets with trees. It would be possible to pass behind the largest of these islands and the Nelson I. shore, which is the route of the telephone cable.

Cockburn Bay. Standing just outside this bay, we decided to skip it. And we think you should, too. The *Coast Pilot* warns that it should be entered only at high tide, and with help from an aborigine. Apparently the only thing it has going for it is the fact that B.C. Hydro brought a submarine power line in there.

There are a couple of unnamed islets between Cockburn Bay and Strawberry Islet.

Strawberry Islet is undeveloped and not particularly remarkable.

You can go either side of it if you like.

So, let's hop over to **Billings Bay** and check it out. The entrance is clear. There is a float with a metal shed at the point where the B.C. Hydro lines come ashore. The house is orange and white and probably belongs to the power company. There is no sign forbidding tie-ups. We have overnighted there. It used to be public and was the Billings Bay Wharf where the steamers serving the coast tied up until steamer service quit a few decades ago.

Billings is the outer body leading to **Hidden Basin**. The name is very appropriate. The entrance is almost completely blocked at all low tides by an islet right in its center. If you decide to enter it, we advise you do it at a high slack water. When there is a change in tide, the current flows through these small passages at a high rate Overfalls can be seen and boats don't climb hills easily. We didn't take the *Sea Witch* in there! So we're going to quote from the *Small Craft Guide.* So if you get hung up, you can bawl out the *Canadian Hydrographic Service:*

Hidden Basin, east of Billings Bay, has an islet in the centre of its entrance that is 30 m. high. The channel north of the islet dries and is encumbered (love that verb!)

by boulders that dry at 3.4 m. The entrance channel south of the islet has boulders in it that dry at 3 m. The south passage is preferred, and should be entered only at or near high water slack; local knowledge is necessary. (If that's the case, then why give us all this advice, huh?) A drying spit, 0.2 mile east of the abovementioned islet, extends from the north shore and considerably narrows the entrance channel in this locality. There are several drving rocks close off the south and east shores of the basin, inside the 10 m. contour line. Anchorage may be obtained in 10 to 15 m. at the northeast end of Hidden Basin. (And when you get in there, guess what you find—a couple of aquaculture layouts!)

Now, if you still want to go in, would you do us a favor and call us and let us watch?

Incidentally, you can hike over from Ballet Bay and look into Hidden Basin.

Hidden Basin Baby

In case you're considering going into Hidden Basin, consider the story of the young couple who lived there in the late 1940s. They were expecting a baby which they planned to have delivered at St. Mary's Hospital in Pender Harbour. They figured they could outwit the six hour wait for high slack and leave the bay in plenty of time to have the baby.

However, babies have their own arrival time, and of course this one decided to come between slack tides. The prospective mother was carried through the trail to Billings Bay and to a waiting boat, which sped off to the hospital in Pender Harbour. This baby girl was determined to set her own schedule and was born in the boat before the family could get to St. Mary's.

The new grandparents, who lived in England, had been concerned about just such an arrival way out in the 'remote wilderness'. They heard about the birth of their granddaughter after the story had been picked up by a Vancouver radio station, which passed it on to the CBC national news, which in turn passed it on to the BBC and broadcast the birth all over England.

Maynard Head has a rock just outboard. This rock has a six foot rod marker in it.

Now, let's check out a favorite anchorage for Americans and a favourite anchorage for Canadians. (How's that for fancy footwork?)

We'll devote a whole chapter to Blind Bay and Ballet Bay.

Outgoing tide at Hidden Basin—no time to try to enter—or leave.

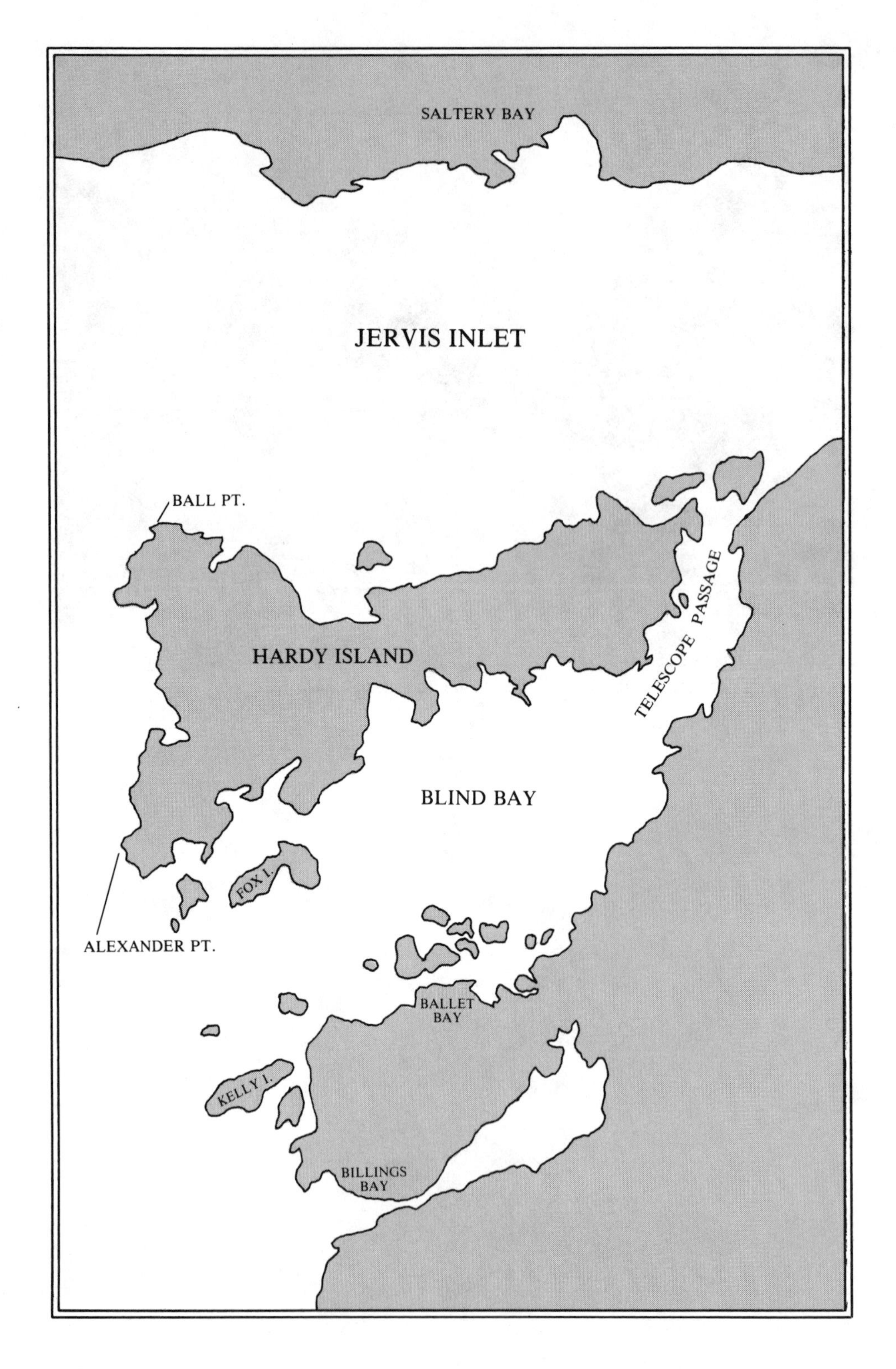
SALTERY BAY
JERVIS INLET
BALL PT.
HARDY ISLAND
TELESCOPE PASSAGE
BLIND BAY
FOX I.
ALEXANDER PT.
BALLET BAY
KELLY I.
BILLINGS BAY

Chapter 7

Between Nelson and Fox Island

Blind Bay

One of the great boons to boaters in this area is the fact that there are three—-count 'em, *three*—charts which cover it. In the big chart book, #3312, chart #2; in the folder of strip charts #3311, sheet #4; or on the big Loran chart of the Strait of Georgia, #3512. This was also something of a nuisance for us—we used all three charts and made penciled notes on all of them and had to spend hours trying to decode all of the information.

This is a treasure trove for gunkholers. There are no public facilities and much of the shoreline is privately owned, but it offers good protection against most of the winds that lash this Jervis Inlet area. It comprises all of the coves and inlets that lie between **Hardy Island** and the shores of Nelson Island on the Malaspina Strait—or western—side, and Telescope Passage entrance on the Jervis Inlet—or northern—side. There are several smaller islands and islets on the perimeter and a few more sandwiched in between the two flanking islands. The popular Ballet Bay is hidden inside Blind Bay.

Kelly Island, which is connected to Nelson Island by a spit at low tides, stands just off the southwest entrance to Blind Bay. It's quite a big island, rocky and forested. A telephone cable lies in the muck behind it. Incidentally, the island was for sale when we studied it on passing. If you want some scenic and rugged real estate you might find it an attractive prospect, if it's still for sale when you see it. There is a little shack or shed, about twice the size of an outsize privy, on the seaward shore of Kelly. It must have a fantastic view down Malaspina Strait. Although the chart shows a rock in the little crevice, we saw a boat anchored near the shore between the northern end of Kelly Island and the islet a few hundred yards to the north, called **Nocturne Island**—so you could drop the hook in this spot outside of the main area of Blind Bay. Nocturne Island is called **'Cod Island'** by the locals. Nocturne is named only on Chart #3512—on the other two charts it has only the number 43 which stands for its elevation.

The southern and southwestern end of Kelly Island have rock faces of granite—in fact Kelly was originally named 'Granite Island.' The island was quarried for the granite during World War II which was used instead of marble, because of its beauty. You can still see blocks of rock that have been stacked onshore ready for shipping.

Looking northwest from Nelson Island across Blind Bay and its bays and islands toward Hardy Island with Texada in the distance. Ballet Bay is at the far left.

Take it for Granite

Granite from Nelson, Hardy and Kelly Islands seems to turn up in most major cities along the coast, and no doubt you've seen buildings made of it or walked on streets paved with the stones and didn't even realize it.

Quarrying the high quality rock began in the 1890s and continued into the early 1960s. It was big business. You can still see the cliffs and remains of quarry operations in Quarry Bay and Deadman's Cove and near Billings Bay on Nelson Island, on Kelly Island (originally called 'Granite Island'), and Fox Island off Hardy Island.

In Victoria, Nelson Island granite was used in the Parliament buildings when they were built in 1917, the sea wall and the Bank of Montreal building. The base of all the better buildings on the coast were constructed of the strong stone, and in Vancouver it was used in the Post Office, Merchants Bank, Bank of Commerce, the Court House, the Hudson Bay Building and the Credit Foncier Building. Statues were made of Nelson Island granite at Convent, Sacred Heart, Point Grey; Harding Memorial, Stanley Park, and in Victoria, Vancouver, Chilliwack, Nanaimo, Kamloops, Calgary, Boise, Idaho and McMinnville, Oregon.

The Federal Buildings in Seattle were built of Nelson Island granite. Cobble streets were made with blocks from Granite Island and Fox Island. The Dominion government drydock at Esquimalt and the UBC buildings at Point Gray also used Fox

There are two areas: one has pink granite and the other has white granite. The white cliffs sparkle in the sun and look like marble.

There are actually two entrances to Blind Bay. The one off Malaspina Strait lies between Kelly Island and **Alexander Point.** The second entrance is through Telescope Passage at the north.

We'll start at the west end and work through the bay. Just northwest of Kelly there are two unnamed dry islets which are equally spaced at the entrance. Residents call them 'Seal Rocks' because they are a rookery. In the summer you may see as many as 100 seals lounging around there. The local folks aren't too happy with the seals. They say that the herring have all been seined out of Blind Bay and so the seals are eating their own weight in fish daily. There is no bounty on the furry mammals. As a result they are increasing and eating all the local fish.

You can pass between these rocks, but most boaters prefer to go around the northernmost one. To the right of the entrance, you will see Nocturne Island, and at the left, **Fox Island.**

There is an arrowhead-shaped islet between Fox Island and **Alexander Point.** A small dry rock stands at its tip. On the southeast face of the arrowhead island, you will see a modern-day pictograph which might amuse you. Alexander Point has a

Granite outcropping on the west side of the island.

Island stone, and the U.S. took much of it for monuments.

Next time you're walking along a cobble street, take a look and see if it might be granite—maybe it's from one of these quarries in the Nelson Island region.

Modern day pictographs.

rock which appears to be the head of Mayan Indian. It is close to the water at median tides.

One of the least-known and most secluded of anchorages in Blind Bay is in the northwest corner behind Fox Island. The shorelands are owned by the Hardy Island Sea Farms which have large installations in Blind Bay, but the land has been left unimproved by the company so that boaters can find a private place to drop the hook and go ashore. The passage around Fox Island is fair. The best entrance to this anchorage is from the southwest. After passing the southern corner of Fox Island, you will find a little hook between an unnamed island and a bay with two coves. There is room for a couple of boats tucked back in behind the hook. The cove to the left is in the shape of a hammer-head on the chart. The other looks like a forefinger. The hammer-head cove is primitive and uninhabited. The southwest shore does not have a dolphin, as indicated by the chart. The wide spot has a depth of about 10 m. Free anchorage for several boats would be possible in this cove. There are some pebbled beaches. There is a trail from the cove through an old orchard to a salt water swimming pool on the outside of the island. This is an ideal gunkhole.

The 'forefinger' inlet has a shallow entrance—3 m. at medium tide—and is also shallow at the end. The center of the area is rather deep. At the entrance there is a rock quarry from which cobblestones were garnered for many of the streets in Vancouver. There is a booming area at the end of it. The inlet looks directly out into the entrance and would be somewhat vulnerable to winds from the south.

There is an islet in the passage between Fox Island and Hardy Island with a small house. The passage is fairly wide and fair, with a depth of about 5 m. at middle tide levels. Just remember, always avoid kelp in narrow passages, just in case it is growing from lurking underwater rocks.

Looking at the geography of the southern side of Blind Bay, we find the entrance to Ballet Bay.

There is a reef between Nocturne Island and Nelson Island, which is an important hazard. There is 1.3 m. of water over it at high tide and it is often not noticed by boaters who want to pass to the right of the island. The reef can be missed by staying close to the east shore of the islet—or by going around the outside.

Ballet Bay

Let's get you into Ballet Bay. The entrance is the route of the B.C. Tel cable. The strip-chart, #3311 Sheet 4, is pretty vague about depths—even more so than Page 2 of #3312. The water (on the charts) is colored blue, which usually indicates very shallow water. The only notations of depth are 1.2 m. and 2.1 m. When we entered at a mid-tide the depth never was less than 14 m. We talked to other boaters who were anchored in the bay and they agreed there was no problem with depth.

The strip-chart we mentioned may be best for this area, although we disagreed slightly about it and decided Page 2 was equally good—and it has the advantage of showing you Telescope Passage besides. You can see that if you follow the route of the B.C. Tel submerged cable, you should have no problems. There is a funnel-shaped introduction created by two islets which stand on drying reefs off **Clio Island**. This island is not named on the charts, although you can tell it is Clio by the numeral '66' on the chart which stands for the elevation. However, it has a sign on it with its name prominently displayed. Follow Clio's southern shoreline until you

In Blind Bay you can see every kind of sea transportation from kayaks to seaplanes.

You can hike to the head of Hidden Basin from Ballet Bay.

Ballet Bay and Hidden Basin

Well, Ballet Bay doesn't exactly look like Swan Lake, so we had to ask a few questions about the name. And the answer was very simple, so we'll share it with you. Harry and Midge Thomas lived in Ballet Bay with their daughter Audree. Audree became a professional ballerina. That couldn't have been easier!

The story of Hidden Basin's name is quite different.

Back in the early days, Hidden Basin was called Billings Bay, same as outside, or 'Billingsgate'. Novelist Bertrand Sinclair stayed for a while with the Hammond family who used to live there, and used the area as a locale for a novel dealing with Chinese smugglers. He named the area and his book, **Hidden Bay.**

His hostess, May Hammond, petitioned the B.C. government to grant that name to the bay and it was done. Sinclair supposedly received an advance on his novel in 1915, but it was never published. However, the novel **Hidden Places** was published in 1919, with the story set in Toba Inlet. The charts of course call the lagoon 'Hidden Basin,' but early islanders still call it 'Hidden Bay'.

Now since you know all this about the names of these two bays, we'll tell you how to walk between them. First of all, check your chart so you don't go the wrong direction the way we did the first time. Then basically, follow the trail which is pretty easy, but seems to take longer than you think it will. For a half mile it goes up over a small hill or two, in the forest all the time. Then you pass by a benchmark set in a little rock wall and suddenly you pop out into Hidden Basin. It's a pretty walk, not terrible exciting, but kind of nice and gentle.

Occasionally you do see a couple of larger boats in Hidden Basin, but they have to enter at high slack water by keeping close to the right hand shore. Back in the 1930s there was a lot more activity in Hidden Bay. There were a couple of guest lodges in the basin then.

There was View Point Lodge at the head of the bay, and Otto Heilkennin's (Captain Henry) Lodge and the Hidden Bay Ranch Resort. They weren't thriving, but they were there.

come to a point on the Nelson Island shore. Off this point is a drying rock which should be visible at all tides less than 3 m. The time to be wary is if the tide is **higher** than that—then the rock is hidden. So now make a right turn and you are in Ballet Bay.

The favorite spot for anchoring is in the mushroom-shaped cove at the southeast corner. On the strip chart, and in Page #2 of #3312, it is the area adjacent to the label 'Ballet Bay.' The hook at the northwest corner of the entrance has a nice house on it and there is a good-sized dock inside the hook.

Depths close inshore are shallow but the area is ideal for stern-tying. Several boats can swing free in the center of the bay and a half-dozen or so can land-tie without crowding. The water is usually fine for swimming.

The shores are not populated and seem relatively untouched.

There is a path leading from the southeastern end of the bay to northern fingers in Hidden Basin. We hiked the trail.

The painted-cloud sunsets from Ballet Bay are famous.

And when the time comes to finally leave Ballet Bay, it is possible to proceed northeast if you're **very** careful. Do not attempt to go between Clio Island and the four unnamed islets just northeast of it. They look like scattered pieces of a jigsaw puzzle on the chart and there are shallow spits and reefs connecting them—with some aquaculture nets thrown in for good measure. One exit can be made by staying close to the northeast shore of the last islet, which is called **Duffy Island** by the homeowners. Go very slowly, preferably on a rising tide. Since one of us is a chicken we often test out new, shallow, scary routes by paddling through them in the kayak first and using a lead line.

Another exit is possible. Those two little islands closest to the Nelson shore—Duffy is north of **Camille**—are separated from an island with a '13' on it (on the strip chart)—called **Partington Island** locally. You can go through that passage. The locals have thoughtfully put bleach bottles on a number of rocks which help considerably. If you decide to take either of these iffy exits from Ballet Bay, you would be best off to do it during a rising high tide and post someone in the bow to look for rocks.

There are a couple of charming sights on Duffy Island. On the northern point of it you will see the remains of an old kitchen stove which was placed there as a practical joke by neighbors. The Duffys promptly put up a sign which dubbed the spot 'Hot Point'. In the summer on the northeast side of Duffy Island near the float you may encounter a buxom blonde mermaid. She sits on the rock with a Mona Lisa smile and does her siren thing. She's inflatable. You may also see a floating plastic alligator with a toothy smile. Its fangs and eyes are painted with fluorescent paint and they glow in the dark. Duffys have a great sense of humor.

There is a home near Duffy Island that at one time was a float house owned by one of Nelson Island's many 'characters'. The story is that the man had a fairly fast boat. In the black of night he would sneak up to log booms, ram the chains and steal logs.

The Nelson Island shoreline of Blind Bay has a number of rocks and hazards, particularly just north of Ballet Bay. There are no peninsulas to offer protection for anchorage.

The Hardy Island shore has several potentially useful coves, but unfortunately,

'Hot Point' on Duffy Island.

The Mona Lisa mermaid on Duffy Island.

Hardy Island Sea Farms, a very large fish farm, has occupied them. The triangular bay between two points which are marked as having dolphins and pilings, is called locally **Big Bay.** The next one is called **Fuel Tank Bay** because when the company bought the property they found large storage tanks from the logging company which had been there previously.

Hardy Island Sea Farms is the company which we mentioned before, the one that set aside some natural area for boaters up behind Fox Island. They are very public-relations conscious and welcome visits from pleasure-boaters. They will be glad to share their local knowledge with you.

On the same shore, behind a sharp peninsula, there is a shallow area with several islets. We have seen boats stern-tied in there.

There is a very active logging camp on the Nelson Island shore as indicated on the charts. You can see the denuded hillside above Blind Bay. Take note of the drying rock on a shoal just north of the log skid. There are oyster strings located shoreward just beyond this rock.

Blind Bay narrows at the northeast end and a narrow passage leads back to Jervis inlet—**Telescope Passage**. This channel is not as threatening as it looks on the chart. (Best chart now is page 2 of #3312, or if you're daring, use #3512.)

Generally, follow the Nelson Island shore as you head out of Blind Bay. Then swing over toward Hardy near the northern point to avoid several rocks at the edge of a reef on the Nelson side. At one point you will see a small fishing cabin on a small islet in the middle of Blind Bay. Then come back over near Nelson Island. Off the northern tip of Hardy Island you will see two islands with shoals connecting them to Hardy. They are covered at high tide so don't mistake them for the pass—stay close to Nelson. In the narrow part of the peninsula on Hardy, there is a Christmas Tree Farm. Chart #3312, page 2, shows two rocks in the passage on the west side. They are exposed at most tides. At the very end of Telescope Passage there is a dome-shaped island which appears as a tiny dot. It is called **'Beehive Island.'** Keep it to port as you exit. We went though at low tide and never had less than 8 m.

Now if you happen to want to come into Telescope Pass from Jervis Inlet, it's pretty easy to find if you're going west from Vanguard Bay—it's simply the first pass you'll find. But if you're going east along Hardy Island, it could be easy to slip into the wrong slot and possibly run aground. So here's our advice: when proceeding east along Hardy look for the big brown house on the northernmost island in the string. It is connected with a smaller island and Hardy by a drying spit. The island is unnamed but the chart shows it is 70 metres high. It would be prudent to go around the small conical island that stands in the entrance, **Beehive Island.**

On the north side of Hardy I., on the Jervis Inlet shore, there are more extensive aquaculture pens, which are also part of Hardy Sea Farms. There would be little shelter in any of the small coves that are not occupied, however.

We think there should be one big fish pen up at the NW corner of Hardy I. It could have a big sign reading '**Ball Point** Pen.'

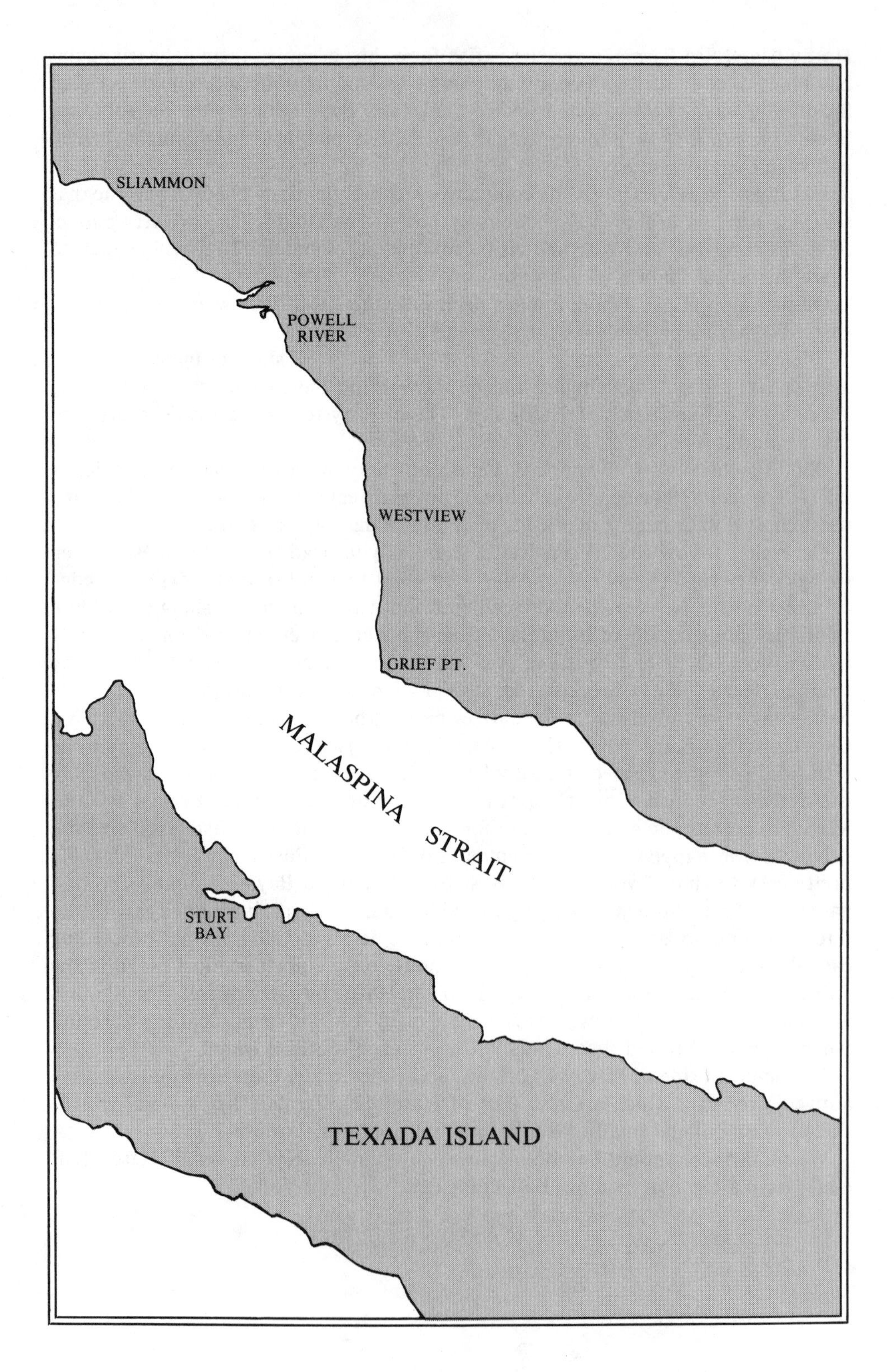
SLIAMMON
POWELL RIVER
WESTVIEW
GRIEF PT.
MALASPINA STRAIT
STURT BAY
TEXADA ISLAND

Chapter 8

Cortes Bay

The Run Up Malaspina

We'll pick you up at the west end of Jervis Inlet and accompany you up to the great boaters' playground, Desolation Sound.

You'll notice that the big chart book #3312 sort of abandons you until you get up beyond Lund. You'll need the folder of strip charts #3311. But they're more convenient to handle than the big book, anyhow. As a matter of fact, we got frustrated trying to wield that cumbersome book in the small cabin of the *Sea Witch* and tore out all of the pages and rolled them up separately. Naturally, they promptly all got out of sequence and the one we wanted was always the last one we unrolled. If you're neat and orderly, you may be more satisfied with the thing all bound.

The strip chart you want is #4 in folder #3311. It will be your guide up capricious and often malicious **Malaspina Strait**. We'll start at Thunder Bay and look at all the features on the Strait up to Grief Point.

Rounding **Thunder Point** you will see some nice summer homes on the shore in Thunder Bay. During the summer weather, they leave small boats out on moorage floats, but there aren't any safe spots, except for temporary anchorage in calm weather.

Evenden Point doesn't even rate a mention in the *Coast Pilot.* We just note it here to show you we're on the ball.

Now, **Scotch Fir Point** is significant. It was named by Captain Vancouver on the 20th of June in 1792. He got his first glimpse of the trees since he left the British Isles, he said. It was the end of an exploration he made in a yawl and launch, all the way from Birch Bay in Washington state. He decided it was worthwhile to bring the big ships this far and he went back to get them. We scanned the shore with binoculars, but couldn't pick out any trees that looked different from the old firs we've always seen. Maybe they've been chopped down.

This point is the junction between Jervis Inlet and Malaspina Strait. It's weatherbeaten and has a rocky face and above it, a thick forest of firs and other evergreens. There is a triangular fishing boundary marker on it. The B.C. Hydro lines come ashore there, but we didn't see where they emerged because we were offshore due to some brisk winds and moderate seas. The phrase 'moderate seas' is old mariner's terminology for 'ornery chop.'

Al bails out the kayak, finally getting most of the water out.

The 'Sea Witch' versus Moby Dick

You are going to think the **Sea Witch** had an altercation with a great white whale. Well, almost, but not quite, although it felt like it at the time.

We had waited for hours to leave the Westview/Powell River government wharf and head down the Strait of Georgia to Blind Bay on Nelson Island. We were on our way back home to Friday Harbor after a couple of months up north researching for this book.

It was a bright and stormy day. There was a doozy of a northwest gale blowing. Even though we had a sailboat capable of handling the storm, we really didn't relish the pounding we and the boat would take—and the computer and printer and everythine else aboard that were sort of precious. Besides, we've done that sort of thing enough that we no longer have to prove we can handle it. We enjoy 'comfortable' sails that leave us exhilarated rather than exhausted.

We kept checking the seas to figure out when we could depart. All we could see out through the breakwater entrance was a panorama of white scud flying off the tops of breaking waves, that usually means winds of 25 to 30 knots. Gorgeous sunshine and blue skies, though. No other boats were leaving or entering the harbor, which gave a pretty good indication of weather conditions. Even inside the breakwater we were bouncing around and the wind was whistling through the rigging.

The forecast was for the winds to drop in the afternoon and pick up again in the evening. All we needed was four hours of relatively decent weather.

Around noon it began to ease off and we decided to check out.

"Piece of cake," we said, as we raised the full main and genoa in light airs on a lumpy sea. The whitecaps were gone. For about an hour or more we ran wing and wing down the Strait.

We kept a nervous eye astern, watching the seas and other boats, the sky, and the kayak. We tow our double Easy Rider for use as a shore boat. It was dancing over the waves at the end of a long yellow polypro line. Another line trailed out behind it with a small fender tied to it—a drogue to keep it from overtaking us in a following sea.

After a bit we were aware the wind had shifted from dead astern to our starboard quarter and was beginning to build. The Strait was showing some whitecaps once again. We dropped the whisker pole and pulled the genny out on the port side.

When we were about nine miles from our destination in Blind Bay, we decided we really didn't need the genny any more—we were getting overpowered. We dropped it, secured it to the foredeck, and continued a little more comfortably.

But the backward glances were disconcerting. Everywhere behind us steep waves were building at an alarming pace. The Strait was now covered with white-caps whose tops were blowing off.

"Look back," said Al above the sound of the wind and waves. "Isn't that charming? The kayak is playing porpoise, diving and sliding sideways down the waves." Usually it followed us a little more sedately.

But at that point there wasn't too much time to admire the kayak. We badly needed a reef. We just had way too much sail up for this building gale.

Reef we did.

Just as we got the reefed tied in, we looked back and were momentarily panicked: the kayak had flipped over! All we could see was the pale gray hull slashing its way through the waves, the little black rudder like a tiny tailfin at the stern.

Over the noise of the wind and the waves Al yelled, "Not to worry—it can float just as well upside down as right side up."

But then another problem caught our attention. The genny had decided it didn't like being on the foredeck and had slipped its secure lines and

Note how stress on the shackle, left, pulled it wide open.

flopped over the side. We now had a forward sea anchor and an overturned kayak.

We were rapidly approaching Scotch Fir Point, a notorious confluence of Jervis Inlet and the Strait of Georgia, where currents and winds and waves can be downright mean. With luck we could get across Jervis and into Blind Bay.

I held onto the tiller and Al crawled forward to secure the wild sail. We were smashing into the waves, getting him soaked to the skin. "It's got to be blowing at least 35 or 40 knots," he yelled when he got back to the cockpit.

We looked back again. The kayak had righted itself. For an instant we breathed easier. Then we realized that the blue covers on both the cockpit compartments were gone! Those two big holes were open to the sea.

As Al attempted to pull the kayak in, it flipped once again. We watched as it rolled over—almost in slow motion. And then, in horror, it not only went over, but down...and down.

The line was so long that the kayak was able to go at least six feet under water. The taut polypro line didn't break, but now the weight of our inadvertent sea anchor had nearly stopped us dead in the water. The waves were pounding us like we were stranded on a beach. We couldn't pull the kayak in. Again it was rolling and playing like a porpoise—only this time an underwater one. And it was no longer 'cute,' it was downright scary. It would swing sideways and then straighten itself out, but it wouldn't surface.

My mind flashed on the fact that yes, indeed, I had paid the insurance, because I was sure we were going to lose the kayak—fast. And we might have to cut the line. We couldn't keep going towing the thing in this kind of a storm.

"Just cut it free!" I yelled to Al over the noise. "I can't keep sailing in this mess!"

"Not yet!" he yelled back. "Let's try and get someplace so we can take care of this."

By now the safest course was not all the way across Jervis to Blind Bay, but instead to turn up Jervis and head into Thunder Bay where we knew we could find some shelter.

We slowly made our way through breaking seas around Scotch Fir, Evenden and Thunder Points. The wind eased as we headed up and into Thunder Bay. We dropped the sail, anchored, and pulled the poor gray kayak up alongside. The darn thing was still upside down, with only an inch or so of its keel out of the water. And it wouldn't roll over, no matter how hard we tried.

We couldn't lift it on deck as it now weighed well over a thousand pounds. After a half hour of struggling we finally coaxed it right side up. We leaned over the side, and began bailing for all we were worth. A half hour later it was floating high.

We checked the damage. The tiny eye riveted on the bow of the kayak, to which we fastened a towing line, was secure. But the brass snap shackle on the end of the tow line itself had pulled apart and come free of the kayak. It was only because of a second safety line tied to the kayak that we hadn't lost it.

Then we saw that everything we had stored inside had washed out. This included the spray skirts, extra kayak covers, beach sandals, and at least a dozen beer cans worth a nickel apiece!

The next day we heard from several fishermen and towboat skippers that the winds during the gale had been upwards of 50 knots.

During the rest of the trip we covered the kayak cockpit compartments with plastic garbage bags tied down with bungee cords. And we never again allowed the kayak to play at the end of a long tether. We kept it snugged up really short—and we had no more trouble.

We realized that even if we had had a conventional dinghy, it would have been in trouble. It wouldn't have looked like a small white whale was following us, though.

You can see the Stillwater Bay hydroelectric plant tower for miles as you head northwest along Malaspina Strait.

At this point, sniff the air. According to Nelson Islanders, if you can smell a pulp mill the wind is out of the west and is coming down from Powell River. This is a worthwhile indicator, because here at the corner of Jervis and Malaspina the winds are crotchety.

Don't worry about **Neville Rock**, it's down there 7.3 m. at least. **Western Rock,** which is off McRae Islet, is 3 m. deep.

McRae Cove

It looks like it would provide shelter from most winds. It is protected by some islets and it has very practical depths: 3 m. at low water in the center and about 1 m. at the shoreline. The *Small Craft Guide* says that "local knowledge is required" to enter the cove, which is named for an early settler. The islets at the entrance string out in a southerly direction and are connected by shoals. There is another big islet off the east entrance. The channel looks fairly straightforward. The big hassle over entering would come if there was a storm in the Strait. It could be very hairy negotiating that narrow passage if the seas are trying to get in there along with you.

McRae Islet is a stony little spine of rocks not far offshore extending in a W. to E. direction. Boats fish the reefs in that area.

Frolander Bay: The shoreline is all built up and has a great number of both summer and permanent homes. It has a nice long curving beach.

The hydroelectric plant in **Stillwater Bay** has a tall white tower, 190 feet high which is a Surge Tank. There is a wide swath cut in the trees from the reservoir lake on the top down to the power plant at the water's edge. Giant culverts lead the waters down to the turbines; they are underground. On the surface, connecting the surge tower and the power plant, you will see a pipeline which must be 3 feet in diameter.

There is another community located along the beach just west of the power plant. There is a dock with a stiffleg crane and booming grounds just east of the power plant.

The delta formed by the Lois River has an Indian Reserve.

Across the Strait, on the Texada Island shore, there are few reference points or indents. **Northeast Point** has a light on a tower on shore 30 feet above the water. It flashes white. There is a windpower rig that maintains it. High on the mountain ridge to the SW you will see a microwave tower on Mt. Pocahontas.

Northeast Bay is a small cove with an islet occupying most of the space. The low islet is surrounded by reefs. It could be a refuge if you got caught on that shore in a storm, but you'd have to be very careful about anchoring to avoid the reefs on shore as well as from the islet. The creek that you see emptying into Northeast Bay is named Russ Creek and it comes down from tiny Russ Lake in the Texada bluffs.

On the mainland shore, **Lang Bay** has a dock which is marked 'public' on the chart. It has no float. It is a fuel-dock for the power plant. There are four big valves at the end of the dock, and sets of dolphins to moor big boats. The beaches are sandy and very pleasant in this bay, and there is quite a community here. At the West end of Lang Bay, near Kelly Point, a long riprap breakwater protects a tideflat where logs are boomed.

Kelly Point has a lot of rocks offshore. They are charted and conspicuous. The beach is a favorite spot for vacationers and residents. The summer community continues along **Brew Bay** which has very attractive beaches. In nice weather you might want to put down a hook, dinghy in and go for a swim.

Albion Point has a shoal that extends out over a quarter mile into the Strait. Much of it would be covered at high water and might pose some danger to boaters who come inshore there to look at the sumptuous homes. Albion Pt. is called **Black Point** by the Nelson Islanders. It has a mom-and-pop store where they go by car to get ice and some grocery items. Typical conversation:

Nelsonite #1: I'm gonna run over to Saltery and go buy some groceries.

Nelsonite #2: Goin' to B.P.?

Nelsonite #3: Naw. I think I'll run in to P.R.

Translation: He ain't goin' to Black Point, he's goin' to Powell River.

Pocahontas Bay on Texada Island is one of those places we wouldn't anchor in for an Onassis dowry. The *Small Craft Guide* says it's okay in case of an emergency and the wind is from the SE. The creek that exits into the flat in front of the old pilings and dolphins is called 'Whiskey Still Creek'. Any guesses as to how it got its name?

How about Rumbottle Creek which drops into **Raven Bay?** That's the beginning of a quarrying area that extends up Texada for a couple of miles. There are loading facilities for marble in this bay.

Back on the mainland side from Albion Point to **Myrtle Point** the shoreline loses its gentle beaches. There are a couple of marine railways in front of homes on the beach along here. **Myrtle Rocks** is at the end of Myrtle Creek and the little community is called 'Myrtle Point'. Myrtle Rocks are rocky outcroppings surrounded by reefs. We'd avoid the whole shebang. The piles that are mentioned in the chart are nothing but bare dolphins. At one time they were holding a loading dock for the steamers.

Back in the 'teens, there was a big wharf at Myrtle Point where a rail line for a logging company ended. By 1919 the rail line was 20 miles long and the firm had 40 log cars and a couple of engines. The logging operation moved out in 1925.

On the Texada Island side at this point you will see some extensive quarries and gravel pits. They extend from a shallow bight called **Spratt Bay** to **Butterfly Point.** There is another giant quarry west of Butterfly Pt. which looks like a super amphitheater with long terraces that look like seats and intersecting ramps.

We didn't investigate **Vananda Cove** and **Sturt Bay** and now we wish we had. It is a fascinating place to see from a distance. One thing about it is that it is so uncharacteristic of Texada Island. All the Eastern extent of this island is primitive and rugged. Here, however, at this deep cleft in the shore there appears to be a small city built up around the quarries. There is even a dock for the 'Texada Boat Club.' We've been told that there isn't a lot to offer visiting boaters. The community has a grade school, one store, one restaurant. As we mentioned, we didn't get to Texada Island, so if you want to learn more about this area, you should read the section in *Northwest Boat Travel,* p.148.

As you near the Marina at Grief Point, you will see the long rock breakwater and a big sign, made up of 2x2s saying 'MARINA'. It's actually Beach Gardens Marina. You can see why they wouldn't want to name it after the point nearby: Grief Pt. This area was once the site of an Indian village with a commanding view of the Strait of Georgia. A farmer plowing his fields in the area found many artifacts, including spearheads, arrowheads and skulls.

There are two long riprap breakwaters and a narrow entrance between them. The marina offers overnight moorage and there is no charge for short visits. They have fuel, ice, water and bait on the dock. There are showers and a pool for visiting

Beach Gardens Marina near Grief Point—sometimes a haven for storm tossed sailors.

Young mooring attendants are ready to help you dock at Westview.

boaters. Off premises sale of beer and wine is permitted. There is a grocery store about a 5-minute walk away. They do not accept reservations for moorage.

Grief Point has a big red and white tower in somebody's front yard. Lots of homes nearby. As you round Grief Pt., suddenly you see the whole Powell River complex. In the distance, the towering stacks are pouring out smoke and fumes. It comes as something of a shock to see a big manufacturing spread after looking at so much pristine area.

Some of the hottest fishing grounds in this area are the waters off the tip of Texada Island at **Grise Point** and on **Alan Bank** and **Oswald Bank**.

We are now at the harbor of an honest-to-goodness city—Powell River.

For boaters, though, the best facilities are found in a suburb of the city called 'Westview', southeast of Powell River. It is about a mile-and-a-half from the mill area.

Westview

It's the tourist hub of Powell River. The government dock is divided into two sections by the ferry ramp. The boats go to Comox and Texada Island. The north docks are primarily commercial. The transient moorage is at the south floats, which you enter between two beacons. Above the marina you will see a number of large storage tanks. There are very helpful young attendants during the summer who meet you as you enter and tell you where to moor. The fingers near the shoreline are filled with fishing boats. There is 850 metres of berthage. Water and power are available on the docks—the AC is 20 amps and requires a 20 amp plug. Other facilities are garbage bins, telephone booths, a derrick and a grid. Fuel and ice are available at the gas dock. At the head of the ramp, there is a fish market which offers sea food and ice at good prices. A half block away, there is a laundromat, showers, public restrooms and convenience store. The 'Infocentre' is right there also, and the attendants will give you the latest scoop on which stores are open, which are closed, what has changed, etc.

There are several shopping centers in Westview, with full service supermarkets. And of course there are banks, gift shops, doctors, drug stores, a liquor store, churches, restaurants, a library, historical museum, tennis courts, recreational complex and all kinds of repair-type shops if your boat chooses to break down.

Ours chose to. Our alternator chose a bad alternative—to put out zero amps. Of course, like everything on a sailboat engine, it was located in a place where human hands could not reach it. Nonetheless, we did get it off and hitchhiked up to a motor repair shop. A couple of very helpful and friendly guys checked it out thoroughly. Then they handed it back to us with a provocative question: had we checked the tension on the belt? The rest of this story is too embarrassing to tell.

'The Tankerman's Friend'

A guy who runs a small tanker around the harbor is called a 'Tankerman.' Back in the bad old days, he could spill diesel or lube oil in the water and not give a rip. What the heck, he could say, the fish ain't locked in hereabouts. If they don't like the taste of the water, let 'em 'vote with their feet' as a great American philosopher recently said.

Nowadays, fuel dock operators as well as tankermen are very much concerned about oil spills. As a matter of fact, we recently were given a specially impregnated paper towel at a gas dock to wipe up spills instead of washing them out the scuppers.

For years now, skippers and fuel dock operators have been using that good old washing standby, JOY, to break up oil spills and gunky bilges. A couple of squirts of the lemon-scented detergent can work wonders. It's called 'The Tanker man's Friend.' Environmentalists are not all that charmed with the idea of folks getting rid of oil sheen in the water with detergents. But then they **are** a bit fussy-fussy, picky-picky.

As long as we're on the subject of household chemicals on boats, here are a couple more.

Buy extra cans of GOOP—you know, the hand cleaner. They don't have it in Canada. They have a substitute that isn't as good, we think. GOOP is great for all kinds of cleanup jobs, not just hand cleaning.

A by-gosh miracle chemical can make the pump for your head work like it's brand new. It's Wesson Oil, or one of its substitutes. A half cup of any, even cheap, cooking oil dumped in the bowl and pumped through will make the leathers and working parts of the pump seem new again. (We got this idea from a book by Bruce Bingham called **A Sailor's Sketchbook.** You should have a copy in your seagoing library.)

Most everything is within walking distance of a couple of miles. One of the shopping centers offers a van pickup at the dock. If you choose to go to the other shopping center, you can catch a cab back to the marina.

If you have time and want to stay an extra day, you can go and take the tour of the gigantic Powell River Pulp Mill. Good thing to do if you're weathered in.

Westview is also the terminal for the ferry to Texada Island and to Comox-Courtenay on the Vancouver Island side.

One further tip: listen to the weather forecasts before leaving the shelter of Westview. Even if the seas are not particularly spicy just in front of the marina, they might be raising Hell above and below the area. Talk to incoming boaters. Spend a little extra time resting and stocking up and wait for good weather. You might not get into trouble out into Malaspina but you could get buffeted around a lot and not find any good place to duck into for miles.

Thunder Bay was the place to stop and 'rescue' our deepdiving kayak.

The Wharfinger Biz

First of all, they're no longer called 'Wharfingers.' That's a shame! It's such a wonderful Old-Englishy title. Now they're called 'Harbour Managers'. Used to be they usually didn't show up to collect moorage. Now they do, even in out-of-the-way docks. Furthermore, the fees are steeper nowadays. They're in line with privately owned docks. Instead of being great, friendly, folksy people, they are becoming more business like. In short, the public docks in Canada are like some of the ones in our Washington State Marine Parks. Visiting boaters often wonder about whether the wharfingers are public service employees or independent contractors.

So here's the skinny. We take the information directly from a copy of the 'Harbour Manager's Manual' put out by the Department of Fisheries and Oceans. Incidentally, the word 'ocean' means something different in Canada than the U.S. 'Oceans' are generally any salt-water body. If you take the ferry from Heriot Bay on Quadra to Whaletown on Cortes, you are crossing an 'ocean.'

Now, you can brag that you are all 'Ocean' Sailors!

According to an act of Parliament in 1978, the Harbour Managers are responsible 'for the operation of the harbour and associated activities.'

The manual points out that the public is to be regarded as 'business clients'. They are told to be 'courteous' and receptive to 'adverse comments or criticisms'. Instructions are to be given in 'the form of a request and a reason...'

They are responsible for, among other things, '(d) accounting for and collection of the charges for berthage, wharfage and utilities...(e) allocating berthing in accordance with berthing policy. (i) ensuring that users dispose of trash and used oil in the containers provided and that the facilities are kept clear of personal property, spare gear, etc. (j) supervising the garbage contractor and such other local contractors as may be employed.'

In some of the ports we have visited the poor old Harbour Manager is going to have a tough time doing (i) and (j) because there are no 'containers.'

Here are the priorities in berthing: (a) commercial fishing vessels; (b) other commercial vessels; and (c) pleasure craft. The rule book says space is allocated on a 'first-come, first-served' basis and no vessel can 'lay claim' to any particular berth. (In reality, you will find 'reserved' signs on many docks.)

Docks can be assigned as 'Commercial' and 'Pleasure Craft.' The manual says, 'However, no active vessel is to be turned away if berthing space is available, regardless of signs. That is to say, a pleasure craft must not be denied a berth at a space designated for fishing vessels if that space, and no other, is available.'

As a fact of life, these Wharfingers are residents of small communities and they have close friends and ties with the fishermen and if they think a gillnetter might be back some night, they will not be likely to give away his favorite spot. Who can blame them?

More rules: 'A vessel must be prepared to berth alongside another vessel or to have one berthed alongside it. Each vessel shall provide fenders. No person shall hinder the free unencumbered passage across the deck of a vessel which has another vessel alongside it.'

And: 'No vessel is permitted to leave a dinghy secured to its outboard side or to leave anything projecting which will prevent another vessel from berthing alongside.'

The rules say that you can't cast off a rafted-up boat without giving notice to the owner or master, except in case of emergency. If you have to move a boat away from alongside in order to get away from the dock and the master is not available, you are responsible for resecuring the boat and adjusting the fenders.

The fee for pleasure boats is set by law at $1.05 per metre per night. There is an additional charge for electricity, of course.

OK, OK, you want to know how much these dudes get in pay, don't you? It's a combination of pay and commission. The bigger and more complicated the job, the higher the pay scale. We don't know just what the range of this is. The commission is as follows:

90% of the first $2,000

80% of the next $2,000

70% of the next $2,000 and so on down to 40% of the next $2,000.

So if the Manager collects $12,000, he gets $7,800 of it.

Now do you still wonder why they have become a bit eager?

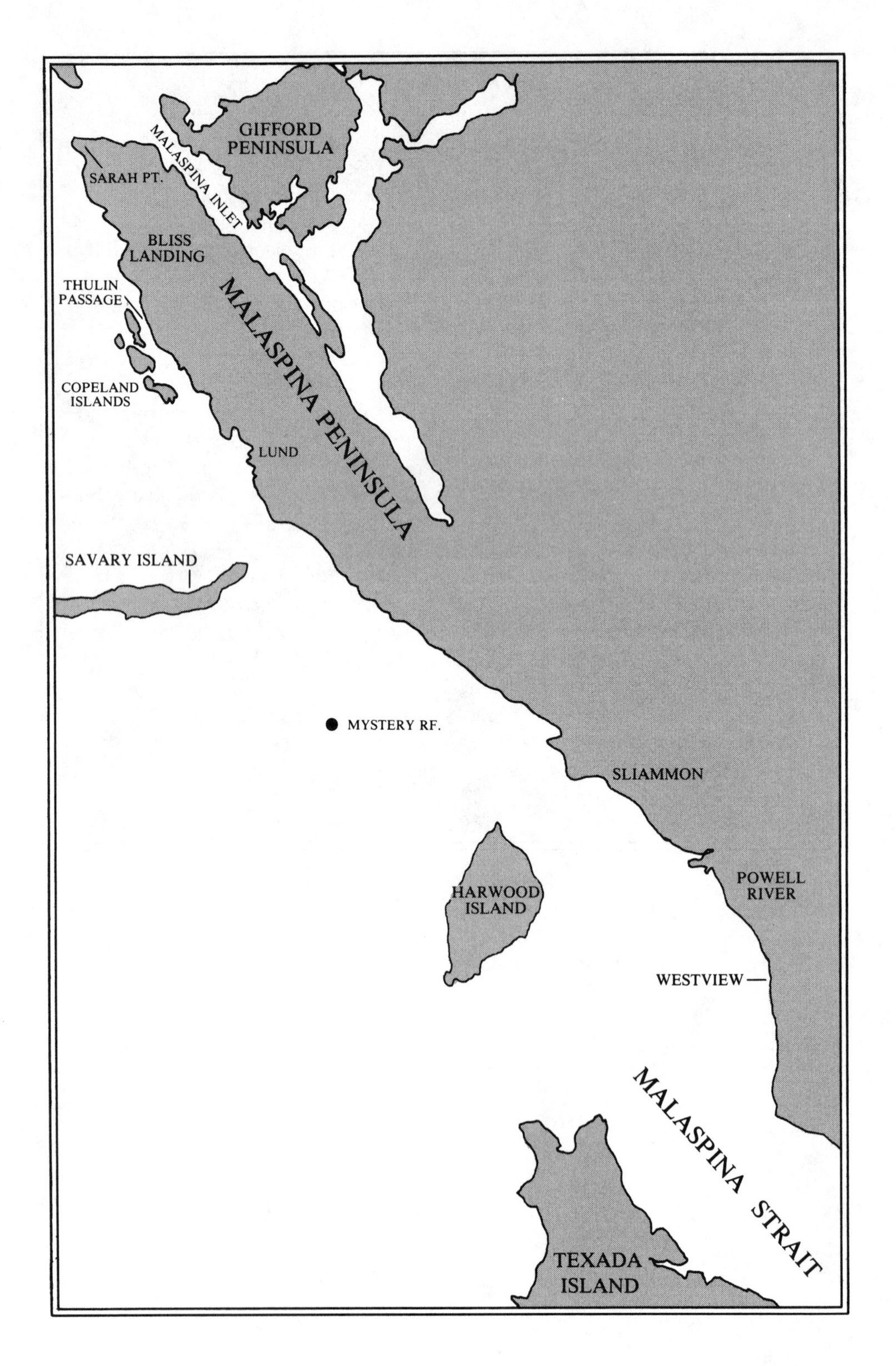
GIFFORD PENINSULA
MALASPINA INLET
SARAH PT.
BLISS LANDING
THULIN PASSAGE
MALASPINA PENINSULA
COPELAND ISLANDS
LUND
SAVARY ISLAND
MYSTERY RF.
SLIAMMON
HARWOOD ISLAND
POWELL RIVER
WESTVIEW
MALASPINA STRAIT
TEXADA ISLAND

Chapter 9

Thulin Pass

Now, On to Desolation

Got all your shopping done? Didn't forget to buy a large bottle of JOY did you? If you're going to bathe in the saltwater, it's the only thing that'll suds up. Of course, it leaves you smelling like a veterinary clinic, but that's the lesser evil. How about clothes-pins? If your on-board clothes dryer is not working efficiently, you're going to need them. Dry cells and film are also out of sight, fiscally speaking, in the stores up yonder.

Mosquito-chaser, too. In damp weather, those little hummers—and the deer- flies and no-see'ums—will reduce you to bony sections.

Thanks A Heap, Pandora!

You read that story about the Greek chick, Pandora, didn't you? In high school. Remember, she was the twit who some Olympian God gave a hope chest to and she wasn't supposed to peek inside. And she did. And all kinds of woefulnesses came down.

You know what was in that box? I'll tell you what was in that box: members of the genus **Culcidae**

MOSQUITOES!

That's what came out of that danged box—Mosquitoes!

Now, nobody knows how many of them were in there to begin with, but however many of them there were, they must have been hellbent to breed in the open air, because there's got to be at least a couple of googols of them now.

And that means that at least one googol is female. Females, you know, are the ones that bite and make lumps that itch.

And every one of those airborne hypodermics are out to get yours truly, Al Cummings!

Up in Desolation Sound, I was bitten by two of them that had Nova Scotia license plates!

So I have made a study of how to do battle with those mini-vampires. I swallowed about a gross of Vitamin B pills on the rumor that they might make me somehow less appetizing to them. It didn't work. I ate onions and garlic until the E.P.A. had an alert out on me—no dice. I practically bathed in repellent lotions, but they would make bombing runs over square yards of coated epidermis until they found one tiny spot I had missed and zappo! They opened a blood bank!

Got some plastic hardware cloth and made screens for the door and the portholes. They used tiny crowbars to pry the cloth away from the wood and crawl in.

I burned mosquito-repellent candles and coils until I couldn't find my way to the head through the clouds. They installed tiny radar sets.

A sympathetic friend, impelled by my wails and moans, bought me an electronic mosquito-banisher. It came from a company of Yuppie Outdoor Rec experts. It consisted of a plastic box the size of a cigarette lighter. It had a small dry cell which fed a solid state circuit. The result was a faint tinny rattling sound. A brochure came with the device. It said that this contrivance was the product of New Age Technology, The sound being emitted was identical to that made by dragon-flies. Dragon-flies, said the sheet, were the predators most feared by mosquitoes. The little wretches would not come within a dozen feet of it, supposedly.

After offering profuse terms of gratitude to my benefactor, I scurried back to the boat. Night was approaching. Squadrons of female insects were being briefed for the night's bombing runs. I climbed into the bunk on the **Sea Witch** and hung the little purring packet right over my head. Somehow I had found new faith—modern science would come to my rescue. I turned out the light and waited. I could hear the comforting ratcheting of the tiny speaker.

Did it work?

Sure it worked. It was a perfect homing beacon for every vengeful female mosquito from Ballet Bay to the Everglades!

I have only one hope left. How much would it cost to buy a used astronaut suit?

Charts, next. You're going to want strip chart #3311 and book #3312. If you have an old #3594, it's a treasure—gives you the 'big picture' of the whole area. You can get the same coverage, at twice the detail, by buying both #3538 and #3541. #3555 and #3559 are also goodies, they are blowups of some of the coves.

Let's hope the forecast holds good. The rest of Malaspina Strait can get awfully lumpy. Westerlies are no longer deflected by Texada I. And by the time you meet those whiteys which have come up the long fetch of the Georgia Strait from the

Weather Predicting

A friend of ours in Blind Bay who is an ex-airline pilot, gave us a bit of weather forecasting information.

"Watch the jets that fly overhead on a clear day. Look at their contrails. If those trails began to disperse quickly and get all fuzzy, it will rain within 36 hours."

We asked, "Why is that?"

"Damned if I know!"

It's like an Indian we know who always could predict when the upcoming winter was going to be severe. He watched the cords of firewood put in by the White Eyes. If they put in a lot of wood, the winter was going to be very cold.

One man told us that his mother always said:

"Never tap the barometer. It makes it rain."

SE, you're talking full-fledged, veteran bumpers. The three offshore islands between Powell River and the Copeland Islands have no hidey-holes.

(Come to think of it, don't read the above paragraphs to your crew. Maybe we should perforate around it so you can tear it out and hide it in your pocket.)

All right, enough of that 'bon voyage' jazz. Let's 'git on up thar!

We're still on Page 5 of #3311, remember.

As you leave Powell River you pass the mill section, where you will notice that the complex is divided into two areas. The one nearest the shore has massive concrete factory buildings and a very high stack, painted red and white and black. There is another area away from the shore which has a cluster of buildings and several smaller stacks. Just south of the plant, there is a small community of workers' homes. The semi-circular breakwater at the mill is formed by ten massive old ships chained together and anchored to huge concrete blocks 150 feet below the 'hulks.'

About two-and-a-half miles west of the mill you come to the **Sliammon Indian Reserve**. You will see a church above the shore facing out over the Strait. The Sliammon Band also have a fish hatchery up on Sliammon Creek. They are very serious about fish propagation.

Sliammon Church

You can't miss that pretty little white church in Sliammon as you sail up the coast from Powell River. It's a landmark—and for more than one reason. You can, of course, see it from your boat and then you know for sure you're off the Sliammon Indian Village.

If you chance to have powerful binoculars, you will notice there is a statue of Christ at the base of the bell tower. He is holding out his hands to welcome worshippers. Okay?

Well, back on Easter Day in 1918 a devastating fire raged from Powell River almost to Lund. Everything in its path burned to the ground, including the Sliammon Church. Everything, that is, except the statue. It remained intact, a trifle scorched, but nonetheless THERE—as opposed to everything around it.

The church was rebuilt, and the statue placed back in its rightful spot. You can almost see it from your boat. A little bit of a miracle?

Farewell to Powell River and its paper mill.

Harwood Island is also an Indian Reserve. There are no public docks or facilities. People from Powell River occasionally go over to the beaches on the island for a day cruise. The beaches are apparently open to everyone. Locals say that **Church Reef** near Harwood lines up with the Sliammon Church.

Scuttle Bay—now there's an inviting name!—is not mentioned in the 1984 *Coast Pilot.* It is apparently of no value to the traveling boater. It would offer no protection in winds from either the NW or the SE. It also goes totally dry at low tides.

Atrevida Reef is a good place to avoid. It is at the outer edge of a shoal extending a third of a mile from the mainland. The rocks peek out at 1.2 m. It is marked by a red buoy, 'Q26'.

Notice now, on the charts, that the shoal from Savary I. extends in an easterly direction about 3 miles from its northern point. **Mystery Reef** is not so mysterious but it is not so easily seen at high tides. It is a cluster of boulders that dry at low tides. It is marked by a flashing green buoy marked 'Q25' and has a radar reflector. This shoal is covered with a good crop of kelp and is a favorite fishing spot for the pros. Come to think of it, Mystery Reef could be a murder mystery in a storm and bad visibility. Our advice: avoid it!

Dinner Rock is a big barren dome-shaped rock. It is clearly evident at all tides. It would pose a hazard only in fog or darkness. You could pass between the rock and the mainland if it were important. It probably got its name from local fishermen. There is a public park just opposite Dinner Rock for land tourists.

The Dinner Rock Disaster

Dinner Rock is a rather nothing piece of real estate sitting out there in Georgia Strait just before you get to Lund. It's just rock and grass and stuff. But it was the scene of a dreadful boating tragedy.

In October 1947 the steamer **Gulf Stream** grounded on the rock during a storm. It ran up on the rock and the stern stayed under water. Five persons were in the stern and they all died as they were trapped and could not be reached. The steamer later slid off the rock and into the depths.

Savary Island

This is a residential area. The beaches are famous for their fine sand and beauty. It is supposed to look like a South Sea island. It does, somewhat, when you look at its northern shore. There is a public dock in **Keefer Bay**, with only 9 m. of moorage and a derrick. We have anchored off the beach and swam there. The water is warm and the beach sandy, but it feels very public to us, and we wouldn't want to anchor overnight because of the winds that spring up. There is a daily water taxi from Lund to Savary from June through September. The Royal Savary Hotel was built on the island in 1926.

When you get there, if you have some spare time, you may want to go ashore and hunt for the buried treasure. According to Beth Hill's book *Upcoast Summers,* there

The Great Transformer

Captain Vancouver named Savary Island In June of 1792 when he was on his voyage of discovery in the Northwest. He said, "About five in the evening we passed between the main and an island lying in an east and west direction, which I named Savary's Island, about two leagues long, and about half a league broad...On the south side of Savary's island were numberless sunken rocks, nearly half a league from its shores, visible I believe only at low water."

The Indians had a different name for this island, and a much more descriptive one. They called it the **'Ayhus'** which was a double headed serpent. Kennedy and Bouchard, historians, point out that from the air, it **does** look like a two headed snake. The legend says that The Great Transformer found a two-headed snake which was trying to get back to its cave on Hurtado Pt. and changed it into an island.

was a trading post on the island in 1870. It was owned by a successful storekeeper, Jack Green. He was murdered by two men who knew he was rich—they had seen him with a big bundle of money. They were caught and hanged, but the murderers swore they never found the loot. So, it may be buried on the island some where. We don't know just where his store was, though.

Mace Point off Savary's eastern tip consists mostly of low rocks and rubbled shoals.

Hurtado Point on the mainland is not very prominent or important. Its only claim to note is the fact that it is the northwest boundary of the Powell River Harbour Authority. Sports fishermen mooch along its steep shores.

Lund

Here is a real bona fide community—not a town, a community. It's population in 1981 consisted of 140 souls, assuming they all *had* souls.

Lund is famous for several things: it is the beginning/end of Highway 101 which goes all the way to/from Chile; it is the site of the famous Breakwater Inn Resort which was built by the Thulin brothers in 1895; it has a lot to offer the boater who needs last-minute supplies or repairs.

Lund Hotel was first built in 1891—what a wonderful structure.

Lund Hotel

The glorious Lund Hotel, originally built by the Thulin brothers in 1891 and which has survived several burnings, served more than just dinner and liquor at the bar. It served as a 'holding tank' for those who imbibed a bit much and couldn't hold their liquor.

Back in the days before the highway from the south reached Lund, there was no way for the Mounties to reach Lund to get their man except by steam launch. So locals handled their own problems. Any man deemed by the bartender to have 'overimbibed' was locked up under the hotel in a small room. The next morning he was released and sent on his not-so-merry way.

A little more trivia: the Lund Hotel is reputed to have the longest bar of any establishment in B.C. (That's only a rumor—we haven't had time to check out all the other bars.)

The new Lund floating breakwater—gone are the oil barrels.

There is a brand new floating concrete breakwater at the public wharf. You can enter by going around either end. Well, it was new in 1988. Gone are the floating barrels. It has 417 m. of berthage, there is garbage collection, water on the dock, lights and available power, and a boat launching ramp. There is a tiny wharfinger's office on the ramp leading up to shore.

The store was built in 1902 and burned in 1957. It was rebuilt and then updated in 1987-88. It is enlarged and filled with much more stuff. There is a big produce section with fresh fruits and vegetables. There is fresh ice cream and they make a good cone. We saw plenty of canned, frozen and packaged foods. The sign at the doorway to the liquor agency says: "Due to the rise of the 'hand being quicker', please wait for the clerk to get the liquor." There is someone on duty at all times to deliver CPR to Americans who first encounter the price of booze in B.C. An antique and gift shop adjoins the store. Of course there is the wonderful old hotel and restaurant, laundromat, showers, post office, boat rental and Esso gas dock. There is also a well-stocked marine repair shop with most necessary items for maintenance and repair of boats. (We know—we needed some things.)

Finn Cove

It was, at one time. a bustling community, with a sawmill, store, and boat building business. **Sevilla Island** in the cove is connected to the mainland by a drying shoal. Some anchorage is possible in the bay. It has a public dock with 98 m. of tieup space mostly used by fishing boats, and no amenities—such as being connected to the land.

The cove a half-mile west of Finn Cove has fish pens in it. A shoreside road-end has been blasted in the rock for logging operation at one time. A tiny island is offshore. It has vegetation on top and is listed as 7 meters high at datum. You can pass inside this small islet, if you allow for the rock off the east entrance to the cove. There is no anchorage because of the oyster strings.

Thulin Passage: It's a high-traffic narrow highway, 450 feet wide at its narrowest point. A lot of fishboats, tugs and monster powerboats ply the area day and night. In years gone by, it was narrowed even more by log booms, but there haven't been many tied up there in recent times.

Copeland Islands Marine Park

These islands are sometimes called the 'Ragged Islands'. There are three islands of roughly equal size in a line from east to west. A fourth, smaller, island is separated

Lund History

We visited with a couple of women who had lived in Lund/Finn Cove/Sevilla Island all their lives—a fascinating experience for us. So we'll tell you some of the things they told us.

Charles Thulin arrived in Lund in 1884, with brother Fred coming two years later. They named the area Lund after the University city near Lund, Sweden, where they were born. In 1895 they opened the Malaspina Hotel, with the first hotel licence north of Vancouver. Fred purchased a 160-acre homestead from Charles Sisil and later pre-empted an adjoining 160 acres.

It had the second post office north of Vancouver, the other being at Gibsons Landing. The brothers also began the settlement at Campbell River and built the old Willows Hotel there.

The Thulins logged the area with oxen. They spread their holdings to include a store in Sliammon and one on a float in Powell River in 1901, and in 1902 built a store in Lund. Three years later the hotel burned and rebuilding began. The Thulins disposed of their oxen.

One of our informants told us that she grew up on Sevilla Island where her father, Alex North, was a boat builder. He built nine 40-foot fish boats, and had the sawmill and store. The store shut down in the 1940s. She went to school in a one-room schoolhouse in Lund. There were about 10 kids in that 'unique community' back then. There are now about 50 school-age children in the Lund area.

Lund used to generate power from a water wheel, but they always had coal oil to use, 'just in case'.

Helen Anderson's family arrived in Lund in 1907 when her dad went to work for the Thulin brothers. There were about seven families who lived on Sevilla Island, mostly fishermen. She said the mission ships would stop in at holiday time and have concerts.

from the center island by a shallow passage. Reefs and rocks associated with the Copelands extend westerly along the channel. Up until 10 or 15 years ago there were people who lived in the Ragged Islets and there used to be wild goats on the islands.

Just for the sake of description, let's name the four islands: East Copeland, Center, West and Northwest.

East Copeland has a light on its east end on Thulin Passage. It's a concrete tower 21 feet high with a flashing white light. Skippers who don't mind being sloshed around anchor in the wide cove adjacent to the shallow passage between it and Center Copeland when there are no log booms in there. It is essential to locate the two rocks in this gap visually before settling down for the night. Otherwise you might find your boat resting on top of one of them at low water, looking like a trophy on a mantelpiece. There is also a rock which dries at lowest tide right smack in the center of this entrance. On the south shore of this island there is a small gap which could be used for a stern-tie anchorage, but it would be exposed to southerly winds on the Strait.

You can squeak through the pass between the East and Center Copelands at most tides, but we would advise careful study of the chart. There is a rock off a reef which virtually blocks the pass. Keep someone on the foredeck who has good nerves and a loud voice. We have seen boats anchored in the south end of this passage.

Center Copeland has a narrow cranny on the passage we just discussed. That's its only cove. You can go around this island if you want to explore by boat. We did it in the kayak. Note the two sneaky rocks marked '+ ' on Thulin Pass near this opening.

There are lovely anchorages in the Copelands.

There is a small, rocky islet just off the east tip of West Copeland, on Thulin Pass. We saw a big sailboat anchored behind it. We asked the skipper how it was during the night. He said it was 'fine'. He was double-anchored, naturally.

A wide and relatively hazard-free cove on the Thulin Pass side of West Copeland is the main anchorage. Some rocky islets protect overnighters from the worst wash from passing boats, however, the boat stilled rocked all night long. *(A cross-cultural note: Americans call the waves created by passing boats 'wake.' Canadians call it 'wash.')* Many boaters drop the hook in little coves on the south side of this island. The entrance to the passage between Center and Southwest Copeland Islands has good depths for anchorage, but there isn't much shelter from northwesterlies. There is also anchorage in a small cove on the west side of W. Copeland, but it's pretty unprotected out there.

There is an unnamed cluster of islets about a quarter-mile northwest of the main Copelands. They are part of the Marine Park. Boats often tuck in there to spend the night. The outermost of these islets has a green-topped tower and a flashing green light.

On Thulin Passage there are four large concrete pylons and one smaller one. On shore, there are pipes sunk into the rocks for log booming.

We searched for the pictograph in Thulin Passage and finally found it. It's about 2-½ miles from Lund. It is between the second and third pylons, heading north, and can be found most easily by scanning the top rock faces in the area for the word 'QUEEN' in white letters. Now look down to find a long slanting ledge that leads into the water at high tide level. This point is just north of a lot of boat-names written on the rocks. The picto is on a little spot with a white face of rock on which the word 'ACTIVE' is printed. Right under the 'E' in the word you will see the picto; only a small portion of it has been defaced, luckily. We feel pretty sure that the guy from the boat named 'Active' was a dork who didn't know about pictographs and just thought it was more graffiti. It is maybe a hundred feet beyond the #2 pylon. It is also right across from the major anchorage in the Copelands. It might be possible, if the light were right, and you had powerful binoculars, to see the red painting from your anchored boat. Also it is right across the channel from the sign marking the Marine Park in the Copelands.

There may be the remains of another pictograph, badly faded, on the same side of the passage. It is on the first part of the rock face opposite the Copelands. Look for an arbutus tree growing out of the rocks about 10 feet above high tide mark. Now look down to find a small pocket in the rock about 18 inches high and about four feet long. We only made out some red smudges. It didn't seem possible to get ashore there to explore it further. Another tip: south of the pictograph rock faces there is a log skid of nine logs.

A shallow cove, known as 'Sharpes Bay,' just west of W. Copeland Island has a marina. It is mostly just a gas dock. A sign announces that it is open from 7 a.m. to 10 p.m. The dock house is on a barge and has a big PetroCanada sign on it. It is named the Ragged Islands Marina.

There is another marina at **Bliss Landing** in **Turner Bay**. One of the problems with this area is that power boats come up Thulin Passage at high speed and their washes are very unpleasant. The marina has two sets of docks. Most of the space is monthly moorage, but some transient space is available. There are a laundry and showers for

An "Indians and Indians" Story

"The houses in the Lund village were raised on stilts and built near the water so that the people could see whoever was approaching. During a particular raid, a couple of Lekwiltok warriors approached the village. Each wore a helmet and armour made from elk hide, so that they were well protected—only their eyes showed through the helmet. Although the Sliammon men were able to fire their bows and arrows at most of the Lekwiltok, one of them got near enough that he was able to sneak underneath a house. There, he tried to pry off one of the floor planks and set fire to it, but the Sliammon heard him in time. As the Lekwiltok warrior looked up, one of the Sliammon men took aim and fired his arrow through the warrior's eye, killing him."

(From **Sliammon Life, Sliammon Lands,** by Kennedy and Bouchard)

patrons. Just west of the Marina, a reef juts out into the opening to the Bay. Three rocks flank the west end of Turner Bay. The outermost has a red triangular marker.

At one time Bliss Landing had a school and store with a butcher shop, hardware, grocery and post office. There was even a government wharf, but it is no more. The Union Steamships landed at Bliss Landing three times a week, back in the 'good old days.' Bliss Landing now has a number of exclusive summer homes.

A cove beyond Turner Bay has some beautiful pink rocks on its shore. There are a couple of homes there.

The passage has high cliffs along the mainland shore. A very slight indent here houses oyster strings.

Finn Cove, a once bustling community, still has its share of docks and boats.

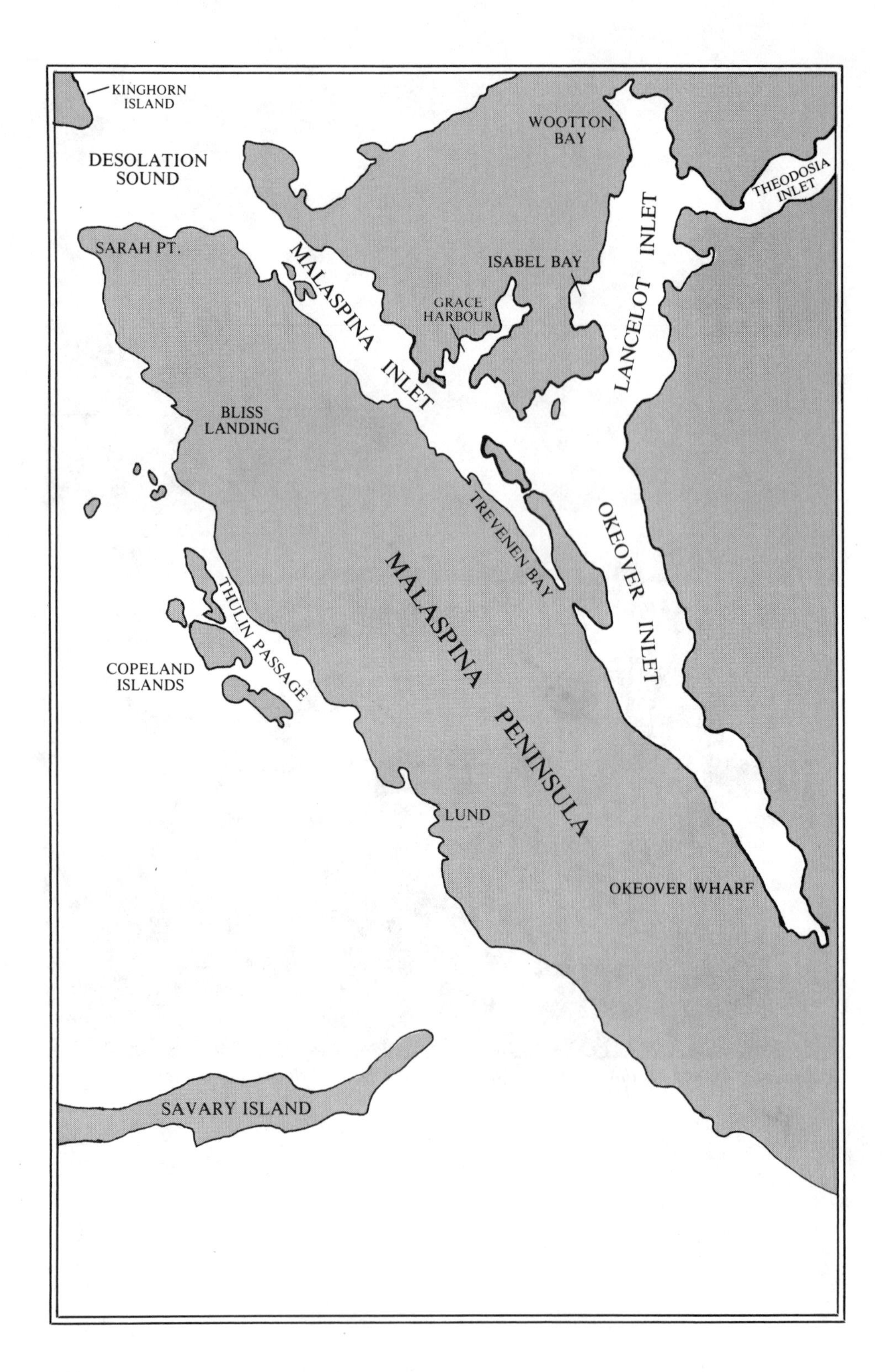
KINGHORN ISLAND
DESOLATION SOUND
WOOTTON BAY
THEODOSIA INLET
SARAH PT.
MALASPINA INLET
ISABEL BAY
GRACE HARBOUR
LANCELOT INLET
BLISS LANDING
TREVENEN BAY
OKEOVER INLET
MALASPINA PENINSULA
THULIN PASSAGE
COPELAND ISLANDS
LUND
OKEOVER WHARF
SAVARY ISLAND

Chapter 10

Grace Harbour

Desolation Sound

Malaspina Inlet Section

It may have been desolate when Captain Vancouver first saw it, but it's sure not desolate now! It's become a playground for boaters from all over Canada and the U.S.

Here's how the Englishman found it:

This (place) afforded not a single prospect that was pleasing to the eye, the smallest recreation on shore, nor animal nor vegetable food, excepting a very scant proportion of those eatables already described, and of which the adjacent country was soon exhausted, after our arrival. Nor did our exploring parties meet with a more abundant supply, whence the place obtained the name of DESOLATION SOUND...

Boy, he must have gotten up on the wrong side of the bunk that morning!

The Desolation Sound cruising area has never been defined geographically. **Desolation Sound** itself is a body of water that, more or less, is the entrance to the larger cruising area. This sound is roughly the area where Malaspina Inlet, Malaspina Strait, Homfray and Lewis Channels all join. Part of this area is Desolation Sound Marine Park. But, when boaters talk about going up to Desolation Sound, they usually mean the waters that surround the two Redonda Islands; and Sutil Channel and Baker Passage, which surround Cortes Island. Some sailors include Toba Inlet.

The government handout says that **Desolation Sound Marine Park** was "established by the government of British Columbia in 1973. The park consists of more than 14,000 acres of high land and 6,350 acres of shoreline and water, and is thus the largest marine park in B.C., as well as the only major park of any kind on the Pacific mainland coast of Canada."

The park boundary runs south down Malaspina Inlet, dips into the Malaspina

Sister Sarah

The point on the north end of the Malaspina Peninsula was named 'Sarah Point' by Captain Vancouver in June of 1792. He dubbed the point on the southeast corner of Cortes Island 'Mary Point'. Sarah and Mary were his sisters. Mapmakers decided to rename the Cortes Island spot 'Turn Point.' Later on, they relented and gave it back to the Captain's sister.

Peninsula to include the Cochrane Islands and a few dozen acres of the shoreline. Then it runs northerly up Lancelot Inlet, peeks into Theodosia Inlet, goes overland north through the Unwin Mountains to Homfray Channel. It then comes back west to include Prideaux Haven, turns southeast to take in Tenedos Bay and then follows the Gifford Peninsula shoreline back to Malaspina Inlet.

Sarah Point: Once you are here, you are standing at the front door of **Desolation Sound**. This spot is famous for its breathtaking scenery as you round the point. You see Kinghorn Island off to port, Mink Island is dead ahead, Zephine Head is to the right. There is even a little cove just around the point without any aquaculture! The high hills have young growth timber on them, meaning the place has been logged fairly recently— scarred areas are recovering. Off the eastern end of **Kinghorn Island** is a floathouse with a whole lot of fish pens.

Malaspina Inlet

It's time for chart #3559, which will give you a nice big blowup of Malaspina, Okeover, Lancelot and Theodosia Inlets. Its scale is 1:12,000 so one inch on the chart equals one-sixth miles. Chart book #3312 has more coverage of the area in several 1:10,000 scale charts. You can also use Chart #3538. It shows everything in a scale of 1:40,000, and is perfectly okay, except for some reason the cartographers have left off a lot of the names of places. For our purposes here, we're using the charts with the most names.

Malaspina heads southeast about 4 miles and then becomes Okeover Inlet, which continues another 3 miles in the same direction. At the spot where Okeover begins, the waters fork off in a due north direction about the same distance—Lancelot Inlet. Two miles up Lancelot, Theodosia Inlet branches off northeast for about a mile and a half.

Stacey Rock is off the entrance to the Malaspina Inlet. It's made up of several rocks, not more than a foot or so above the water at about mid-tide. Watch for these guys.

Myrmidon Point for all its glamourous name (one of Achilles' armies) won't show you much. There are some reefs and an islet west of it that should be avoided.

Just before Beulah Island, on the south shore, is a cove where **Hinder Creek** empties into the bay. There used to be a sawmill there, owned by a man named Parker. We called it **Hinder Cove,** because the next two coves down are loosely called **Parker Harbour.** The name doesn't appear on any of the charts, however. We found out through 'local knowledge.'

There is a small peninsula with a private dock marked on the chart, in the cove formed between northern **Beulah Island** and the peninsula. There is a dock that shows on the chart. Although it's private, a sign on the dock says 'Welcome to Parker Harbour'. There is a big home on the point and an older cabin on the beach. The beach at the end is marked as a shell fish lease. This could be excellent moorage if northwest winds didn't curl in. We called this cove 'Parker Harbour North.'

You can go down the inlet between Beulah Islands and **Josephine Islands** in a fairly straight line. Stay a little closer to Beulah in the beginning, then swing a bit toward Josephine Islands to avoid all the kelp-marked shallows. The big island southeast of Beulah Island (it is unnamed but we called it Beulah Island, also) has a sign that says 'Caution: Mariculture area, slow down and watch your wash.' The same sign appears on the Josephine Islands side.

Josephine Islands are remarkably high—50 metres—and crested and heavily wooded. For such a small island the larger of the two has a considerable rise. It's separated by a drying strip and kelp in a shallow passage from the small northern islet with just a few trees on it. It seems that the flood current runs faster close to the Beulah Island shore more than it does to the Josephine Island shore on flood. We saw about 2-½ knots of flood. We couldn't find the kelp bed indicated northwest of little sister island. We did locate shallows with our depth sounder—it read about 8 m.

The little hook almost due north of Josephine Islands and southeast of **Hare Point** looked good. But it seems to have a rocky bottom and might be difficult to get your hook in. Beyond Hare Point you can see shoals that go quite far out in the channel.

Just beyond Beulah Island is a beautiful little cove that hooks back behind the peninsula and it has a lot of shelter and room for moorage in six m.— could be ideal. We named it 'Parker Harbour South'. Happily it was not taken up by aquaculture.

If you wish you can go over to the Gifford Peninsula side of the Inlet and follow that down. Whatever, watch out for **Cavendish Rock, Cross Islet** and **Rosetta Rock.** Rosetta Rock extends out quite a ways and supposedly dries at 2.8 m., although we never have seen it no matter what the tide. There is a good healthy bed of kelp off the rock.

Thorp Islet is a tombolo, surrounded by reefs marked with kelp and lots of aquaculture. Shallows extend from Thorp Islet a considerable distance to the northwest. The shoals are all marked by kelp. The southeastern approach to this islet is blocked to some degree by oyster beds.

Neville Islet on the other side of the inlet was apparently missed by the surveyors who wrote the *Coast Pilot.* Easy to see why—it's a nothing.

Cochrane Islands

The Cochrane Islands are part of Desolation Sound Park and it looks like anchorage is quite possible behind them. However, we decided against anchoring there for several reasons: the wind would have put us on a lee shore and it was too early in the day, anyway. They consist of two islands roughly the same size with a scattering of small islets in between.

The southern entrance to the Cochrane Islands has a short oyster string just offshore but it is not intrusive. There aren't any sandy beaches back in here but it's a very pleasant place and there are some rocky beaches. The reef that extends from the island is marked by kelp. As you can see, a wind blowing down Malaspina out of the north would whistle right through here. So it is not the best of all possible anchorages unless you're in a southeast wind situation.

The waters behind the islands are divided by some reefs and rocks that block easy passage from one to the other, although it would probably be possible with care to go behind them at high water. Entering the northwest lobe you have to go quite a ways around the kelp beds in order to get back inside. Somewhat limiting the access is a string of oyster beds which come out from shore. The water is quite deep until you're into the shoals. The current floods through here at a good rate also. There is an oyster lease sign on a reef on the southwest shore on South Cochrane Island so you can't pick oysters. The reef off to the west of the southern entrance has some kelp surrounding it where it juts out from shore. There are no trees to stern-tie to although moorage is possible down in the southwest corner behind the South Island.

Between **Kakaekae Point** and **Scott Point** there is a little cove that we explored. The center is too deep for easy anchoring, but you could drop the hook farther in and stern-tie, although the winds might follow you in. The winds in this area seem to either come up or down Malaspina Inlet and then follow into each little bay. Just off Scott Point there are two tiny tombolos.

We ducked into the next bay which trends quite a ways back. It also dries at low tide. It's shaped like a reverse question mark. At the head of the bay are several logs which could either be part of an old log skid or may have been blown ashore at high tide. The water was warm and the beach wasn't too bad. There is another small bay, also too shallow for anchoring.

Grace Harbour

The Provincial Park sign on the **Jean Island** shore announces that you are now in 'Desolation Sound Marine Park'. You are in lovely Grace Harbour.

Grace Harbour is a well-protected basin about a quarter-mile across. The narrows entering the northerly inner basin are fair if you stay in the center.

Before you enter the inner basin, you will find there is good anchorage to the north of Jean Island—just watch for the shoals. On the northern shore, inside a small island, there is an old cabin on piles. It was weatherbeaten and picturesque, with an old orchard behind it and a lovely view. We peeked inside and found a couple of beds and an old stove. A small sign on the door said, 'For Rent, Grace Harbour Inn.'

This little island may be the same one that was used as a rostrum from which speakers would deliver speeches to the people of the Sliammon, Klahoose and Homalko Bands who would gather in this bay for a sort of winter carnival, a century or so ago.

The water was very warm for swimming here. There were lots of rocks around, but the cove was great for kayaking. Farther along the same shore was a nice camp-

'Grace Harbour Inn' awaits the hearty souls.

site. Two large power boats were anchored between Jean Island and the shore in plenty of water. The chart shows a drying reef at low tide, but there is a channel close to Jean Island you could maneuver at high tide.

The navigable width of the little entrance to the inner basin is about 100 feet across. Winds do funnel in through the entrance, and although it may blow a lot, there seems to be not much more than a ripple across the waters. The basin is tucked in behind forested hills with rocky shores except in the northern tiny bay where there is a small amount of beach and a campsite above it. Beyond the campsite there is an outhouse and then a trail leading to the lake beyond. The approximately half-mile trail is well marked. It goes past a few bogs and a stream from the lake to the harbour, then past an enormous tire and a few remnants of earlier logging machines. About the time you think this is a long half-mile, there is a jog to the left, marked by a wooden arrow on the ground. (Let's hope it's still there to guide you.) This little trail leads to the lake itself. In early July the lake is warm, slightly brownish, with not too much slime on the rocks. It is a wonderful place to bathe or swim. Just to the left of where you enter the lake you can see a beaver dam under the trees, a feature which keeps the lake fairly high.

Swimming is good in Grace Harbour itself, with temperatures ranging into the high 60s and low 70s late in the summer. The biggest bugaboo about this harbour is the enormous number of small, non-stinging jellyfish here: 'Jellyfish Harbour,' we call the place. It's not fun to swim among them, not because they hurt, but because they feel so awful. Powerboaters say they can't run their generators for more than a couple of hours without having to clean out the strainers because of the way the jellyfish are sucked in. You can jig for small cod in the harbor and even set your crab pot. There are signs as you enter the harbor saying that shellfish are contaminated here.

There are a couple of summer homes on **Moss Point** which is the southeastern entrance to Grace Harbour. There is also a sign that reads 'Okeover Resort—483-4682—at the top of the wharf. Fine camping, dining, tenting, also general store.' The arrow points back to the right—more on that later.

Grace Harbour is a destination for kayakers.

Did You Hear Somebody Saying 'Gloop?'

Little Burial Islet at the mouth of Trevenen Bay in Malaspina Inlet isn't named on some of the charts, but with 'local knowledge' you'll soon know what we know about it.

Seems a man bought a pig to put on the island to 'rototill' it for him. The first night it left in the middle of a storm. The theory was that 'spirits' of the dead Indians drove the pig off. They also scared the settlers out. Now if you can believe that, you might also believe another old-timer: "When the tide goes out, there is a hole in the rocks where you can hear a mysterious voice crying out, 'gloop! gloop! gloop!' It also does it when the tide comes in." There goes your neighborhood!

Isbister Islands are connected at low tides. There is a small passage between them and **Coode Island.** The middle of the three Isbisters has a white sign painted on a rock announcing the fact that it has an oyster lease. There's a big cream colored A-frame house on this second Isbister Island and it looks out over the aquaculture on the Trevenen Bay side. Indian skulls were found on these islands in the 1930s.

If you have any hopes of going down into **Trevenen Bay** and exploring, forget it. The whole bay south of Isbister Islands is cut off by nets extending nearly clear across the waterway. There is a channel between the big yellow mooring buoys at the end of the nets with a black can buoy farther on. It might be possible to pass between but we didn't see anyone to ask about them— and besides it blew us away to see the whole inlet covered with aquaculture. Maybe by now they've moved on, because they do that now and then.

Little **Burial Islet,** just opposite the Isbisters on the Malaspina Peninsula side has oyster buoys on either side. It is supposedly named 'Burial Islet' because Indians were buried there.

Lion Rock dries at low tides. It is not marked. It is on a rather indistinct line between **Edith Island** and Coode Island. It is the junction point between Malaspina, Okeover and Lancelot Inlets. We noted that at low tide Lion Rock, which is really two rocks, is marked by a gull sitting on each rock. We are not certain if these are government gulls so they might not be there when you come by. If they're gone, you can find it by looking for the kelp beds.

In **Okeover** Inlet, Coode Island is adjacent to **Coode Peninsula**. There is a narrow and shallow strip between them. An aquaculture installation fills the void. Along the northeast shores of Coode Peninsula, you will see signs proclaiming that it is oyster lease land and there are a number of oyster strings close to shore. Coode Peninsula was named after Captain Trevenen P. Coode, Royal Navy, captain of the *Sutlej*. We have the feeling that Trevenen Bay was also named for him.

Boundary Rock has a sign calling attention to 'Penrose Bay Marina'. The chart does not mark this marina. It simply shows a dock. A road from Okeover Park leads

'Cougar' Nancy has lived in Okeover Inlet most of her life.

'Cougar' Nancy

"Cougar" Nancy Crowther arrived in Okeover Inlet with her family in 1927. She's never left. We met her a couple of years ago and spent several interesting hours with her at her property as she discussed early life in the area.

About her name, of course. Yes, she admits to having killed cougars—and bears and wolves—but only if they killed livestock. She first killed a cougar when she was 14 because it attacked her. But while cougars are bad and bears worse, she said wolves are the most aggressive.

When her family first arrived, they ate only clams, as did most of the original settlers, she said. The family eventually had goats—"they were our meat and milk." They also raised chickens, apples, pears, plums, grapes, rhubarb, strawberries and other produce.

"Mother insisted we acquire phonetics and my brother and I took correspondence courses, until they needed us in the school to bring the enrollment up to ten so they could keep the school open. My parents took a course in 'how to survive in the country' because they knew the 'hungry 30s' were coming."

When we asked Nancy about the pictographs in Okeover Inlet she said, "Oh, yes, they were painted by the Larson brothers, Frankie and Eddie. Some people named Barrow were up here in their boat and when the boys heard they were hunting for pictographs they went out and painted them."

Later, we found in reading Beth Hill's book, **Upcoast Summers**, a compilation of summers of cruising by Frank and Amy Barrow in the 1930s, she writes that the Barrows had met the Crowthers—in 1933—more than 50 years before we met Nancy. At that time she was 14—and had just shot the cougar. The Barrows did go over and look at the pictograph, but they hadn't heard about the Larson Brothers. Most anthropologists tend to think the pictographs are genuine, however.

down to it. The marina has both transient and permanent moorage. The owner said that some folks take their boats to Desolation Sound, cruise a couple of weeks and then leave their boats at his dock while they fly back to the Seattle or Vancouver by float plane to catch up with their work. That accomplished, they fly back north for more cruising. He said it was cheaper than running power boats back and forth and saved a lot of time. Good point.

Okeover Public Dock

It has 72 m. of moorage and a phone booth right at the head of the ramp. It also has a derrick and offers 20 amp power—quite unusual for such a remote public dock. It adjoins Okeover Provincial Park and has a boat ramp. This is a major kayak-launching spot, with a ramp right next to the dock. Cars can drive to the park and put in their small trailered boats there—it is the farthest north road on the Sunshine Coast—an extension of Highway 101 which goes to Lund. Okeover Park has campsites and pit toilets. Take your own water. We found a little stream with only a trickle of fresh water in the park. But it's a lovely park, we camped there for a couple of weeks one time. All trees and beach and warm swimming and very few people.

Okeover Resort, which is near the dock, has a wonderful restaurant and a small store called, charmingly, the 'Mickey Mouse Store.' It offers a few staples, such as milk, butter, bread and fresh home-grown vegetables and ice, and a small number of repair items such as patches for rubber rafts. The store is managed by a woman named Youtah Heins, who is also the wharfinger. She is a very eager and helpful person who monitors channel 16 and is willing to help boaters who need emergency services. Her store also has a paperback book exchange and souvenirs, and she wants to get yacht club burgees from all over. You make her very happy if you drop off your yacht club burgee with her.

Okeover Inlet public wharf—a popular spot to launch kayaks—or to stop and have dinner at the nearby restaurant.

Now this is our idea of a houseboat.

There are pictographs across from the public dock on a sheer rock face about eight feet above high tide. They are also above a little rock ledge. They are on the right side of the rock face. Someone has done some coloring in red crayon on a rock about 3 feet above high tide line. There is also some kind of marker about 20 feet to the right of the pictograph—it is a white circle with a cross inside it.

Farther NW in the inlet, you come to a Sliammon fish pen installation where coho are raised. The workers greeted us when we hailed them from a distance and asked if we wanted to come and visit. On the shore, you will see an old shack mounted on a barge.

Oyster strings are all along the eastern shore of Okeover Inlet down to Hillingden Point, so there is no possible moorage.

Freke Anchorage, which is down at the end of Okeover Inlet is not really a small boat haven. There is no protection from winds from either direction. The Sliammon band has a small community there on the tideflats.

Hillingden Point represents the beginning of **Lancelot Inlet.** It has a sign on a juniper announcing that the area is part of an oyster lease. Another 100 yards or so from that sign is another sign mounted on a piece of yellow styrofoam.

The unnamed cove in Lancelot Inlet that is marked by the charts as having log booms has an old log skid. But it, like so many of the old logging areas, is filled with mariculture pens.

A small bight on the southeastern side of this cove offers a small area for stern-tying. You would have a spectacular view of the junction of Lancelot, Malaspina and Okeover Inlet. It would be susceptible to winds from several directions, however. Above this cove, you will see hundreds of acres of devastated timber.
timber.

Bunster Point has a small cove just south of it with a fabulous house boat. It appears to be part of another sea farm.

Thors Cove has another of the legendary names of the Lancelot Inlet. Did Thor have anything to do with the knights of the round table? Like all the other bodies of water, this one has mariculture installations—one in each wing of the cove. The end of the cove has a nice beach and some homes. The nook behind the island in Thors Cove would have been a very nice moorage but it is completely blocked off by the sea farm. But if you want to anchor in somebody's front yard, you could drop the hook at the end of the cove.

You can go between **Thynne Island** and **Bastion Point**. If you choose to do so, note the shoals on the mainland side and rocks on the island side. Thynne Island is an historical site. It was named after (according to Walbran) "Louisa, Countess of Harewood, 2nd daughter of Thomas Thynne, 2nd Marquis of Bath." On June 27th, 1792, Archibald Menzies and Capt. Vancouver "...breakfasted on a small island about the middle of it (Lancelot Inlet) wooded with Pines." Actually, the two weren't very happy as they had just returned from an unsuccessful attempt to discover whether Theodosia Inlet led to the Northwest passage.

We kayaked to the island, ate our lunch, and then looked to see if they left any royal napkin rings or ale flasks or whatnot behind. But we couldn't find any relics of their visit.

Wootton Bay

This place looks as though it might be good for anchorage but there isn't a lot of protection. It is important to note that wind can come over the Portage Cove neck at the end of the bay. Often when there is no wind at all in Okeover or Malaspina Inlets, there will be a sharp blow in the end of Lancelot. There is no protection at all as you come along the western shore of Lancelot into Wootton Bay.

One lobe of Wootton Bay is close to Portage Cove—only a few hundred yards across land. This land is privately owned, however. It has a beautiful green meadow extending down to the waterfront. There is a fence across it and NO TRESPASSING signs are posted. The owner has apparently been bothered by too many small boat owners and hikers who want to cross his land over to Portage Cove. As a matter of fact, the whole corner of Wootton Bay is posted. A little to the right of the neck is a cove where the upshore is posted. There were a couple of boats anchored in there.

An interesting note: in the center of both open spaces in the Bay, we saw light green patches in what should have been deep water. Since the area is not very attractive to boaters, we didn't explore the spots. If you intend to anchor there, you might check to see if there are any unmarked reefs in there. We talked to the owner of the property at Portage Cove and he said he didn't think there were unmarked rocks, but the light green was suspicious.

The name was given to it by Capt. Pender of the *H.M.S. Beaver* in 1863. Henry Wootton was Postmaster General of British Columbia. This bay also has an alias: it was labeled 'Brazo de Bustamente' (Bustamente Arm) by Valdes and Galiano in 1792. Josef Bustamente was captain of the *Atrevida,* a Spanish exploring vessel.

Grail Point off Susan Islets has a few altar-shaped rocks that might possibly make someone think of the 'Holy Grail' but we doubt it.

Susan Islets

They are nice little wooded rocks maybe a half-acre in size, with a reef off to the left

Senors Galiano and Valdez

Captain George Vancouver and his retinue weren't the only explorers around the area back in 1792. While Vancouver was busy charting and surveying for England, there were a couple of Spaniards out there too. At this point, both England and Spain had made claims to some of the territory, but the Spanish were later treatied out of North America north of Mexico.

Commander Dionisio Alcala Galiano, skipper of the **Sutil** and Commander Cayetano Valdes of the **Mexicana** had been sent from Mexico to complete earlier explorations of the Strait of Juan de Fuca, begun in 1790. The two met up with Vancouver on June 28, 1792, at the entrance to Toba Inlet, and began to explore together.

The English and the Spanish cooperated in many ways, both of them naming islands and channels and points. However, while they filled each other in on much of what they had found, both sides occasionally—and no doubt purposefully—left out some important facts when communicating about their discoveries.

side, as indicated in the charts. We went into the bay behind and found it could be a good anchorage if there was no southeasterly blowing. We have friends who say it's their favorite anchorage in the whole area. It appears to be the site of an old homestead. The smaller of the two Susan Islets has a rock pyramid on it, with a couple of scrubby trees. Rounding Susan Islets the water is a fairly steady 18 m. It drops abruptly to 12 m. when you pass the larger islet and then to 8 to 10 m. as we moved into the center of the area behind the islets. It was 8 m. at almost high tide. There were no surprises, the water gently shoaling to 7 m. as we approached the shoreline. There was a nice little cove that had signs on shore noting another oyster lease. We felt it would be a shame to block it off to boaters.

When you're dealing with Lancelot and Grail, obviously **Galahad Point** would be next. Except there wasn't much of a point to it, and we just kind of went by slowly as the water began to shoal up for the entrance into Theodosia.

Across the entrance to Theodosia Inlet from Susan Islets you will find another aquaculture area.

Theodosia Inlet

To the right on entering Theodosia Inlet there is a small island, actually a tombolo, which is sometimes used for picnicking and/or camping. The flats in that whole cove are pretty much occupied by oyster strings.

As you enter the inlet—going fairly fast on an incoming tide with the current, or fighting it as the case may be—you can see the kelp beds to your left. There are also long strings of kelp off the tombolo to the right. After you pass the narrows the inlet opens up to quite a wide bay with snowy peaks in background—a very pretty sight. The shorelines here are marked with aquaculture lease signs. Around the tombolo just past the entrance on the left side is a drying sandy (muddy) flat where we got oysters a couple of years ago—before the oyster lease signs were put up.

There is a log booming and sorting operation inside Theodosia on the right side. The end of the inlet seems to be undisturbed. Many places back in here look like they would make excellent moorage because the depths are proper and it looks protected. However, these are all booming grounds. While you might be able to stay there for two months without anyone bothering you, there's a possibility a tugboat skipper might decide he wants to put a boom right where you are and you might have to move. They might even roust you out in the middle of night. Chances are they wouldn't put a boom where a pleasure boater was, though. Those guys are usually pretty nice.

There's a bunkhouse area with modular buildings and an earthen dam and dock, and just beyond are pilings that are part of an old dock. A little nob far inland to the left looks like an attractive cove for moorage, however it's very shallow—4.5 m. at high tide. You could only anchor there if you were certain there would be no low tides. In effect, almost all of this reach at high tide looks like a great big bay, but it is nothing more than a giant tideflat the last two-thirds of the way in. We understand there are streams at the head suitable for kayaking or canoeing if you choose. When you get past the area of the logging camp, that is the edge of the tideflats.

Some friends of ours who were in a small sloop went ashore, met some of the loggers, the cook and nurse. They said everyone was friendly, glad to meet people, and enjoyed visiting. You can walk the logging roads after they quit work at six.

The camp is run by MacMillan Bloedel. Logging has been going on in Theodosia for years and years. Our friends also said there were far more jellyfish there than even in Grace Harbour.

Around the early 1900s Theodosia was a logging and farming community of some 5,000 persons. A logging railway was constructed in Theodosia Arm that eventually reached 31 miles, the longest railway in the Powell River area. The operation apparently closed down in the late 1930s as the marketable timber was exhausted.

Isabel Bay

We almost hesitate to tell you about this spot, it is so lovely and should only have a couple of boats in it at a time to be properly appreciated. Maybe we could work out a 'take a number' system.

Don't try to cut between **Madge Island** and the peninsula—it goes totally dry and it's pretty rocky. The entrance is to slip down between **Polly Island** and Madge and then take a right around Madge and head up into the little bay. The southerly bight in Isabel Bay is now aquaculture, so you can't anchor in there any more.

We anchored in Isabel Bay at high tide in about 8 m. of water and stern-tied to Madge Island to a dead tree trunk. It looked stout enough when we tied to it, but the next morning while we were untying our line the darned thing pulled loose and tumbled off the cliff! In a previous time, we anchored and stern-tied to the mainland side of the cove. There is not a great deal of room and you do need to stern-tie.

There was one other boat in the bay that was at the head of the harbor, a Catalina 36, and it looked like it had the only other good anchorage, or rather the nicest one. At high tide we kayaked between all the reefs and rocks. On the way back and just outside of the anchorage, we found a wonderful rocky ledge for bathing and skinny

There may not be a lot of room, but it's beautiful in Isabel Cove. That's 'Sea Witch' on the right and 'Tan Barque' on the left.

This shack still stands on Isabel.

dipping in the water which was 72 degrees.

On shore, it's all rocky, but the head of the bay is the easiest place to land a dinghy. There is an old outhouse in pretty good condition built out over a stream at the head of the bay, primitive but effective waste disposal, eh? The stream does not show on the chart—this is at northern end of bay. We walked up the bank, into the woods and across the stream. There was practically no trail, but we found the remains of three old shacks or cabins. There was also a rock terrace retaining wall.

We walked over to Madge Island which joins the mainland at low tide and found the remains of what is probably old logging equipment. There were also rusted cables around on the rocks. Something looked like a huge rusted conveyor belt. From the island we could see the Catalina sailboat at the head of the harbor was aground—sitting in mud and weeds. (It's a good idea to take the time to check depths and tides when anchoring.) They weren't in too bad shape, just a foot or two out of the water and they floated free in about an hour or so after the low. This is an exceedingly well-protected harbor, absolutely beautiful, and one of our favorite gunkholing places—not anywhere nearly as many jellyfish as Grace Harbour.

As you go out, especially at low tide, beware of reefs all around Polly Island. You can go between Polly Island and the mainland, there is plenty of water.

Running down from Isabel Bay past **Stopford Point,** there is nothing exceptional. The cliffs are of diagonal granite, not very high. There is a point south of Stopford Point where the chart shows moored boomsticks. There were none there as we went by. The next place is an unnamed open bay with Edith Islands on the southwest side of it. The bay was too deep for anchorage and there were no nice beaches. Nevertheless it was pleasant, with a rocky shoreline.

Edith Islands are connected by a drying spit to the mainland.

Salubrious Bay, between Edith Islands and Selina Point, is not listed that way on chart #3559, but it appears, out of nowhere, on Page 13, Chart #3312. It's not in the *Coast Pilot,* either. Obviously the name was dreamed up by a real estate developer who bugged the cartographers enough to get them to put it in the new charts. *Ain't that a scandal to the jaybirds?* It has quite a few homes in it. There are some boats on private mooring buoys. The Edith Islands side, where they connect, has a lot of logs strewn around shore. The beach in the far northern bay has aquaculture, blocking it off. There's another shell beach facing the entrance with a big beautiful home. Along the waterfront on the western side there is a remarkable high dock with what would have to be a long ramp to a float, but there was no float or ramp.

Selina Point is moss-covered with trees and fairly steep. **Selina Rock** does indeed have a crop of kelp off it as the chart indicates. Between there and a line to **Moss Point** are three clusters of rocks, each surrounded by kelp. It'd be wise to keep a wide berth when going from Selina toward Moss. In a tiny little niche inside Selina on the west side there were a couple of boats tied off between the little islands on the tide flat—a powerboat and sailboat both double-tied to both shorelines.

Now, back up Malaspina Inlet to **Zephine Head,** the northwest corner of Desolation Sound Marine Park. It is sloped and has a number of lichen-covered faces and is forested to the top. The rock off the point covers at medium high water: 2.2 m.

This is the view as you round Sarah Point—breathtaking!

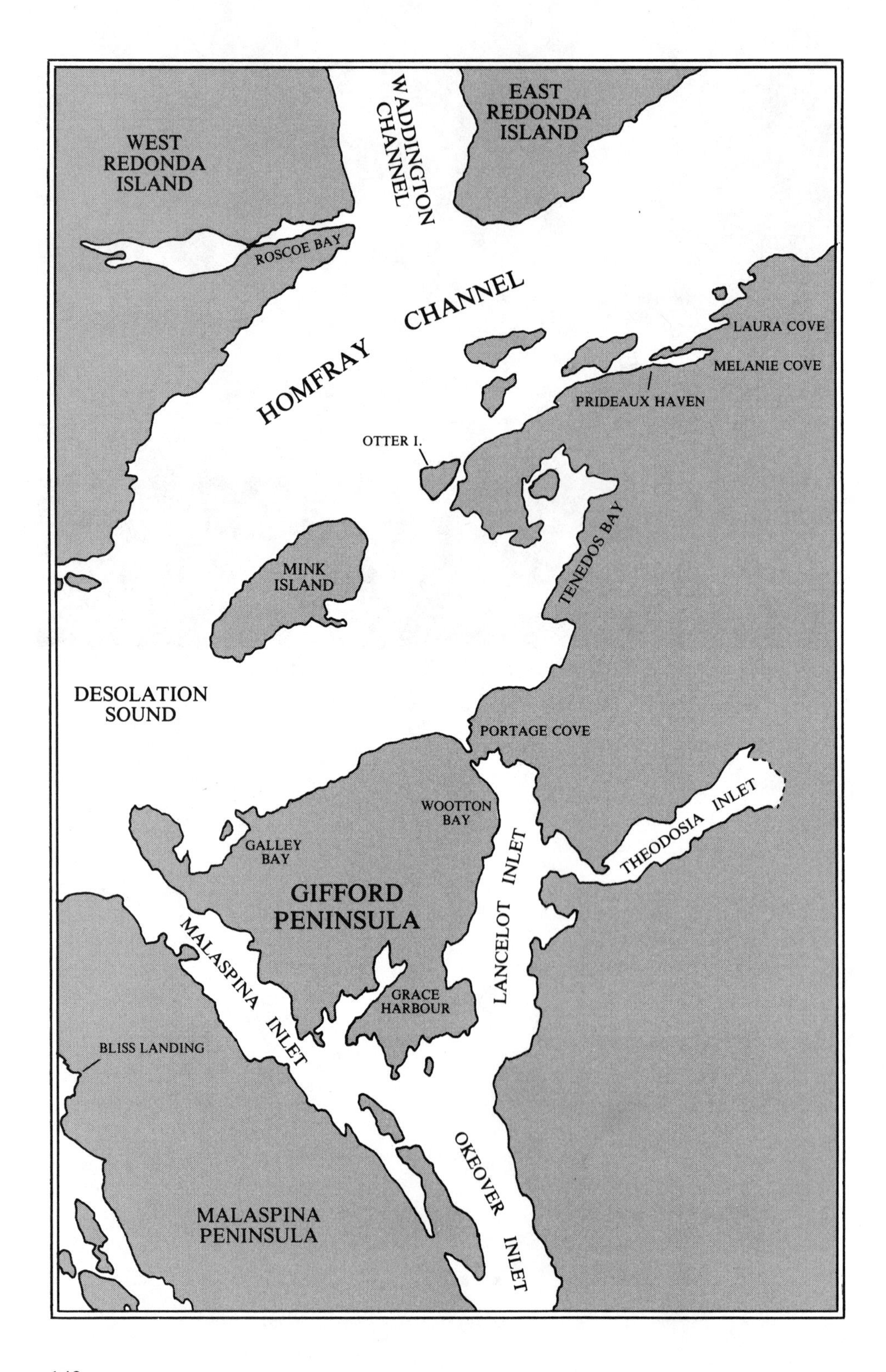
WADDINGTON CHANNEL
EAST REDONDA ISLAND
WEST REDONDA ISLAND
ROSCOE BAY
HOMFRAY CHANNEL
LAURA COVE
MELANIE COVE
PRIDEAUX HAVEN
OTTER I.
TENEDOS BAY
MINK ISLAND
DESOLATION SOUND
PORTAGE COVE
WOOTTON BAY
THEODOSIA INLET
GALLEY BAY
LANCELOT INLET
GIFFORD PENINSULA
MALASPINA INLET
GRACE HARBOUR
BLISS LANDING
OKEOVER INLET
MALASPINA PENINSULA

Chapter 11

Galley Bay

More Desolation Sound Marine Park

On the northwest shore of Gifford Peninsula, around the corner from Zephine Head, we come to another anchorage in Desolation Sound Marine Park. We are still using the big chart book, #3312, page 12, or you can use #3559. Naturally, all the time you're traveling around Zephine Head, you're pinching yourself about this fabulous scenery here in Desolation Sound. And no matter how many times you've been there, you still revel in the beauty around you.

Galley Bay

Entering Galley Bay from the west side you will see a big sign on the west shore saying 'Home Sites For Sale'. Another sign under it says 'No Trespassing'. The first little cove supposedly has a breakwater, but we didn't spot it. We did see an interesting house on pilings, a kind of fishing cabin. You may see some relatively permanent liveaboard-type boats in this bay. There are good depths for anchorage all through the bay—if there is room.

The peninsula forming the east side of this cove has a reef with kelp beds. It dries at 4.4 m. so it is not visible most of the time—be careful not to bump into it.

There are two major drying rocks in the center of the bay, east of the little peninsula. They are marked with kelp, according to the charts. We didn't spot the growth. The inner rock was showing, but we did not see the outer rock, which covers at half tides, although we did spot the pale green water it was undoubtedly hiding under.

The wide area at the head, or southern portion, of the bay is not attractive as an anchorage because of its 17 m. depth close to shore and the aquaculture.

There are a couple of little niches with beaches, exposed to northerly and northwesterly winds. A stream comes down to one little beach with green fresh-water algae. In the eastern lobe there is a house with a long dock at the entrance and several other docks at the eastern end. The fairly large unnamed island on the north side is a popular moorage in 5 to 7 m., although there are some reefs. You could stern-tie and be careful of reefs. On one corner of that island a somewhat flattened log has lodged between rocks—it looks like bench to sit on.

This deer found a way to outwit the Mink Island wolf.

Galley Bay has long been a settled area. A school was built there in 1914, according to a former resident who now lives in Lund. The school was closed down a little more than 30 years ago. She said her family took up property at Galley Bay back in the teens. They had 200 fruit trees at the time. Most of the residents were loggers or fishermen, but it was not a large enough community to warrant a stop by the Union Steamship boats.

During the 1960s Galley Bay was discovered by hippies who returned to the land, forming a large commune. However, it did not flourish as not many of the members were interested in the hard work it took to keep such an idea afloat. Locals still tell stories of the young women of the commune swimming nude to visiting anchored yachts where they bummed cigarettes.

Mink Island

It's just a little over two miles across Desolation Sound waters to Mink Island, a 900-acre privately owned island. Chart #3559 will no longer help, and you'll need Chart #3538 or page 9 of Chart #3312.

The only good moorage is in the bay at the eastern end of the island, and it is a lovely spot. Even the large outer bay is well protected. Most boats in the harbor stern-tie because the center is too deep for good anchoring. There is a rocky island far inside the bay, which becomes a peninsula at low tide. Water in the bay is usually in the low 70s for good swimming. The owners of the island, who have a home and float at the head of the bay inside the small island, have done some selective logging of cedar trees. There is another private home and float near the entrance to the protected harbor. The owners have posted several signs about 'NO FIRES'. Since the land is private, boaters should respect this.

Once, while kayaking at low tide along the rocky bluffs just outside the small island, we found a deer huddled up in the rocks. We guessed that a wolf on the island probably cornered the deer who plunged into water and swam to safety at high tide. Later that day, after the tide had come in, we paddled back, and the deer was gone. We hope it made it safely to some other shore.

Going along the east side of Mink Island we saw a short logging road about a quarter mile south of the Curme Islands. There is another cabin in a tiny bight on the northwest shore of the island.

Curme Islands

Here is a cluster of rocks and islets off the northeast shore of Mink Island that is an incredible one-boat moorage. The passage between them and Mink Island has a rock, marked with a ' + ' sign on the chart. It is called 'Cork's Rock,' because a lady nicknamed thus failed to follow a boat that was to escort her boat safely through the area. She discovered the rock the hard way.

There is a unique little moorage opportunity between the two larger northern islands. The northwest entrance is the better of the two—it is about .3 m. deeper than the northeast. Both passes are extremely narrow and shallow. You would have to make a double tie here. We visited the islands by small runabout at low tide and found a sailboat double-tied in the little cove. It was very shallow in both the passes and the rocks were covered with oysters in very clear water. A friend advised us that if we were going to pick the oysters we should toss any starfish we find above the high tide line. He said they eat the oysters, so if people are going to eat the oysters they should get rid of the starfish. Makes sense.

Another time we saw two small power boats rafted together inside the narrow

The Curmes are ideal for kayakers like Craig and Connie Steenbergen and their children, Matt and Martha.

Portage Cove is beautiful, private and not a good moorage.

passage at the point where it turns to the northeast. The boats were tied four ways to the rocks.

For a number of years a professor from a California college used to bring his friends up to the Curme Islands and they would help clear areas for camping and picnicking.

The Curme Islands are a favorite place for kayakers and canoeists. They usually paddle there from Okeover Inlet, haul their boats up high on the rocks, and set up camp. It's very isolated and lovely, and the water is warm for swimming. Because it is so shallow in between all the rocky islands, there is little large boat traffic, and it is a real find for the hardy.

Portage Cove

Back across open water south from Mink Island, you will find Portage Cove. We mentioned it when we discussed Wootton Bay, as you may remember. This cove may be entered safely only at high water because of a reef that narrows the entrance. Once inside, you would find that there is no swinging room for an anchor—a private float takes up the center area.

There is a very interesting remodeled old house on shore. It belonged to the original homesteader. The present owner has worked very hard to make the neck between Wootton and Portage a grassy meadow. He has carefully nurtured the old fruit trees planted by the original owner. There is a small house on the land just behind the main house—it is occupied by a caretaker when the owner is away.

The gentleman who owns the land is somewhat famous for a reason that makes him a little uncomfortable. He discourages kayakers and canoeists who ask to portage across his property as the Indians used to. He points out that permitting access would quickly make it a custom among visitors and he would not be able to protect the fragile environment from careless hikers or sightseers. He is a warm and generous soul, and he does not relish being inhospitable, but he has learned that it is important to be firm about the matter. (However, we do know he let a pregnant woman and her friends go across when there was a storm.)

Incidentally, he told us that the fruit trees on his land were planted by the first owner—a homesteader—not entirely for the purpose of providing fresh fruit. The province required that homesteaders begin at once to 'prove up' their land by adding something permanent. Nothing could be more of a declaration of the intention to live out your life in a spot than the planting of fruit trees.

Besides, it was the easiest way of meeting the requirement. In those earlier days a canny trader came around to all of the new landowners with a barge filled with starter fruit trees which he sold to them. It was a classic case of supply and demand.

He also told us the name 'Portage Cove' was based on the fact that Indians did indeed portage their canoes across the little isthmus. He has found an Indian midden in the area.

Tenedos Bay

Only 2.5 miles northeast from Portage Cove you will find yourselves in one of the most popular parts in Desolation Sound Marine Park—Tenedos Bay, also known as **Deep Bay.** It's got to be a name applied by the Spaniards—something about a 'fork' *(tenedor, Sp.)?*

Approaching Tenedos Bay you pass some hazards off to the north: **Ray Rock** and two drying rocks. One is due west of Bold Head and the other just off the entrance to Tenedos. This rock is evident only at low tides, and then does not clear by a lot. Favor the mainland side of the entrance and you will be perfectly safe.

Just inside the entrance to Tenedos, you will find—by looking, we hope— another drying rock a hundred yards or so off the northeast corner of Bold Head. Note that **Bold Head** is roughly shaped like a claw-hammer. The rock is pointed to by the claws.

One of the favorite moorage spots in Tenedos is just north of two tiny dry islets just off the middle of the claw. The shelf at this point is narrow. You can also anchor with much less protection in the southerly part of a passage around an unnamed island on the western shore of the cove.

The other end of that passage is a very handy and sheltered moorage. You proceed around the island in a counter-clockwise (go 'anti-clockwise' if you're Canadian, of course) until you come to a narrowing of the pass where the rocks all but block the transit except for shallow draft boats at high tide. We anchored in here and loved it. At low tide the island is joined to the peninsula by a rocky beach.

In the northern cove of Tenedos Bay you will find a garbage float—always a welcome sight—and we're sure that you will thank the Parks Department for providing it.

Most boaters prefer to go down into the head of the bay, which is the indentation off to the east. Notice the rock which dries at low tides in the shallower water at the

Swimming is great in Lake Unwin.

head of the bay. We usually anchor over to the right.

The reason this is such a favorite place is that a creek comes down from **Unwin Lake** and forms a picturesque series of small waterfalls between the lake and the bay. Campers and kayakers often pitch their tents on the grassy flats above the bay. This was the site of a homestead many years ago. In fact, when we first started visiting Tenedos Bay back in the 1960s, there were still remains of the cabin. There are some fruit trees and flowering plants around the flats.

Boaters who have been to sea for a week or so without access to a fresh-water shower trek up to the lake and take baths. It is considered polite to converse loudly among yourselves as you approach in order to warn bathers to dress for the occasion. Although, in truth you may find some of the skinny-dippers are something less than modest and blithely continue with their ablutions in plain sight. (Men: take note, this is not to be counted on.)

As just about everywhere else in the area, Lake Unwin was the scene of logging operations in the 1920s. It was also the scene of many bears. One of the early settlers told us they would go out on the lake in a boat and row to a spot where they could pick blackberries—usually the bears were already there. "But they would see us and go the other way," she said.

The stream from the lake also has several different, well-screened by trees, small

Oh, how good that freshwater shower feels!

waterfalls and rocky bath tubs. They are perfect for a warm shower or bath or even doing the laundry. We found a spot that had pre-soak, wash and rinse pools.

Incidentally, the shores of Lake Unwin are not very conducive to swimming at the point where the path comes out at the water; there are old logs and algae-covered rocks on shore. If you skirt along the beach a few hundred feet to the right or to the left you will come upon some relatively clear rocks which are more inviting. The water is usually several degrees warmer than the saltchuck in the bay, which averages in the low 70s in the summer.

On to Prideaux Haven

Leaving Deep Bay and heading for Prideaux Haven, keep in mind the hazards. Make a nice wide curve to the right around Bold Head and all its offshore rocks we noted earlier, and proceed north. Several small indentations on the shoreline here will not tempt you to moor, probably. The water is very deep and the protection is minimal.

Looking at the chart we were a little unsure about going behind Otter Island through the narrow pass, until we were told there was nothing to it. A kayaker friend of ours said that it "looks like you could jump across the cut between **Otter Island** and the mainland." It is certainly narrow, but deep and passable at any tide. There are high cliffs on either side and not a lot of width, but there is no problem. It is a very scenic little trip. Some rocks intrude into the channel, but there are no shoals or reefs. Currents flow through the pass and may speed you up a couple of knots or slow you down.

This same passage widens out in the northern end and there is room for several boats to anchor there. It is a very popular spot among the old-timers. Be advised, however, that this narrow high slot can funnel winds from Homfray Channel. This is an excellent little moorage for a number of boats if they stern-tie.

On the outer side of Otter Island there is a little cove with a sandy beach and a big forbidding rock in the center. That rock shows on the chart as a little yellow dot. If you turn directly north coming out of the pass you could hit **Sky Pilot Rock** which bares at about 1.2 m.—be careful.

Sky Pilot Rock, halfway between Otter Island and Morgan Island has a religious significance—ministers are often called 'sky pilots', you know. In fact, the mission ship that used to call at Pender Harbour was named the *Sky Pilot.* The rock is not very interesting otherwise. The chart indicates it is marked with kelp, but we didn't see any. We understand a fair number of 'boat pilots' have discovered this rock the hard way.

Outside the Prideaux Haven complex, there are two islands that are very scenic but do not offer much in the way of amenities to a passing boater.

Morgan Island has no coves or indents. It is a typical domed island, heavily wooded. There are some reefs off the northeast shore which might be of interest to cod fishermen. There is a small islet due west of it and on a line with it a few hundred yards farther, you will see **Pringle Rock** which is a reef usually visible except at very high tides—it dries at about 5 metres above the datum level.

Melville Island is tadpole-shaped. There is a small indent at its tail on the southern shore. A reef and a rock lie just off its head to the south. It was probably named after the author who had a thing for white whales. A tiny islet just off its nose might be called 'Ishmael'.

Mary Islet is located to the east of Melville, separated by a very narrow channel. It has reefs associated with it on both ends. The reef to the east extends out to **Grass Islet,** which is named on #3312 Chart, pages 9 and 11, but isn't even noted in the *B.C. Coast Pilot.*

Before entering Prideaux Haven, you might want to poke into **Eveleigh Anchorage**, which is the cove between the island and the mainland. It might be considered an 'overflow' area when the more popular spots inside the complex are crowded. The most attractive spot is the shallow indent on the Island's southeast shore, it would provide lee from westerlies. The chart shows a drying isthmus between Eveleigh and the mainland. It does dry, believe it.

When you see the term 'Anchorage' used in a chart, you can be pretty sure it applies to commercial craft and log tows, which have difficulty entering the narrow passages into the inner bays of Prideaux Haven.

Prideaux Haven

Prideaux Haven is the popular boaters' paradise behind the protection of **Eveleigh Island**, and inside Scobell, the William Islands, and Copplestone Island. Page 9 of Chart #3312 gives a good overall view of this area, but Page 11 gives a 1:6,000 scale which is wonderful. Chart #3555 has the same scale, but it shows depths in fathoms rather than metres. We advise that you use one or the other for the greatest peace of mind in navigating these narrow and often shallow waters inside.

Al draws the line.

Oh, Where to Draw the Line?

We debated for a long time about how far we ought to go beyond the Redondas and Cortes Island for this book on Desolation Sound. We finally decided that people loved to visit Desolation Sound for not only the beautiful scenery, but the fact that **the water was warm.** With that as a criterion, we decided to draw the line inside the narrows and rapids that lead out of the area, because beyond them, the water changes constantly and the temperature drops significantly. We also arbitrarily snubbed Toba Inlet because it has so little to offer boaters. Frankly, we realized that if we were not careful to draw the lines somewhere, we would be suckered into covering Ramsay Arm, Bute Inlet, Okosillo Channel, Calm Channel, Hoskyn Channel and all of Quadra Island—and we would be poking around up there for the next few years!

Another contributing factor: we made this great decision while sitting in the tiny cabin of the **Sea Witch** while moored in Prideaux Haven where we had been holed up for a week because of torrential rains!

Boats tuck in every little cove in Prideaux Haven.

Prideaux Haven impels writers to thumb through their Roget's *Thesauruses* for adjectives. Most folks agree that, second to Princess Louisa only, it is one of the choicest spots in the whole B.C. Coast. It is truly beautiful.

Boats bound for Prideaux from the south usually proceed past Morgan Island to the south, following the north shore of Eveleigh Island, rounding Lucy Point and staying along the Eveleigh shore, avoiding **Oriel Rocks**; the highest parts are visible at all tides. Note here: there is a rock, marked with kelp, off **Lucy Point** so pass a little wide of the actual point shore. This course will take you into the main body of Prideaux Haven—a sometimes pristine anchorage.

In the larger area of Prideaux there will be another welcome sight: a garbage barge. This main bay has anchorage in 12 m. for hundreds of boats. It is the gathering spot for the larger power boats, which unfortunately often run their generators all night long. There are usually some teen maniacs in fast outboards and on water-skis who slalom among the anchored craft. You may want to go down into the shallow inlet south of Copplestone Island or in the small cove off the reefs of William Islands. The main bay in Prideaux Haven is not one of our treasured spots.

Melanie Cove

One of the choice alternatives is Melanie Cove. You enter it by passing the garbage barge and heading for **Melanie Point.** Stay slightly off the point to avoid a narrow reef and you will come into a long channel leading to an oval-shaped body of water. The bottom is around 6 to 7 m. and holds well. It is easy to stern-tie to shore.

Some say the east end of Melanie Cove had the famous 'Flea Village' described by both Vancouver and Menzies. That's the abandoned Indian village which was possibly located on the tiny island at the head of the cove. When the explorers went ashore they were attacked by hordes of fleas—not Indians—who had left their village to the rampaging insects. **We** doubt that this islet is the spot, however, it's too small. There is also a fresh water stream along the southeastern shore of Melanie, just a tiny bit west of the island. There is a trail from the head of Melanie to the head of Laura Cove which is part of an old logging road.

Laura Cove

There is a sort of Prideaux Haven Annex: Laura Cove which lies east of the Copplestone Islands. It's our favorite. To enter this anchorage, go back out between Lucy Point and Oriel Rocks and pass between Scobell and the William Islands—staying center—and proceed to Copplestone Point. Or, if you want to play it safe, go out around Scobell Island and Paige Islets and head due east to **Copplestone Point**. (Do you suppose that's an old spelling of 'cobblestone?')

Just off Copplestone Point prudent boaters (except 'old hands') usually put someone up in the bow to watch for light green water covering lurking rocks. A rule of thumb: stay halfway between Copplestone Pt. and the unnamed point on Copplestone Island and keep a sharp lookout for the rock just off the course to the right. As usual, it's wise to enter a new anchorage on a low, rising tide. It's much easier and safer to find the rocks that way.

Matt Steenbergen explores the ruins of "Old Phil's" cabin in Laura Cove.

Al finds the benchmark in Prideaux Haven.

Laura Cove is usually the last to fill to capacity in the high-traffic days of summer. The bottom is from 7 to 10 m. and it is an ideal place for tying to shore. When we were there, there was a rope swing tied to a tree just opposite the entrance. Boats with kids on board anchored under it.

There once lived a hermit on the shore at the northeast end of the cove. Old Phil's cabin has been almost totally destroyed by time. It has toppled down and is slowly becoming rotten boards. There are still cherries on the trees, apples, and the remains of flowers and bushes he planted when he homesteaded the place.

For those boaters who prefer to row or paddle and camp out, or for kayakers and canoeists—and for small craft crews who just like to picnic or sleep on shore, there is a veritable paradise in this area. It is the spacious drying areas behind Copplestone Island and between the eastern end of the main Prideaux Haven anchorage and the western end of Laura Cove. In sunny weather, the shallow water on those rocky ledges can become almost hot-tub temperatures. There are a number of grassy slopes and flats that are perfect for tenting. It has a further advantage in that the big boats cannot enter the area because of the shallow water. There are sand dollars on the beaches, oysters and clams.

Incidentally, the tide gets higher in Prideaux Haven than in any other place around. It reaches as much as 5.7 m. above datum at higher high water. Chart #3555 shows there is a bronze benchmark set in a low round boulder 5.4 m. above datum near the easterly tip of a small cove on the southwest shore of Copplestone Island. There really is—we found it—it was dated 1966.

Phil & Mike

Back in the late 1920s and the 1930s, when Muriel Wylie Blanchet was cruising around Desolation Sound in the **Caprice** with her five kids, she often stopped in at Prideaux Haven and visited with Phil, the old Frenchman in Laura Cove, and Mike, another hermit, in Melanie Cove. On one of her visits she said her family had gone into Melanie to enjoy the warm swimming.

"...then it clouded up and started to rain. The mountains back of Desolation Sound seem at times to be a favorite rendezvous for clouds that are undecided where to go. They drape themselves forlornly on all the high peaks, trail themselves down the gorges, and then unload themselves as rain on the sea at the mountains' feet."

Isn't that beautiful?

They visited with Phil at his little cabin in Laura Cove, which is now a tumbledown shack, on several occasions. Mike had built a little cabin in Melanie and had flowers and apple trees, paths and terraces, vegetables and apple trees. There are no visible remains of Mike's place—except a few scrubby apple trees. There was a trail between the two coves, if the men chose to visit each other by land. Or they could row from one cove to the next.

Originally a logger in Michigan, Mike had built his cabin on pre-empted land after he had nearly been killed in a fight with a fellow logger. He wanted to get away from people at that point. So he built a cabin, filled it with philosophy books, handlogged the nearby virgin timber, and planted apple trees on his terraces.

He sold his timber. And he would row three miles to Deep Bay where he would sell his apples to other loggers.

One year when the Blanchets arrived in Melanie Cove, they found his cabin occupied by someone new. They went to see Phil and he told them that Mike had been getting crazier all the previous year. Early in the spring Mike had been shooting at people and had even threatened him, Phil said. The police finally had to take him away and he died the following winter in a home in Vancouver. The family mourned their roughhewn, gentle friend.

Roffey Island

We were interested in this island because it seemed to meet some of the descriptions of Flea Village in Vancouver's diary. We kayaked over and explored the area. We decided that it was too big and there wasn't any set of giant stepping-stones to land that could be bridged with their technology. And there weren't any maple trees visible. We still aren't sure where it is—you decide.

The cove behind Roffey Island has a lot of protected water, but it also is a minefield of rocks and reefs. If you were daring enough, you could squeeze down through the northeast entrance, in between the kelp beds, and drop the hook in about 4.5 m. A mean-looking reef cuts across the passage behind Roffey Island. The cove created by the reef to the south of the island has good anchoring depths, but it would be exposed to winds.

We didn't see any boats in the area when we visited, but the coves in Prideaux Haven weren't full either. No doubt hardy souls will venture in there and anchor when the Park is full.

We met some other kayakers behind the island. It would make a great place for camping. There are mountains of oysters on the rocks.

Kayakers grab the rope swing in Laura Cove.

The Canadian Coast Guard is on hand to help visiting boaters.

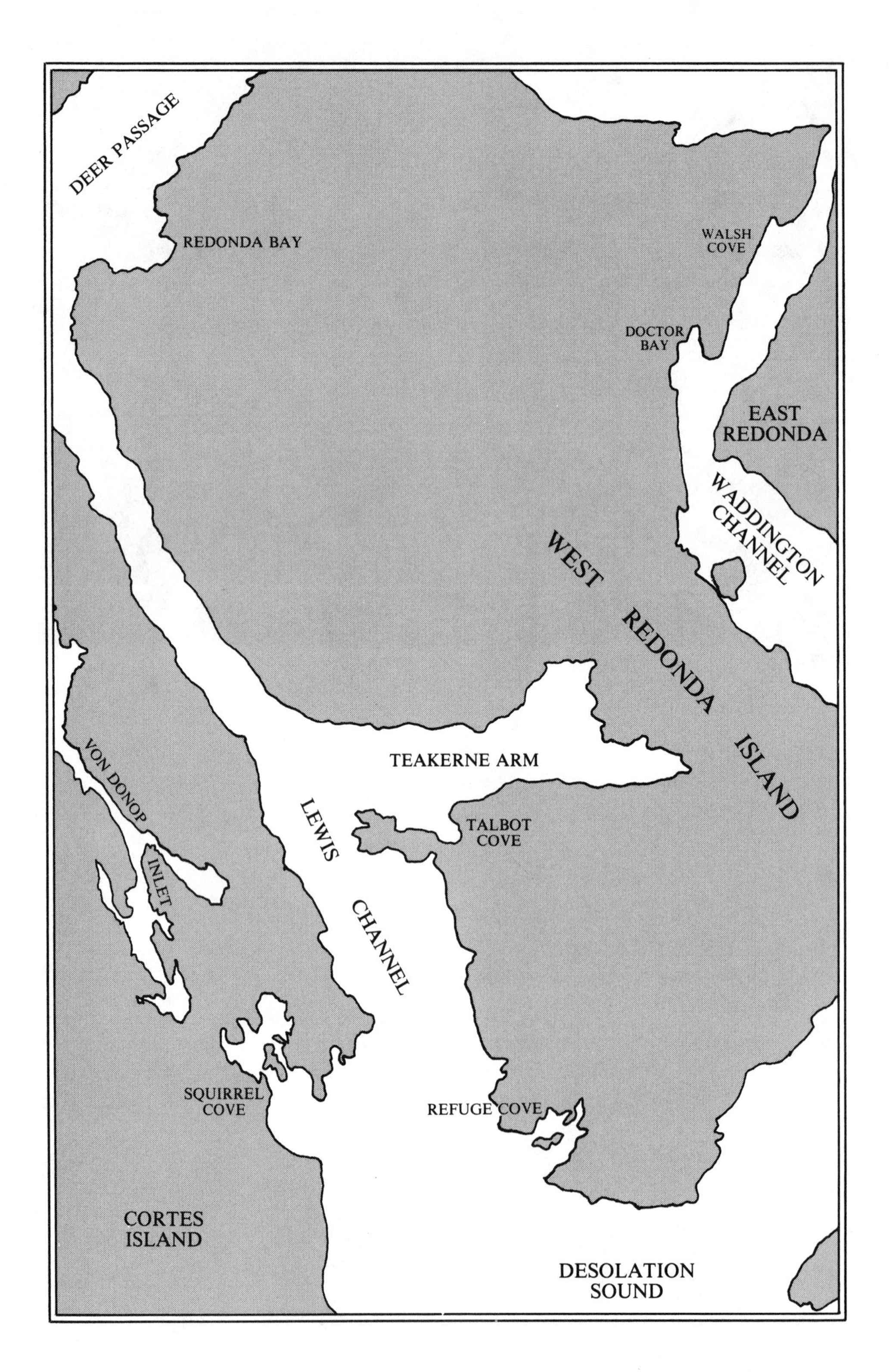
DEER PASSAGE
REDONDA BAY
WALSH COVE
DOCTOR BAY
EAST REDONDA
WADDINGTON CHANNEL
WEST REDONDA ISLAND
TEAKERNE ARM
VON DONOP INLET
LEWIS CHANNEL
TALBOT COVE
SQUIRREL COVE
REFUGE COVE
CORTES ISLAND
DESOLATION SOUND

Chapter 12

Laura Cove

The Northbound Highway—Lewis Channel

Decisions! Decisions! What sort of pathway through the Desolation Sound area would make the most sense? Which way from Prideaux Haven would the reader like to go? We have to do a do-si-do around three big islands.

Then we hit upon a novel notion. We would pretend that you were running low on vittles and wanted to go stock up. Voila! (That's French for 'shazam!')

We're going to take you, hopefully not kicking and screaming, to Refuge Cove for fuel and victuals. Thus, stocked and stored, you should be ready for the next bunch of gunkholes.

It makes sense, doesn't it? So, we'll do it even if it does make sense.

Set your course for Refuge Cove. If you've got chart #3555, which was great for Prideaux Haven, you'll find it invaluable for the rest of this chapter. Except, of course, you'll still need either Chart #3538 or pages 8, 9, and 10 of Chart #3312 in order to get there.

You'll go along the north shore of Mink Island and head for the south corner of West Redonda Island. But before you get all the way to Martin Islands, we want you to turn around and look sort of northeast toward Horace Point on the southern tip of East Redonda Island. See how the land slopes down from a high mountain? OK, did you read *Winnie the Pooh?* If you did, you'll recognize that ridge very definitely as 'Heffalump Head'. If you didn't read *Winnie the Pooh,* too bad for you!

There are two islands just offshore that look like they broke away from the larger island some time in the dim past. These are the **Martin Islands.** If it's 'nasty' out in Desolation Sound, you might appreciate a little lee by taking the channel north of the islands. There are no worries in this channel. You will notice that you can't go between E. Martin Island and W. Martin Island as there just isn't any water. There are some extensive oyster strings along the Redonda shoreline in here.

The light on the unnamed corner of West Redonda Island is called the 'Refuge

Refuge Cove is indeed a refuge, with a grocery store, fuel dock, laundry, and other amenities.

Cove Light'. It's a tower 21 ft. high with a red top and a flashing red light. You then hook back due north and run down the cliffed shore.

Refuge Cove

As you enter the cove on the right side there is a welcome 'ESSO' sign. There are several houses on the right side and a small island to the right. Usually there are several boats anchored in the bay, but most tie to the government wharf which is generally very busy. The anchorage itself is open to southwesterlies, although the dock area seems fairly well protected.

The outermost dock is the ESSO dock of **Refuge Cove Marina** where they have fuel, propane, CNG and water. After you fuel up, you have to move to the government float to tie up while you do your shopping. The government dock offers 178 m. of moorage and no amenities, and sometimes you have to wait to moor. There is no garbage disposal in this cove.

There is a good grocery store, with a deli and dairy section, liquor, ice, fresh fruits and vegetables, ice cream, canned goods, frozen meats, books, magazines, fishing supplies, film, batteries and ice. There is an adjacent building which houses a laundry and shower; a hamburger stand is across the path and a fascinating gift shop is up the stairs. All in all, Refuge Cove is a good stop. Telephone service is by radio telephone only.

There is a small cove at the head of Refuge Cove. Its entrance is narrowed by two rocks which dry at .6 m., we saw them. There is very limited anchorage in this cove because of the private mooring buoys. There are a few homes on the shores. A longish, virtually impassable, creek connects this cove to **Refuge Lagoon**, which extends some 2 miles inland. We didn't explore it, because we would have had to portage our kayak and we felt lazy that day. Incidentally, in B.C. the word 'portage' is pronounced as in French, 'por-*tawj*'.

Early settlers in Refuge Cove, many of whom were hand loggers or fur farmers, had a dance hall in the rear of the store. As in many communities, settlers from miles around would row to the dances and dance the night away. Refuge Cove was also the site of the first school in the Redondas in 1914. Apparently the school was closed in the 1930s and 1940s and reopened again for the last time in 1949-50.

There is a very big oyster installation in the channel next to the unnamed island in the cove. There is plenty of room to pass north of that island, despite the aquaculture.

Replenish The Oyster?

Aquaculture in the Sunshine Coast and Desolation Sound area is a subject for often-heated debate. Some of the old-timers are dead set against it, others think it is the wave of the future. We heard both arguments and listened carefully. One important distinction may have escaped the fans and foes. There are two kinds of aquaculture: oyster culture and fish propagation. You can tell the difference by the appearance. Fish pens are structures built on pontoons which hold nets in which the fingerlings are allowed to mature without escaping or falling prey to predators. Oyster culture is characterized by long strings of colorful ball floats.

The advocates of aquaculture talk about the future food needs of the planet. And they have some fish industry people who believe that with the present immense pressure by foreign nations as well as our own on the fishing grounds, the future of the wild salmon is not promising. Pollution and 'reclamation' of spawning areas also threaten the fish supply. It may be that in the next century fish will have to be farmed like potatoes.

However, the other, and more expansive field of aquaculture, oyster farming, does not seem to us to be addressing a critical need of the future. We have been in too many bays and bights in the B.C. cruising area to have any concern about the future crops of oysters. There are literally billions of them, piled up on rocks sometimes two or three layers deep, on almost every shoreline.

It would seem that selective harvesting of the natural supply of oysters would make it an almost inexhaustible resource. Only the most minuscule share of the crop is taken by boaters and residents. The starfish and gulls take a much heavier toll on their numbers.

It may be that cultured oysters are chiefly of value to fine restaurants and gourmet packaging. As such, the farming of oysters has a contribution to the commerce and employment of the area. And with the waning of another natural resource—timber—-jobs in those areas are scarce.

But we don't think that the argument that we are some day going to have to feed the underprivileged of the world with bivalve delicacies is going to hold water—to squeeze a metaphor.

The waterfall at the head of Teakerne Arm is an attraction for boaters.

Now, let's leave Refuge Cove and do a right up Lewis Channel. For this you'll need chart #3538 or page 8 of Chart #3312.

Junction Point has a 29 ft. tower with a green band and a flashing green light.

Joyce Point has a cove which is filled with oyster strings. No great loss here. It would be lousy anchorage, anyhow. The island in its entrance is a little low forested hump. Just off its eastern shore it has a couple of dry rocks.

Teakerne Arm

Teakerne Arm is a popular stopover place, even though it offers little in the way of good anchorage; only mediocre scenery and little privacy. Talbot Cove, the waterfall at the north head of the arm, and **Cassel Lake** above it are the big attractions. The waterfall is a good photographic subject and the lake is a delight for saltchuck-weary boaters.

As you approach the entrance to Teakerne from the south you will notice a mountain to the north with a titillating name, and a glimpse of a waterfall about three-fourths of the way to the top and just under the peak.

Talbot Islet has some low trees and brush and dried grasses on it.

Talbot Cove

There is one large head at its southeast extremity, and it is a booming ground. It offers better depths for anchoring than the other parts of the Cove, but it offers no protection from winds which come from the northwest down Lewis Channel. When we visited, the sections of breakwater which are normally installed in the cove were stored there. They consist of low iron A-frames mounted on logs with a screen of timbers which goes from the bed of the float to the top of the 'A'. The breakwater has a sign on it saying 'No mooring inside of breakwater'. The south face of the cove is squared off and has booming areas on it.

There is a rock in the very center of Talbot Cove. It uncovers at about 3 m. You can locate it by looking toward the center of the flat shoreline on this face. It is out from the shore on a line parallel to the face and extending from the northernmost point of the cove.

The best-protected anchorage is in one of the several small niches in the southwest head. You will be out of the fetch from Lewis Channel and behind Talbot Islet. Here the waters are deep. You will have to drop the hook in between 15 to 23 m. and put a line to shore.

We met some kayakers from Bend, Oregon, on the rocky tombolo at the west end of the flat shoreline. It seemed to be an ideal place for camping.

The famous waterfall is at the head of the north lobe of Teakerne Arm. Anchorage is difficult at this spot. Water is very deep right up to the shoreline and there is no protection from winds which curve into the arm from Lewis Channel. Many boats do stern-tie near the falls, but their anchors are hooked in very deep water and their sterns are close to the rocks on shore. There were campers on shore on a low rocky ledge just west of where we moored. It would be a great place for kayakers.

Somewhat better water depths can be found at the little nook indicated by the reef southwest of the falls. We dropped the hook in 25 m. of water and took a line ashore to tie to a tree.

Then we kayaked over to the shore where there are usually a couple of shore-boats up on the rocks at the beginning of the path. In case you are there alone, you will find the spot by looking up at the rocks on shore on the small squarish point just west of the falls. You will see a square slab of concrete marking the point. Near the slab you will see a couple of big eye-bolts sunk into the rock for holding boom cables.

The path runs up the slope to the top, along an old skid road. There is a fire-pit and camping spot on the rock just above the landing place. You will also see a number of old rusty logging cables across the path, leading down to the water.

As you climb the path, you will find the cables running along it for most of its length. At the top of the trail you will come to a big flat rock-outcropping. There is an old winch abandoned on this rock. It looks fairly complete and you may want to take some pictures of it. If you are a beachcomber, you might speculate on how to get the thing out of there and sell it. It doesn't look like it has been used in years. It probably was hoisted up there by a bulldozer during logging operations. It also looks like it is valuable enough to merit hiring a helicopter to lift it out.

The path has been well-trodden. It looks like someone has gone to the trouble of cutting steps in the rock.

On the flat rock surface, you can look down into the gorge at the bottom of the falls. Occasionally there are people splashing about in them. There is no barrier or warning on the rocks, and it would be a dangerous place to play 'chicken.'

The view is remarkable from up on the rock.

From the top of the falls, you will be surprised at how small the creek is. There is not a great volume of water cascading down the falls—at least not by August. Above the edge of the falls there is a small pond, which looks rather tranquil. It has a lot of old waterlogged timber on its bottom. There is a big old tree which has fallen across the neck of this pond and you could walk to the other side of the pond on it, if you were so inclined.

Skirting along the pond, a path follows a narrow rocky ledge which is only slightly threatening. It eventually comes out on another rock tabletop which is just above the best place to bathe. There is a long incline of smooth rock which dips down into the lake. When it enters the fresh water you will notice that it is slightly slippery from algae and you will have to hold onto the exposed rock above it.

When we visited, the water was about 4 degrees warmer than the saltwater below, but this is enough to make it very inviting. If you get there when it is vacated, you can take a bath. You would probably hear hikers approaching so you could scamper back up the rock and dress for visitors. One of the nice features is that the rock is clean and you don't have to brush off leaves and dirt to get dry.

There is not much of a temptation to try to haul a boat up to the lake. From the vantage point of the bathing beach you can see that the shoreline is all clogged with old snags and logs. The only beach that might be worth investigating is at the north-east extremity where there seems to be a small island and grassy spot nearby. It

Cassel Lake is another great place to bathe.

would probably take a lot less energy just to swim to it rather than lug a small boat all the way up there.

Teakerne Arm is shaped like a fish-tail. The east head is taken up almost completely by log booms. The shoreline between the two heads is also often blocked by booms. We saw a number of boats tied up to the booms and facing up into the entrance.

There were early settlers at Teakerne Arm who grew great fruit and vegetable crops.

Now, Back to the Highway

Now let's head back north up Lewis Channel, which is a water highway for commercial and pleasure boats.

Going north in this channel you can see the difference in topography between the Redonda Islands and Cortes Island to the left. The thousand metre peaks on West Redonda look like Alaskan views. Cortes is low and cliffy along the shore.

One of the few notable elevations on Cortes is **Cliff Peak** which is opposite the entrance to Teakerne Arm. It is about 450 metres high and has a high mesa on top.

We tried to find the tiny Indian Reserve on the Redonda shore near Teakerne, but all we saw was a rather narrow beach.

We didn't see any log booms on the eastern shore of the channel where they are marked on the chart.

Two creeks come down from the tops of the mountains on West Redonda Island. The northernmost of these can be made out by looking for a shoulder on the west face of the peak. Just below this, you will see a narrow curving path through the trees. You probably won't be able to see the creek itself—there are no visible waterfalls.

Just east of the creek exit, you will see a tiny sandy beach. We saw a sailboat anchored there. We couldn't believe it. It must be a very bumpy moorage because of the wash from the passing boats.

And now it's time to change charts again. For this section you can use Chart #3541, or page 17 of #3312.

The light on the east side of Lewis Channel is on shore below great mountainsides. It looks like a miniature. It is listed as the 'West Redonda Light' in case you want to log it. It's 23 feet high and has a red band and a white light—unusual!

Looking up **Calm Channel,** you will see a series of V-shaped divides which look like a giant river coursed down between them. They may have been created by massive earth-moving glaciers. The scene is worth a photo.

The northwest corner of West Redonda Island just before Redonda Bay has no name, but there is a tiny islet just offshore. Rounding that brings you to Redonda Bay.

Redonda Bay

At the head of Redonda Bay you see the extensive logging operation with stifflegs, skids, bunkhouses, heavy logging equipment and a float. The Government Wharf noted on chart #3555 is no longer there, although the list of Federal Facilities still notes it.

There is a rock in the center of the bay, called **Deceit Rock**. The hydrographic service contributes to its deceptiveness by not giving us the depths over it.

Jo's turn to find the datum marker at Redonda Bay.

A second, equally ornery, rock lies inshore from it and its depth is not noted. The two rocks line up with the old pilings that were a dock at the south end of the head.

The area which held the old cannery and the town—where **Lillian Russell Creek** enters the cove—now is dominated by oyster strings. There is an old tug boat anchored there which is possibly housing for a caretaker.

Lillian Russell Creek comes down out of the mountain from **Ellis Lake.** It is

Crack the History Books Again

In the early 1800s there were two Salish Indian villages on West Redonda with about 100 persons each. Near Deceit Rock there was a summer village. We think we found the remains of the circular stone fish trap at the mouth of Lillian Russell Creek that we had heard of. The rock placements—which we could see at about mid-tide—certainly looked intentional.

Redonda Bay was once a thriving community with a cannery, homes, post office and a school. It was even a steamer stop, beginning in the early 1920s. All that is left of the cannery is just a mass of pilings, and an old boiler on the shore.

Later on, there was a corrections camp housed above the bay, but it is no longer there. The buildings were left vacant, according to a logger we talked to. Vandals came in and trashed the houses, taking doors and windows and destroying anything of value. When the logging company took it over, they had to bulldoze the old houses and burn them.

Sunsets are lovely from Redonda Bay.

There was extensive logging above Ellis Lake in 1988.

fresh, clear water and there is a very shallow dam just above the high tide line which can be used for a quick bath—if you can stand the clouds of blackflies. There is a benchmark on shore near Lillian Russell Creek. It is set in rock near an old tree with silvered roots. It is noted on the chart at 15.49 feet above datum.

There is a caretaker's cottage for the logging company on the shore, with a little fenced vegetable garden in front of it. Housing and workshops for the loggers are on the hill above the caretaker's place.

We got a ride with a truck driver, Pete Hana, from the logging camp. We went up to Ellis Lake but we were on the west side of the lake and very high above it, so we had no chance to go find the petroglyphs we had heard of, which are supposedly on the lake's eastern shore.

Although there is good depth and holding ground near the head of the bay, anchorage would be subject to northwesterlies. You might get permission from the logging company to tie up to their float, however.

We will continue our journey around West Redonda Island, a fascinating trip down Waddington Channel, in the next exciting chapter.

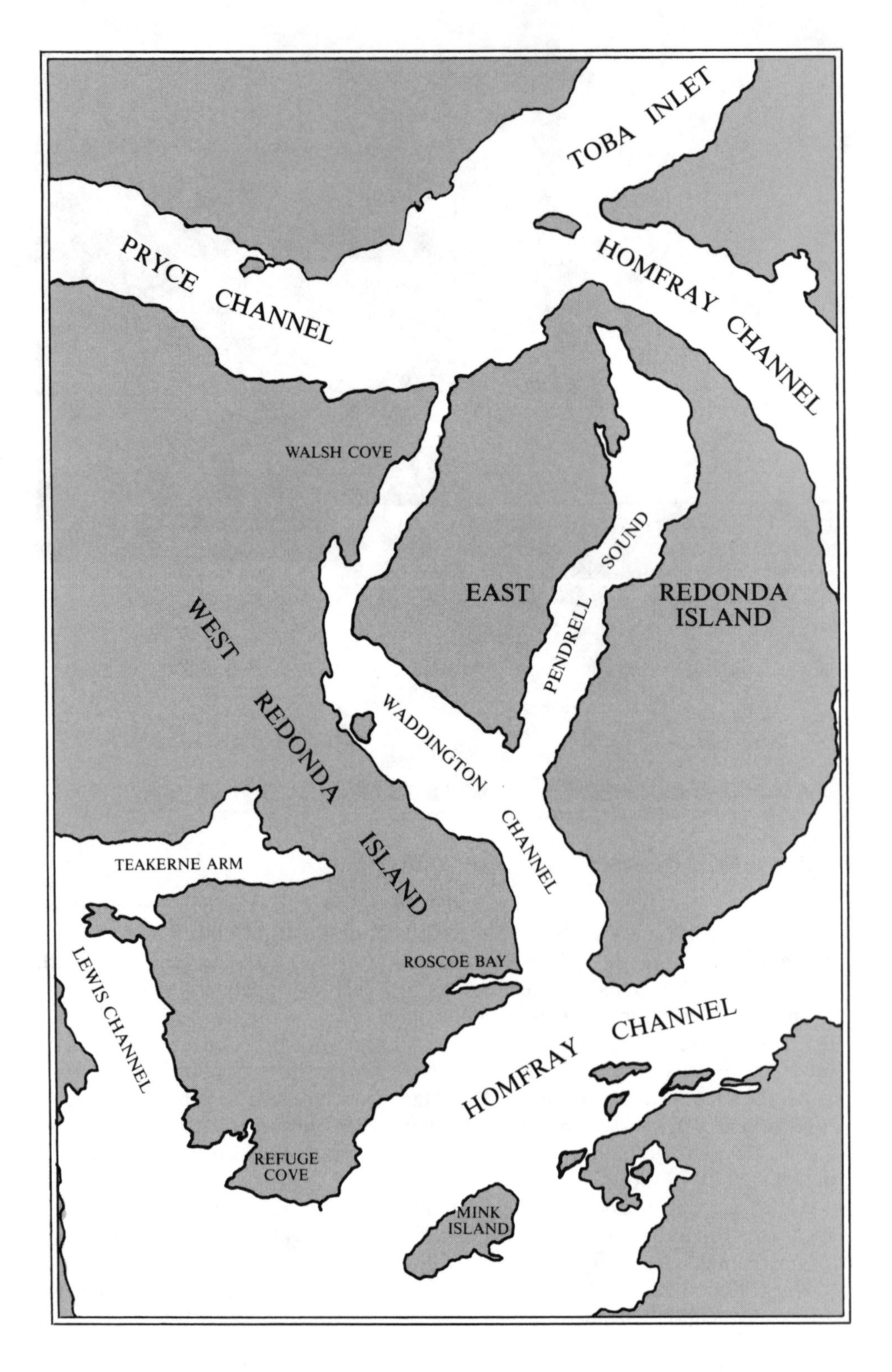
TOBA INLET
PRYCE CHANNEL
HOMFRAY CHANNEL
WALSH COVE
SOUND
EAST
REDONDA
ISLAND
WEST
PENDRELL
REDONDA
WADDINGTON
ISLAND
CHANNEL
TEAKERNE ARM
ROSCOE BAY
LEWIS CHANNEL
HOMFRAY CHANNEL
REFUGE
COVE
MINK
ISLAND

Chapter 13

Some Neat Spots in Waddington Channel

First of all, we have to get to **Waddington Channel** from Redonda Bay. Right now we're on Chart #3541 and/or #3312, pages 16 and 17.

Just for tidiness sake, let's look at the shoreline on **Deer Passage** that leads to it. The relatively straight western shoreline of West Redonda Island, north of Redonda Bay, has no features of interest to passing boaters. A creek comes down the mountainside from a small high tarn into the passage about two miles north of Redonda Bay. It does not have a beach or delta visible onshore.

Connis Point at the junction of Deer Passage and Pryce Channel has a little circular island off it. This islet has low rock faces on all sides. It may be passed close to the south.

Ready for a little history? Okay. Connis Point was named after...guess who?..a *dog!* It was a Skye terrier who accompanied Captain Pender aboard the *H.M.S. Beaver.* He also named a rock and an islet after this pooch. Maybe these are places where he had to take the dog ashore for a pit stop.

We are now in **Pryce Channel**. The West Redonda Island shoreline here is very steep and is heavily forested with second growth. In patches, the timber has been clear-cut recently.

In 1892 the Redonda iron mine, 'Elsie', was located on Crown Grant land on the north shore of West Redonda. It was short-lived, however, even though 626 tons of magnetic iron were shipped to an Oregon smelter the first year it was worked. In 1920 more than 8,400 tons of limestone rock was shipped from the same area. There are no visible remains of the 'Elsie' iron mine.

There is a little bay at **Gloucester Point.** We ducked into it for a look-see. We didn't see the line of rocks shown on the chart. We saw a sailboat anchored off a pretty sandy beach on the west head of the bay. It was clear why the skipper chose the spot. There was a glorious view up Toba Inlet, and we heard land birds in the trees near the beach. We wouldn't want to spend the night there, though. Any wind from the north would be troublesome and the wash from passing boats in the channel would roll you.

As you near **Dean Point** you see the tower of the entrance light. It is 20 feet high and has a green band and light on top. Directly across Pryce Channel you see a waterfall.

This is another wonderful panorama of the country north of Desolation Sound. Up near Toba Inlet you will see lots of snowfields and glaciers.

The water here is a fascinating milky green color as the glacial fresh water from Bute and Toba Inlets mixes with the salt water.

Across Pryce Channel we saw a big tank mounted on a barge. It was in the outlet of a creek where there is a log skid and a large booming ground. Above it is a large logging operation with yarding still in place. It has logged a swath clear up to the top.

Around the corner from Dean Point to the right, there is a rock that remains exposed at all tides. This is the rather narrow entrance to Waddington Channel.

Waddington Channel

Old Alfred Waddington must have been a remarkable character. He may deserve to have a movie made of his life.

Alfred Waddington, Dreamer

If some screenwriter wanted to do a film about a dreamer, mover and shaker, he ought to read the story of old Alfred Waddington, one of the richest and most adventurous men of B.C. in the mid 1800s. In 1849 he emigrated from England to California. Finding a lack of challenge there, he moved to Victoria in 1853.

After five years of exploring the Desolation Sound area, he became fired with a dream. He felt, for some reason, that the port of the future was at the end of Bute Inlet. This would be the terminus of a road that would eventually stretch east across Canada, a royal highway for carrying the treasures of the Northwest back to the centers of industry.

He gambled almost all of his considerable fortune on this enterprise. He watched the wagon road inch through the forests and up the valleys until April 30, 1864 when the Chilcotin Indians attacked the workers' camp. Of seventeen men, only three escaped. The Indians destroyed his tools and provisions and put an end of his project.

In 1868, he had a new dream—to build a railroad from Eastern Canada to the Pacific. He returned to England to lobby for it. Two years later, he returned to Victoria with promises of funding. He sold his plans for the railroad to the Canadian Government.

He died of smallpox in 1872, when he was 76 years old and never lived to see the success of his dream, although the railroad was built.

The line is now known as 'The Canadian Pacific Railway'.

The channel which bears his name runs about nine nautical miles in a boomerang-shaped course between the two Redonda Islands. Even though it has a narrow entrance the currents, which flood to the north, seldom exceed one knot.

There is a rock almost in the center south of the entrance which pinnacles up to about 2.4 m. This is a favorite cod fishing spot. However, when we fished it, the cod decided to go find another spot. Skunked again.

The Indian Reserve is another small beach on East Redonda just short of the point and near the cod rock.

Butler Point is the north flank of Walsh Cove on West Redonda.

Walsh Cove

Now this is a place you have to visit! Particularly if you are interested in pictographs.

The cove is located behind two wooded islets connected by a spit: **Gorge Islets.** There is only one actual niche in this bay and it is too shallow to anchor. It was blocked off by a cable and logs for some reason. The waters are deep offshore and stern-tying is tricky.

We anchored in Walsh Cove in 15.2 m. of water, about 100 feet from shore. We took a line to the rocky ledge and took up the slack in our anchor rode. We were then only about 20 feet from the rocks and we were in about 9 m. The water temperature was 70 degrees, Fahrenheit, that is— and swimming was great.

Converting Centiheit to Fahringrade

When the weatherman in Nanaimo says the temperature is 40 degrees and you're perspiring like a love-child at a family reunion, you **know** there is something a-kilter with their thermometers. What has happened is that the mad scientists have not only made dirty words out of 'inches' and 'feet,' they are messing around with temperatures. They have a new-fangled, probably Communist-inspired, thermometer which has '0' as the freezing point of water. They call it 'Celsius.' It was named after a Swedish astronomer. That's right—an astronomer—not a physicist! He thought you should start measuring temperatures from ice! Well, what do you expect from some dude who spends his time peeking into little optical tubes!

So, thanks to this spacey Scandahoovian, the Canadians are measuring heat in some off-the-wall system that requires a Yankee to have a degree in math.

Here's the formula: Paste it up somewhere along with your 'liters to gallons' recipe.

C = (F-32) x 5/9ths

F = (Cx9/5) + 32.

So—at what temperature does a Canadian cook boil turnips?

Celsius = (212 degrees - 32) x 5/9.

180 degrees x 5/9

100 degrees Celsius.

SO: never order turnips in a Canadian restaurant— they'll be tough!

It was a spectacular moorage. Across the channel we saw the high mountains of East Redonda Island. There is a dry watercourse that runs down the face of one of the mountains. There is a sort of squarish head on the mountain to the northeast. We saw about 15 boats in there, and only three were free anchored in deep water.

In the cove that is blocked, you will find some old machinery which has been abandoned and now is encrusted with barnacles and oysters. Up among the trees on a low bank there is an old iron bed frame near a stream. A few yards up the creek there was an old pipe which had been planted in a tiny pool to provide a water source. It was only trickling when we found it, but when we shoved a small stick through it, it began to run better. Then we scooped out the debris that had filled the little sump and the 1-1/2 inch pipe and the flow became quite full. If it is plugged up when you get there, please clear it out so other boaters can get fresh water from it.

In the trees above the cove we found some large old cedar stumps with slots cut in them. The hand loggers used to cut notches in the bases of the cedar trees and then insert 'springboards' in them to stand on so they could saw the trees off about 10 to 12 feet above ground. The trunks often 'bulged' at the base and were not good wood, so they cut above them. In many forests you can find these remains of hand-logging days.

Logging wasn't the only interest in Walsh Cove. In 1913, a beautiful pink granite was discovered that was said to be similar to the celebrated Baveno granite from the vicinity of Lake Maggiore in Italy.

The **Gorge Islets** in Walsh Cove have one little detached rock to the south which has 2 or 3 trees. The Southern Gorge Islet is elongated and has a bluff face toward the channel. There is a drying rock off to the east of the channel side. The long island is very pretty and forested—well worth exploring. You can swim there from your anchored boat or dinghy as the water in between these islets is very warm, particularly on a sunny day when there has been a low tide. On the islets, and also on Butler Point, there are strawberry plants, chives (or wild onions) and thyme—remnants of Indian encampments. Seems they carried these plants with them and planted them wherever they set up a temporary village.

False Pass behind the Gorge Islets is not entirely false. It can be dangerous, however. There are reefs that extend out from both shores which nearly block it, but the reefs are staggered so it is possible to go through at all tides. We saw two power boats slowly and carefully picking their way through at a .5 m. tide.

Bluff Point marked on the charts is something of a mystery. Neither it nor Gorge Islets are mentioned in the *Coast Pilot.*

Doctor Bay

South of Walsh Cove about 1-1/2 miles you come to a high bluff and headland. This is **Bishop Point**. The Channel makes a deep pocket here—Doctor Bay.

There is a large natural grotto in the cliff just beyond Bishop Point and just before Doctor Bay. It is a triangular pocket in which a long flat rock looks like an altar with live flowers growing on it.

Entering Doctor Bay there is a small hook in which small power boats can anchor. There are some nice beach areas in the head of this bay. However, the bay is pretty well choked with fish pens. A sign says it is a 'SALMON REARING FACILITY'. The shop and house of the installation has a satellite dish. We saw a number of boats

Christopher Malloy is a great picto-finder.

More "Indian Pitchers"

We found the pictographs in the rock faces just inside Butler Point in Walsh Cove. There are four major groups of them. The first group is just to the right of a fringe of trees and extends back behind them. Two sets of pictos are on surfaces that face the same direction— south, down Waddington Channel.

In the second set of pictographs there is no convenient ledge on which the artist could have stood. There is a small crevice just below the paintings and a very small arbutus tree growing out from it. There must have been a larger tree for him to stand on when the pictures were made, or possibly there was an outcropping of rock then which has since fallen away. It is at least 20 feet above high tide.

Around the curving rock face there is a picture of tiny fish which seem to be jumping out of the water. In one of the panels you will see two sets of inverted Vs with a line across the top. These may be fish drying racks.

There is another group of pictures hidden by a small arbutus. There are a number of trees on that particular point so you couldn't see the pictographs from the water. This group is just opposite a tiny black offshore islet—it is totally covered by mussels.

There are several panels in the area which are associated with a burial cave, summer fishing grounds, and possibly shamanism rituals. Several paintings were clearly done with brushes, as opposed to fingers, according to Doris Lundy.

Plastic pipes hold the oyster spat.

Supposedly the largest oyster culture facility in North America.

tied to a pier, but couldn't decide whether they belonged to workers or friends of the company. A sign implied that visitors are 'not welcome,' 'keep away', etc. It's a spot not known for its hospitality.

The prim little light on Waddington Channel on the West Redonda Side is about 23 feet above high tide. It has a green flashing light. It is right across from **Shirley Point.**

Allies Island

The oyster culture facility at the bay near Allies Island is the largest in North America, according to workers who talked to us. The sign calls it 'Mariculture.' There are two spreads, each a quarter-mile across. These have one-inch tubes filled with spat, suspended in enormous strings marked with black plastic balls.

The workers said they are happy to help boaters who want to moor in the area. They said to come down the fairway between the two culture areas and hail somebody. If you want to anchor on the north side of the cove, or anywhere else possible in there, they will escort you. This area is good except in northwest winds. The fairway between the lines is obvious. It is best to stay about 20 feet away from the line of black buoys along the clear path. The yellow buoy in the center is tied to a concrete anchor and does not form a hazard. Yellow buoys mark most of the outer areas. The company is called 'Pacific Aquafoods' and has its home office in Lund. There are from 5 to 20 employees on the place depending on the time of year. They move the spat, care for the oysters, and maintain the place.

A cove just south of Allies Island hooks back in and looks like a neat place for anchorage except in a southeast wind.

Another potential anchorage is a small bight a quarter-mile north of Alfred Island. We have seen boats in there.

There is an oyster string and a lease sign on the shore behind **Alfred Island.** We got the name from Bill Wolferstan's book, as the island is not named on any chart, and even the *Coast Pilot* calls it unnamed. A big old fallen tree juts out into the passage between Alfred Island and West Redonda. There were some speedboats anchored in the channel. The west side of Alfred Island cove has a reef extending from the Redonda shore. It would be visible at all tides. There are two shallow coves on the west face of Alfred Island and the one closest to the island has a reef that extends. Passage between the little island and Redonda was no problem.

Behind Walter Point on the East Redonda side of Waddington Channel there is a small cove. We saw a couple of sailboats stern-tied in this cove. The cove is shaped like a left mitten. The thumb and hand are separated by a steep rocky cliff. We talked to one of the skippers. He said their hooks were in 10 m. of water. They were in the finger section of the mitten. They said they had stayed in the moorage before and loved it because of its isolation.

Pendrell Sound

At this point, we're going to leave good old Waddington and take a little side-excursion up Pendrell Sound. This is a most unique area for several reasons, including water temperatures and unexpected winds which blow up or down the channel. Since the waters are warmer than most making the region ideal for the production and collection of oyster spat, the *Coast Pilot* advises that to avoid damage to the spat collection gear, speed in the north half of the sound should not exceed 4 knots.

Walter Point is very attractive. It has some rock faces and clusters of evergreens. If you want to take one picture which epitomizes the Desolation Sound area, you should shoot Walter Point in the morning sun. As you come out around the point and head up the sound, you are once again treated to the glorious scenery of this area. **Mt. Addenbroke,** the highest peak in the Redondas at more than 5,200 feet, has a visible glacier in a crevice toward the summit. There are icy creeks below it.

As you come around the point there is a niche with a rock at the entrance which covers at 3.4 m. It is quite narrow but it might be possible to tie in there in case of an emergency.

Going up Pendrell Sound, staying on the western shore, you can see that **Mt. Bunsen** on the western shore has been denuded by logging. It's quite a blight in an otherwise beautiful area.

About half way up Pendrell Sound on East Redonda Island we understand there was once an old gold mine. We couldn't determine the exact location.

Pendrell Sound Water Temperature

Because of unusually warm waters in late July and August especially, Pendrell Sound has become a productive area for oyster culture.

However, freaky northwest winds in the summer of 1986 caused an 'upwelling' of deep cold water to the surface. It killed much of the oyster spat. The area is no longer considered as reliable for oyster culture, according to marine biologist John Keays. Usually water temperatures reach around 25.5 degrees degrees Celsius (78 degrees Fahrenheit) in the Sound. About August 15 of 1986 they dropped from 2 degrees C. (73 degrees F.) to 18 degrees C. (64 degrees F.) in three days and the larvae died. He said some of the oyster growers moved from Pendrell to Pipestem in Barkely Sound.

Keay also said that while pleasure boaters are concerned with good moorages being taken up by aquaculture farms, the oysters growers are concerned that pleasure boaters don't pollute the waters with sewage and garbage: it works both ways. While salt water kills off viruses in time, oysters can't be sold if there are high coliform levels in them as a result of pollution. Disease is a principal concern. And of course the pollution affects the natural growing oysters that boaters can pick as well as those grown in the aquaculture farms.

On the eastern shore, in a cove, there is a sign which says 'Oyster Storage Permit/Please avoid walking on area below 8 ft. tide level.' All along the shore you will see little stocking-shaped bundles of oyster shells which apparently hold spat. Incidentally, there are a number of bullet holes in the sign. *Everywhere you go—critics!*

In the widest part of Pendrell Sound off to the west there is a lagoon and a niche behind an island. If you anchored in this spot, you could look across the Sound at a spectacular view of the mountain—a deep divide with a frozen creek at the summit and a running creek below. These are below two glacier fields which are now visible. There were about a half-dozen powerboats in this cove anchored in 6 to 7 m. There were two more stern-tied on the shore south of the cove. The winds coming down off the glacier are much colder than they would be in other parts of the Desolation Sound area. It's too bad that this cove doesn't have a name. It could be called 'Mountain View Cove,' for instance. We felt it was the best anchorage in Pendrell Sound. A narrow creek leads up to the saltwater lagoon behind this cove. The passage behind the island itself is fair and there was a large houseboat-type boat stern-tied to the island and anchored in the passage.

Beyond this moorage, about a quarter of the remaining distance to the head of the sound, we saw some white plastic pipes—probably 4 feet in diameter in a tiny bay. They may be part of the apparatus for spat propagation.

In a small niche just beyond this, we saw a small power boat in an area not much more than three times its own dimensions. It had an elaborate anchoring arrangement—two stern lines and a bow line. The two stern lines were out at right angles to the hull to trees on each shore.

There is a cluster of oyster strings in a niche beyond the shoulder in the last wide section before the head of the sound. On this shoreline, you will see a rock face with beautiful black striations. Back in a niche near the western end of the head, you will see an old ruin of a barge up on shore. It is possibly used as an underwater storage area for oyster shells containing spat.

There is a tiny finger at the head on the western side. It's wide open to the winds, but it has some shallow water for a hook if you stern-tie.

There is some truly beautiful scenery at the head of Pendrell. A bluff is all moss-covered and has a crown of evergreens. Snow capped mountains rise in the distance.

Returning down the eastern shore, you come to two islands which stand close off-shore. The area is devoted to aquaculture—oyster farming. The approach to the islands is blocked off by the strings. The temperature of the water in the area of the oyster beds was 65 degrees, much colder than in most areas.

There were supposed to be pictographs on these islands, but the oyster strings kept us from going in closely enough to see. We didn't see anybody around to ask for permission.

Following the eastern shoreline, we found that there are more spat areas, but they do not involve lines or buoys. In places, you will see markers: plastic bottles or pieces of styrofoam suspended from tree branches onshore which must indicate where the spat beds are. We also saw many string bags of oyster spat.

A creek bed leading down from the mountain north of the point marked 'aquaculture' is now dried and appears it may have been used as a skid road for timber many years ago—the bed is strewn with scrap logs.

In this area, some kind of blight has apparently hit the trees along the shore. There are hundreds and hundreds of tall dead trees.

A sign on this shore says: AREA RESERVED FOR OYSTER SEED COLLECTION/ALL VESSELS MUST REDUCE SPEED TO MINIMIZE WASH. It is signed: The Commercial Fisheries Branch of the Department of Conservation and Recreation. If you have a fast boat, slow down please.

The shoreline where the four creeks empty into the sound up near **Durham Point** becomes level and has some pebbled beaches.

Okay. We're back now in Waddington Channel.

Church Point has no explanation for its name. There is no beach area on which a church could have been built. It might have been named after a Mr. Church. It is rounded and has a few scruffy trees and moss slopes.

Just before you get to Church Point, up in a niche on shore, is an enormous log. It must be 5 or 6 feet in diameter and 20 feet long. If it ever floated it could be a menace to even big ships. We wonder if it will be there when you come by.

By the way, if you were on Chart #3541, you'd best slip back onto Chart #3538. You can still stay on page 9 of Chart #3312.

Now, me hearties, it time to visit another famous hangout:

Roscoe Bay

There is a resident eagle that usually sits in a tree on the left hand side as you enter, and he regards this popular spot as his own private reserve. Since he lives on

When the tide is out, the door is closed. Gerry Carlstron shows how shallow it is.

Marylebone Point, you can think of him as the Marylebone Eagle. We didn't get a picture of him. The fink listens for the sound of film advance in cameras and takes off when he hears it.

As you approach the entrance you will see a small dead-end off to the right and the main channel to the left. The water in the entrance is quite deep— over 33 m. At high tides, the entrance looks wide open and very fair. At low tides, you'd swear there wasn't anything in there. Even at high water there are some hazards. As a matter of fact, there is a door which opens and closes with the tides.

We favor the left hand side of the entrance at the first narrowing of the channel. You see a very prominent reef off to the right—that is the shoal area that almost dries at low tide. The water shoals up quickly as you approach it. We entered at about a 2.6 m. tide. At about 100 yards from the first narrow we had 20 m. under the keel. As we approached the second narrow, the depth dropped to 15 m. This was off a smaller reef to the right.

At about 150 feet from the second narrow it held at 12 m. Passing that first shoulder of rock, we trended toward the right and got 9 m. Nearing the big reef, we had 6 m. At the rock we had 4 m. Just beyond the reef it got down to about 3.5 m. So—keep to the right of the channel even though the rocks off that side seem formidable. The good rule of thumb is: stay about ¾ of the way to the right as you enter. And, unless you've been there before and know the area well, go through on a rising tide.

Despite the fact that the entrance to Roscoe is a little dicey, it is a popular anchorage. The fresh-water Black Lake just above the head may be the reason. It is possible to row to shore and walk up the path to the lake and take a bath on a rocky beach. It

It's a popular rendezvous spot.

is a B.C. Forest Service Recreation Site and there are four campsites—consisting of picnic tables and fire pits. There is an outhouse but no garbage removal. 'Bring it in, pack it out.' Roscoe Bay is one area that has water shallow enough for free anchoring.

On the north shore at the widest part of the bay, you will see a clearing with some remains of an old log camp and a hill with grassy terraces. We call it 'The Yellow Brick Road'. A stream enters the bay at this point. You will see on shore a few abandoned machinery parts—for example, an old engine or dynamo mounted on an iron base. In the woods behind the creek exit there are apple and cherry trees, lilacs and other flowers. We found some split rails above the creek—all signs of an early homestead. On one of the shoulders of the grassy mounds we found some worked rock points—including one rather crude arrowhead.

Along the northern shore at the widest point you may find a waterfall with good fresh drinking water—it's a little hard to make it flow into your container, however. Closer to the head of the bay on the north shore, you might find a rock with what looks like the sculpted face of Socrates—a friend who pointed it out calls it 'William Shakespeare.' We still think it looks more like Socrates. What do you think?

On the shoals on the southwestern shore, at the shallowest point, we found delicious small clams in the gravel. This is also the place to park your dinghy when you walk up to the lake to swim.

So leave the dinghy on the shore, walk along the path which follows the little stream from the lake to Roscoe Bay. The stream used to carry logs from the lake to the bay when logging was going on. There are the remains of logging machinery in the stream, which is not navigable. However, the path to the lake is fairly level and

Pete and Doris Wakeland toted their boat up the lake.

wide and many people carry rubber rafts or kayaks up to Black Lake for paddling.

To find the bath rocks, just stay on the path—past the beginning of the lake which has too many logs around for swimming. You can put your shore boat in there. Anyhow, go up the trail on a gentle slope and when you see a small trail to the left, take it to the first of the shores. Then you go downhill a bit to the lake. There are several good places along the rocks to dive in.

Or you can go farther along the trail and find yet more private beaches. Wherever you go, we can assure you you'll be pleased with the bathing/swimming areas you find.

We're going to drop you off for the night here. Don't forget to set the hook hard. When you leave, make sure you head out on a rising tide if possible—or at least near high tide.

You might want to post a lookout if you don't wear swim suits at Black Lake.

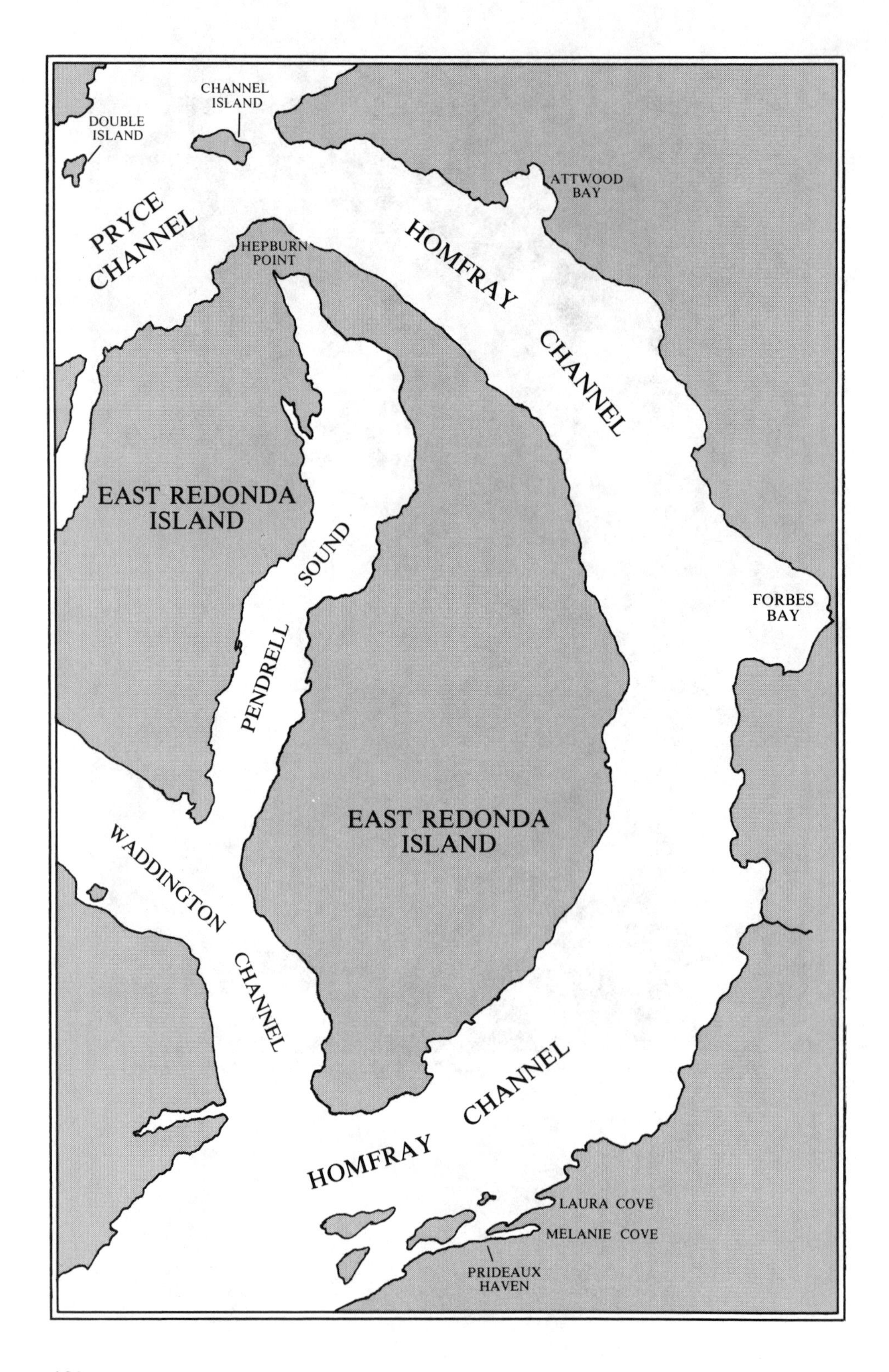
CHANNEL ISLAND
DOUBLE ISLAND
PRYCE CHANNEL
HEPBURN POINT
ATTWOOD BAY
HOMFRAY CHANNEL
EAST REDONDA ISLAND
PENDRELL SOUND
FORBES BAY
EAST REDONDA ISLAND
WADDINGTON CHANNEL
HOMFRAY CHANNEL
LAURA COVE
MELANIE COVE
PRIDEAUX HAVEN

Chapter 14

Von Donop Inlet

"The Back Forty"

That's the way we think of **Homfray Channel**. You will find many fewer boats along the eastern shores of **East Redonda Island**. There are some decent anchorages and one very magical place that we want you to see.

Looking at the profile of East Redonda Island on out-of-print chart #3594, you get the impression of some humongous amoeba about to divide. Pendrell Sound almost chops it in half. Better get out charts #3538 and #3541, and pages 9 and 16 of #3312.

We're going to roust you out of your bunks in Roscoe Bay, when the door opens, and take you up Homfray Channel to the foot of Toba Inlet.

First, a little sightseeing junket. Around the corner of Marylebone Point, and south about a half-mile, you will see a remarkable fissure in the cliffs. It is in the first small bight. There is a face of beautiful pink rock—maybe granite. We first saw it from across Desolation Sound near Mink Island. The sun was shining on it and we thought it looked like a giant neon light.

Now past Horace Head and you're on your way. (Jo's dad and brother were both named 'Horace', so we saluted as we sailed past.)

Brief history lesson here. Homfray Channel was named for Robert Homfray, an eccentric engineer. He designed, among other vessels, the steamship *Great Eastern,* built in 1858. It was the largest vessel ever built until near the turn of the century. Before his death he had his tombstone erected in the Ross Bay Cemetery, with all the particulars on it except for the date of his death, which was added the day he died, Sept. 19, 1902.

By the way, the *Coast Pilot* says that tidal streams in Homfray Channel seldom exceed 1.5 knots, the flood stream flowing south throughout most of the channel but north in the south part. The speeds and the boundary between the north and south flowing flood streams are greatly influenced by winds.

There is a marginal anchorage on the south end of East Redonda. We saw some boats anchored in the little pocket behind a reef and near the beach on the head of the cove. They may have been overflow from the crowded Prideaux Haven area.

Price Point, across the channel near Roffey I., is not significant.

On both shorelines in Homfray Channel you will find the exits of at least two dozen mountain creeks. In seasons with some rainfall you will see plunging creeks and waterfalls. On the East Redonda Island side, a number of them have produced beaches and deltas. These would be worthy of exploring, if you had the time. Old Indian bands needed fresh water for survival just like modern day folks. There should be middens and other traces of encampments. Most Indian villages were built near the mouths of streams.

Lloyd Point is unusual because it is low and marshy and almost seems to be lake scenery. There is a low bight behind the point. The scenery above it makes it a good picture opportunity, we think.

Lloyd Creek itself comes tumbling down through some exposed rocks into a small niche just beyond Lloyd Point.

Here's a 'f'rinstance'—the bay near Lloyd Creek on the mainland side. It deserves a name, as far as we're concerned. We're going to give it one: **Lloyd Creek Cove.** How's that for creative nomenclature?

Lloyd Creek Cove is south of an unnamed point that is surrounded by rocks and reefs. It has depths that are very great and that drop off sharply at the shore. It would be a very difficult place to stern-tie along most of the head. In the very north end of the cove, behind some rocks, it might be possible to find marginal anchorage. There is a beach onshore. We decided it would be a nice place for kayakers to camp.

On the north side of Lloyd Creek Cove there was a backhoe and some logging gear. On the beach nearby there is a massive log float. Some boom logs are scattered along the shoreline. This would be very exposed to southwest winds.

The next point has a cove behind it and on the point there is a big wooden box built on top of the rocks. We wondered about it. Go explore it, Tiger, and let us know what it is!

At a creek about a mile north of Lloyd Creek, there is a meadow and a house with several outbuildings. It looked deserted—the front door stood open. There were no

The house north of Lloyd Creek looked lonely.

boats on shore. There is a small dock beside the stream. It is noted on the chart.

There are some interesting sculptured cliffs at **Bohn Point.**

We couldn't even *find* **Booker Point** across the channel on the East Redonda shore. We did see a house with a blue roof up on a small promontory. Above it was a glacier high on the mountainside. South of the house there is a clear cut area with a white stiffleg crane up on one of the high logging roads.

This particular portion of East Redonda Island is pretty fantastic viewing. But to make the most of it, you have to get your boat out over the number 726 m. (2,396 feet) on the chart. It's just below the 50 degrees 15' line of latitude. (That's just outside Forbes Bay.) Now look west to Mt. Addenbroke, which is marked 1590 m. (5,247 feet) on the chart. When you're looking up at Mt. Addenbroke from this position, you are looking up nearly a mile while sitting on a boat which is on water about a ½-mile deep! Gives you a great feeling—the kids would probably say, 'awesome'!

Archibald Menzies kept a great journal of his trip up this part of the area, and we'll let you know how he saw things in June, 1792. He was traveling with Peter Puget and Joseph Whidbey in the *Discovery's* cutter and launch:

...I accompanied (Puget and Whidbey) as the rugged and wild appearance of the Country was likely to afford some variety to my pursuits...

(Translation: "I was bo-r-r-red!")

...a high conspicuous Mountain to the Westward...on the opposite side of the Arm was named from its figure Anvil Mountain. We now found the Arm taking a turn round the bottom of this Mountain to the North Westward & was contracted to about a mile & a half wide with rocky shores and high steep mountains wooded with Pines on both sides; those to the Northward had their summits chequered with Snow...

Early on the morning of the 28th we again set out & soon after passed a Bay (Forbes Bay) with some low land round the bottom of it & a large stream of fresh water emptied itself into it which collected from the Mountains over it in rapid torrents.'

Forbes Bay

At this point you will need to turn to page 16 of Chart #3312 in order to follow along. But Chart #3541 is still just fine if you're using that. Entering Forbes Bay there is a pleasant little grass and lichen covered slope—possibly a nice place to camp. A gently curving shoreline leads into the bay from the north. In the head of the bay you will see the tideflats associated with the creek delta. That is the Indian Reserve. This is a very big bay—it must be a mile across. As you enter you will see a fishing boundary marker about a third of the way down the north shore.

Since Homfray Channel is not a very popular body there is a great likelihood that you would have much of the area to yourself. This head of Forbes Bay is very pretty; low grassy shorelines and a creek. We saw a small power boat anchored in the confluence. (How about *that* word? This is gunkholing with high literacy!) This creek is the southern boundary of the Indian Reserve. No signs of habitation, though.

Winds can enter Forbes Bay through a saddle in the hills behind it, as we discovered. We dropped the hook and tied to an upright log on shore in the southeast corner down near the creek. Our bow was aimed into the prevailing wind, but we were

"Hey, Mom, what's this?" asks Martha Steenbergen.

uneasy about anchoring on a lee shore. So we decided to play our hunch. Even though it was fairly late in the afternoon and the nearest protected anchorage was Prideaux Haven, we hoisted anchor and left. We were glad we did, because later winds came up from the north and caused other boats in the area to move, we heard.

There is a waterfall in a creek leading down to shore in a niche just north of **Foster Point**. A little south of that some hardy soul has built a cabin up on shore and has a float in front.

Homfray Creek is listed as a community that has been abandoned. It is in a delta formed by the creek which comes down in a saddle between two mountains. There is a grass covered meadow on the delta but we couldn't see any ruins or indications of habitation. We didn't go ashore, incidentally. We were feeling lazy that day.

Attwood Bay

The south head of this cove is filled with an extensive fish pen. The limits of the nets are marked off by yellow buoys in the cove.

There is a waterfall coming down from the river in the eastern end of the bay. There is a logging road below the stream.

Along the shoreline in about the center of the bay there is a sheet metal float house and some boom logs. The house has a sign saying 'PRIVATE FLOAT'. Visiting boaters have painted their names on the front of the float house. Behind the house, there is an old shack on shore. Another logging road and stream enters the cove just beyond the float house. There is a log skid and a yellow truck on shore.

We visited with a woman who now lives on Cortes who worked at the logging camp at Attwood Bay in the 1920s. She told us:

I would get up at 5 o'clock each morning and ring the gong to wake up the men in the bunkhouse—and every time I did it I'd think about quitting. But I really liked the work. I cooked three meals daily. Breakfast was hotcakes, bacon and eggs, and porridge.

I would start in February cooking for five men, fallers and buckers. Then it would increase to 10 to 16 men later in the spring.

We had radio-telephone contact and could hear both sides of the conversation—we knew everybody's business.

This same woman said she had grown up living on float houses while her dad had hand-logged at various places.

He could cut the trees so they would go straight downhill into the water. We'd row to Squirrel Cove once a week for groceries, and we ate wholesome good food. We had our own gardens, orchard, pigs, chickens and cows, which bellowed night and day. It was a good life. We'd can 70 quarts of cherries, put up a cask of sauerkraut for the winter, get deer meat, fish before daylight.

We saw a couple of small power boats stern tied to the rocky shore on the northeast side of Attwood Bay. There is anchorage there, and that looked like the best spot, but there wasn't room for more.

We were reading depths of 100 m. just off the shore on the north end.

There is a reef with drying rocks which extends in a southerly direction from the point at the northern entrance to the bay. Next there is a round head that extends north behind the reef and a rocky headland to the west.

Now look back at East Redonda Island for a bit. The eastern half of the island is a Provincial Ecological Reserve. That means camping, fires or disturbance of animals or vegetation are prohibited. So don't go ashore on the eastern half.

At one time the Klahoose Indians lived on East Redonda. Later there were loggers and early settlers on the island. There are no settlements on the island at the present time.

The north shoreline on the channel is a favorite fishing ground. The mainland side of Homfray Channel from Attwood Cove up to **Brettell Point** is pretty much unrelieved.

Here, at **Hepburn Point**, you are at the three-way junction of Homfray Channel, Toba Inlet and Pryce Channel. The scenery up Toba is breathtaking in some weather conditions. In sunlight, it looks like pictures of Norwegian fjords. In low-lying clouds, you can almost see Viking ships coming into view.

Channel Island is dome-shaped and gently sloped.

Double Island in the distance, has two humps, one taller than the other.

At this point, in going back over our notes on our exploration of the area, we have some nagging by our consciences for not making the trip up Toba Inlet. We have never been in that body. We decided that it didn't have enough to offer the vacationing boater to merit exploration. We are not alone in this opinion. A number of our energetic friends have made the trip and they all say the same thing: "Absolutely magnificent!" "Not a single worthwhile anchorage or gunkhole in the whole sound."

We can tell you that Walbran says Toba Inlet was named by the Spanish naval explorers Galiano and Valdes on June 27, 1792, the day before Menzies took the trip. They named it 'Canal de la Tabla' because they found a sort of strange table (tabla) of planks, carved with hieroglyphics by the Indians. By a Spanish chart engraver's error 'Tabla' became changed into 'Toba,' and this error has since been perpetuated on the charts. Galiano in his journal always refers to the inlet as 'Canal de la Tabla'.

However, all is not lost. Archibald Menzies went up the 'Arm' and we'll tell you what he saw:

...About Noon we came to a naked point where a large branch turned suddenly off to the Northward with two small Islands in its entrance wooded like the rest of the Country with Pines. Soon after leaving this point to prosecute our examination in the Northern branch, we met with Capt. Valdes in the Spanish Launch on his way back from the head of it; he readily shewd us his Survey of it, & told us that it terminated in shallow water surrounded with low land about eleven miles off, & that he saw Mr. Johnstone with his boats on the preceding day in the Western opening we had just passed... We continued our examination in the Northern branch which was soon after found to take a turn East North East & went in that direction about nine Miles to its termination preserving its breadth all the way which was in general about a mile & a quarter wide.

On each side were high steep Mountains covered towards their summits with Snow which was now dissolving & producing a number of wild torrents & beautiful Cascades. As we advanced the country became more dreary & barren, large Tracts were seen without the least soil or vegetation, exposing a naked surface of solid rock, of which the mass of Mountains appeared entirely composed—the Woods became scrubby & stunted & the Trees were but thinly scattered except in Valleys & near the water side. It was observable however in these stinted situations, where Vegetation was making as it were a slow beginning, that Hardwoods such as Birch Maple Medlers Whortle berries & were most predominant & not Pines the general covering of the Country.

In the dusk of the evening we passed a number of Fish stages erected (by the Indians)...Next morning... we soon reached the head of the Arm which we rounded out in very shallow water, extending so far from the shore that we could not Land tho allured by the prospect of a pleasant Valley with a considerable track of low marshy Meadows backed by a forest of Pines & high snowy Mountains from which a number of foaming torrents fell into the Valley & formed a considerable winding Stream that glided gently through it.

On our way back from the head of this Arm... we found ourselves greatly assisted by a strong Drain or Current setting in our favor apparently occasioned by the great number of Torrents & Waterfalls which were observed rushing down the sides of the Mountains from the melted snow & these afforded such a considerable supply that the Water was perfectly fresh & of a whitish colour for several miles.

The Grotto looks intriguing and mysterious.

Maybe we'll explore Toba Inlet for our 'second edition', but even so, we'll never match his prose.

Now, we want to take you to a fantastic place. It's on the northwest shore of East Redonda Island, about halfway between Hepburn Pt. and Dean Point. We call it 'Wolferstan's Grotto', because we read about it in his book. It can give you goose-bumps.

'Wolferstan's Grotto'

Note that there is a square cove about a mile west of Hepburn Point. A stream empties into Pryce Channel there. We have it pencilled in on our charts as 'Grotto Cove'. There is a pebbled beach here and it would make an ideal camping spot for kayakers. The rocks on the face are tinged with pink.

Continuing west, you will find a big reef that comes out from shore, marked with '(2)'. Now, between the cove and the reef, you will find the cave.

It is in a rock face, half hidden by a high slab of rock which Wolferstan calls the 'Shield'. You can find it by looking for two large fir trees and one medium large cedar just a few feet above the high tide mark.

The cave is very startling. At first glance, from the boat, it seems to be endless. It may be as much as 30 feet across, 20 feet high and 20 feet deep. Since it is high above the water, it is not possible to see the floor of it, so it may be deeper. Also, the base of the entrance is covered with low brush.

The reefs just east of the grotto have small fissures and caves. This is a very interesting shore. Several niches are filled with drift logs—in one crack, there is a giant tree root. In the north side of this cove, the rocks are black with mussels. There are many overhanging rock faces that create scooped-out areas.

Now, figuratively-speaking we are going to do a Mary Poppins and take you to Squirrel Cove for the big trip around Cortes Island.

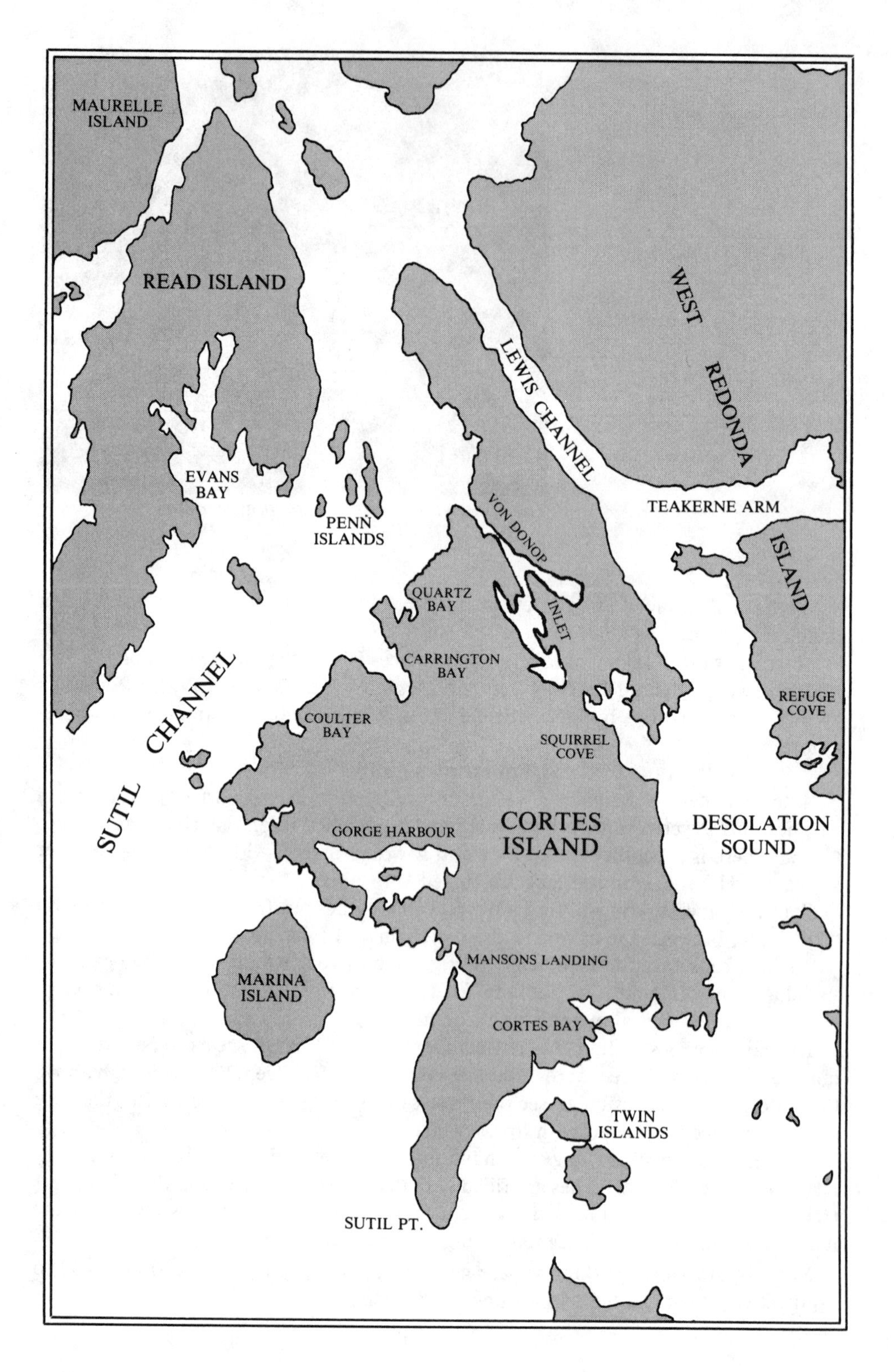
MAURELLE ISLAND
READ ISLAND
EVANS BAY
PENN ISLANDS
WEST REDONDA ISLAND
LEWIS CHANNEL
TEAKERNE ARM
VON DONOP INLET
QUARTZ BAY
CARRINGTON BAY
SUTIL CHANNEL
COULTER BAY
SQUIRREL COVE
REFUGE COVE
GORGE HARBOUR
CORTES ISLAND
DESOLATION SOUND
MANSONS LANDING
MARINA ISLAND
CORTES BAY
TWIN ISLANDS
SUTIL PT.

Chapter 15

Around Cortes Island

Wonderful old Cortes Island! It's a gunkholer's paradise. Nature has nibbled at its shores and created dozens of bays and coves and hidey-holes. Some of the best-known anchorages are to be found on its western side, along with its little-known but prized stopovers. Cortes Island was named in 1792 by Galiano and Valdes after Hernando Cortes, the conqueror of Mexico. The island to the southeastward is named Hernando and the island to the westward is Marina, after his mistress.

It is a good shopping area because it's served by the ferries from Vancouver Island and has a good network of paved roads. You can drive to most of the ports on the southern shores of Cortes, so it's a good place to meet crew members who come by car.

To circumnavigate Cortes Island in a seamanly manner, you'll need Chart #3311, sheet 4; Chart #3312, pages 8, 10, 17, and 19; and Chart #3538, which we think is the best and easiest to use.

Squirrel Cove

The southern approach is fair, but the northern gate at **Boulder Point** has a couple of detached reefs which should be noted. The outermost one dries at 3.7 m. above datum. They are quite close to shore, however.

Squirrel Cove is the stopping and shopping center in Desolation Sound and has a well-stocked store. There are other stores at other bays on Cortes Island but they are mostly 'general' or 'Mom & Pop' stores. There is also a wonderful protected moorage 'inside.'

The store does not have its own dock, so boaters must tie up at the government wharf and walk to it, either along the beach, which is the shortest way, or along the road. The wharf has 123 m. of space. It does not have water or power, but it does have garbage facilities, which are very important. They ask you to separate cans and bottles from other kinds of garbage and put everything in plastic bags. There are two floats and a derrick on the main dock. Usually there are a number of small boats owned by the locals on the floats. You may have to raft up or wait your turn. There is no fuel dock in Squirrel.

What's on Cortes?

There are about 700 folks on Cortes Island, and like most islanders, they are a hardy, independent group. Many are lifetime residents.

Early settlers, mostly English, Scottish, German or Swedish folks, homesteaded the land. They planted orchards and vegetable gardens, logged by hand or with oxen or horses, eventually adding steam donkeys and trucks. Early roads on the islands were often cowpaths and logging roads. Steamer service began in the early 1900s, with stops at Mansons Landing, Squirrel Cove and Whaletown. Now roads connect all the communities on the southern two-thirds of the island, while logging roads crisscross much of the northern section.

There is a Community Hall a couple of miles from Mansons Landing which is the center of island activity. There we found a library, a part-time doctor's office, a post office, thrift shop and play school. The coffee shop is open when the post office is open. The hall is also used for carpet bowling, dances, community activities, a theatre group, the Cortes Island Singers, and for classes sponsored by North Island College.

Where there were once seven or eight different one-room schools on the island, there is now one school, built in 1979, with well over 100 students and two school buses to transport them. There is even a place on the island that rents videos.

Jewelry from Cortes Island artisans.

There is a phone booth at the shore end of the dock and another phone at the store.

The store is well-known for its capacious walk-in cooler room full of fresh fruits and vegetables. It's like being a kid in a candy store to find all that wonderful produce—especially if it's hot out. Then you can cool down while picking out dinner. You can find just about everything else you need, including liquor, frozen meats, breadstuffs, canned goods, ice, propane, and gas for your outboard if you want to carry the tank to the store. There is a gift shop in a little building nearby. It has lovely jewelry and gift items made by local artists and craftsmen.

There is an old wreck up on shore just west of the store. It is the after section of a large steel boat, badly rusted and with grass growing out of the deck. It is marked on the chart with a tiny black triangle and line for a mast. There is a conspicuous large rock on the shore just west of the wreck which is noted on the chart by a tiny circle on the beach.

The Old Klahoose Herring Trick

This note is taken from **Sliammon Life, Sliammon Lands** by Kennedy and Bouchard.

"One year the herring didn't go to Squirrel Cove to spawn, so a Klahoose man named Marshall Dominick...tied together a male and female herring with a piece of string and towed them in the water from the place they were spawning, all the way to Squirrel Cove. And the other herring followed. Marshall Dominick was able to do this because he was a twin; twins are related to the fish, his people believed, and therefore have some communication with them."

A picturesque Klahoose Indian village is about a half-mile west of the dock. You will notice a white Catholic church—St. Peter's—and a cluster of about a dozen homes, all painted in bright colors: blue, green, yellow, tan. Most of the residents moved there from other villages in 1939.

The Squirrel Cove anchorage area is beyond **Protection Island**. The safe channel is to the west of this island. The channel to the northeast looks inviting but it has a number of troublesome rocks and reefs at its inside end which would rule it out to all but people with good local knowledge. By staying close to the little hook of Protection Island at the narrows in the preferred channel you can pass at all tides with minimums of about 6 m.

On beyond the narrow entrance, the cove widens out with fairly deep water in the center of the area. There are two distinct anchorage areas, both of them popular. The outer body has a couple of tide-flat hooks which are not useful. The northern

Willy Joseph—Klahoose Indian

We visited the Squirrel Cove Indian Reservation a couple of years back and looked up Rose Hanson who introduced us to one of the older Indians in the band—Willy Joseph. At first he was rather reticent to talk, until it turned out that he and Jo had the same birthdate—August 15. The years were different—his was 1911, and we won't mention hers.

He was born at Church House on Calm Channel and was a fisherman for years. As a child he gillnetted, worked the fish traps and reef-netted. In 1927 he seined. He had eight brothers and never married. In 1926 he fished at Alert Bay. "That's when the fish were pretty cheap: 2 cents each, chum were 10 cents and sockeye were 25 cents," he said. Then he chuckled. "I haven't eaten fish for over 20 years."

Willy Joseph left Church House in 1939 and moved to Squirrel Cove where there is a Klahoose reservation. He said there are now less than 100 Indians on the reservation. After he quit fishing, he was a logger. Now he is crippled and doesn't work anymore.

Willy Joseph, patriarch.

hook has three reefs which front it. You will see a cabin on shore between two sections of mudflat. In that area, there is also a log-strewn beach which looks like the aftermath of a logging operation some time in the past. A path through the woods that leads to the store begins there if you like to paddle ashore and walk. There is also a path at the head of this cove that is the portage trail to Von Donop called, the 'Von Donop Nature Trail'.

The inner harbour area is limited by the northern end of Protection Island and a finger that protrudes out from the eastern shore of the Cortes Island side. There are two islets which offer shelter from the winds that can occasionally scoop down over the low profiles of Cortes Island. The larger of these islets is heart-shaped and has about a dozen trees on it. The passage behind it has one shoal point which can get down to .3 m. At datum, that rock would be sticking up .3 m. We cleared in 6 m. by staying about 100 feet offshore of the islet. A reef extends out from the south end of this islet. The area behind the islet has a shoreline which is part of an Indian reserve.

There is a peninsula which divides the anchorage into two sections. The large lobe to the west has a lot of good anchorage area. We saw several large boats anchored in there. The smaller lobe to the east of the peninsula has a creek which leads up to the lagoon. This body has a couple of pebbled beaches and a nice meadow for camping.

Canoeists camp in Squirrel Cove Lagoon.

Squirrel Cove Lagoon

This is a saltwater lagoon which is about a ½-mile long and 1/8-mile wide. It is connected to the main Cove by a creek about 100 yards long. This is a fascinating little creek. At low tides, it is a low waterfall running through rocks. At high tides, it looks like a channel with very strong rapids. Water rushes into and out of the lagoon at speeds up to 10 knots. The narrows is active at all times, except for a five or ten minute period of slack. The depths at high tide must be no more than several feet in the deepest point. The overfalls of the rapids are impressive. Small boats going into the lagoon may be trapped there for hours waiting for an ebb unless their owners want to carry the boats out of the lagoon across a narrow rock and mud flat with large boulders that make such a portage difficult.

The entrance to the lagoon is quite narrow, probably not more than 20 feet across. The current rushes

At high tide, it looks almost like a passage from Squirrel Cove into the lagoon.

through there with considerable overfall. It probably only remains quiet for a short time before it begins to reverse. We went into the lagoon in our kayak **with** the current which must have been flowing at least 10 knots. We were shot through it like a rocket. On the lagoon side there were eddies and countercurrents which spun us around and tossed us out into the more placid lagoon itself.

There is a small wooded island south of the entrance with drying flat rocks. We swam there and bathed in relatively warm water—about 70 degrees.

The south end of the lagoon ends in a marsh with several logs across the end of it and a muddy flat. Proceeding up along the eastern shore of the lagoon we came to a grassy meadow where some people were camped. They were canoeists who had portaged from Von Donop Inlet into Squirrel Cove and then into the lagoon. Off to the north west there are three small islets The first is the biggest with three trees on it: one arbutus and a couple of evergreens. The other two have grasses on top but no trees. There's a marsh at the north end of the lagoon and it too is muddy and grassy.

Coming back out of the lagoon

At low tide—it's clearly a creek.

proved to be much more difficult! The current was still against us at 6 to 8 knots because there was a heavy overfall, a lot of white water. We tried several times to paddle UP the river but could not make it and each time were pushed and swirled back into the lagoon. We considered portaging the kayak by carrying it along the boulder-strewn, muddy shore for about 100 yards. But just as we started, a couple of teen-agers in wet suits came to our aid and waded waist-deep through the rapids to get our boat back to the cove itself. Whew! We noticed they were helping several other boaters out of the lagoon. Nice kids!

There is a square-shaped lobe to the east, behind a small narrow islet that rises to 4.5 m. above low tides. There is a big old log raft near the shore. On the east shore of this lobe, you will see a tumbledown shack on a barge which does not float at high water. On the shore beyond the shack, when we visited last, there was an old clapboard float house with a big sign proclaiming 'HOMADE BREAD' for sale.

Certainly not your average bakery.

'Homade Bread'

The old floathouse in the southeast cove in Squirrel Cove has a large sign advertising 'HOMADE BREAD', and boy does that sound good after you've been eating biscuits fried in the cast iron fry pan for the past couple of days!

But before you can figure out how to get to the floathouse on tired-out logs, two curly-headed teenagers come zipping up to your boat in their old outboard— taking orders. Be prepared to fend them off as their boat doesn't carry fenders, they haven't learned where the brakes are, and they aren't worried about THEIR hull.

They go around to all the boats moored in Squirrel Cove and take orders for bread and cinnamon rolls for the following morning. Then they deliver next day, somewhere near the time you asked for it. Pretty neat arrangement.

After we tasted the goodies—their baker dad doesn't scrimp on the sugar—we paddled the kayak over to visit. It wasn't too easy to climb up the logs to the house at low tide, but we did it, only to find out the baker was fast asleep. After all, he had gotten up at midnight to start work. So we talked to the boys—in whispers—in the floathouse kitchen.

Bill Randall is the dad, Chris and Ben are the boys. They've been living there and doing the homemade bread bit for a couple of years. The boys attend school at Mansons Landing on Cortes.

What the kids didn't realize is that their dad's bread is famous all up and down the B.C. coast among boaters, and lots of people go to Squirrel Cove just for that reason alone!

Here's a heartfelt wish for their success—for two reasons. First, they bake a good product. Second, this story will seem somewhat dopey if they aren't there when you get there.

Chris Randall helps sell his dad's baked goods.

After you leave Squirrel Cove and head south down Lewis Channel, you will discover there is a long curving beach extending south from Squirrel Cove. Just north of the point marked on the chart as **Seaford** there is a big and bare clear-cut. The once-thriving community of Seaford no longer has a wharf—only one piling remains. It consists now of a half dozen homes along the island road.

Tiber Bay

It's a desolate and forbidding place, but it has some very dramatic scenery. It is a little indent created by two unnamed islands and a clearing rock. The chart mentions 'Percy Logging', but we didn't see any activity or machinery in the area. The chart also indicates a boat launching ramp, but we couldn't find it. We did see an old log skid, however. Telephone and power cables enter the water here. Just under the terminus of the northernmost power cable there is a very impressive house partially screened by trees. Behind it is a house that looks like a store-front. Farther south, there are several beautiful homes.

You will discover, when you go out around the unnamed islands, that there is a real estate development here. This small cove would be only a temporary anchorage unless you could expect little or no winds. The islands are connected to Cortes Island by a long sandy spit—winds could sweep over it from Georgia Strait. A sign an-

Memories of Seaford

At one time there was a post office, school and wharf in Seaford where the Union steamers stopped. Nellie Jeffery, who has lived on Cortes most of her life and grew up at Seaford, tells:

"The 'Union' boat was a big part of our lives. My parents had a flagpole with a light which they'd turn on when they wanted the ship to stop. It brought our mail, groceries, and carried the people coming or going up and down the Coast.

My father pre-empted 160 acres at Seaford and also worked as captain on the **City of Lund** boat at Lund. I started school in September just before my fifth birthday so there would be enough kids in school. They had to have 7 or 8 students in grades 1 through 8 in order to have a teacher.

When we were growing up we didn't have bikes—the water was our life. We always had boats of some kind, punts, or rowboats. There were no jails. If people did anything wrong, no one knew it."

nounces that the tidelands have a shellfish lease and warns 'No Trespassing'. The southernmost of the two islands has a tall snag with two eagles looking out over the water. They look like they own the place. On the isthmus that connects the islands to the shore, there was an old abandoned cream-colored van.

Mary Point is gentle and sloping and has a discernible point. The third bight west of Mary Point is very deep and there is a driftwood-strewn beach.

We have been told there is a big eagle's nest on a point west of Mary Point. We searched but didn't spot it. We saw a couple of eagles soaring over the area, but they didn't go home while we were watching.

There is a rock off one of those bluffs, which bares at one foot above zero tide—it may keep you away from a thorough search.

The **Three Islets** off the entrance to Cortes Bay are in reality just drying points on one big reef. They are barren and covered on top with lichens and grasses.

Just outside the entrance to Cortes Bay there is a deep bight with a wide curving beach. It has some tideflats. There is a very picturesque house up on stilts in that cove.

Just before entering Cortes Bay you can look out over Desolation Sound to the Redonda Islands and see all of the glaciated mountains and it looks like Alaska scenery. Cortes Island is relatively flat.

Cortes Bay

There is a handsome red light as you enter Cortes Bay. It must be about 20 feet high with an occulting red light. On the left shoreline you see some very interesting rock faces. They are in a lot of small niches—looking like rock alcoves with green trees nestled into them.

There is a big sign on the port entrance that says 'DAMMIT PLEASE SLOW DOWN!' So much for word-mincing!

Cortes Bay Marine Resort is elaborate and popular.

On the northern shores there are big signs with warnings about fires—'FIRE HAZARD...NO FIRES...NO TRESPASSING!' *A skoshie paranoid, aren't we?*

Inside Cortes Bay there is a government wharf and a private marina. The government wharf is directly opposite the entrance to the bay. It has power, water, garbage disposal, and berthage space of 159 m. There is a telephone nearby. The house above the wharf has a red roof—the same color as the ramps—it possibly belongs to the wharfinger? There is a small church at Cortes Bay called St. Saviour-by-the-Sea.

In the south corner of the bay is Cortes Bay Marine Resort. It is an attractive marina with a series of stairs and decks leading to a store, showers, and a restaurant, the 'Wheelhouse.' There is moorage, gas and diesel—no propane—a laundromat, showers, cabins, and a store which carries groceries, fresh produce, books and magazines, hardware, tackle, T-shirts and sweatshirts, ice, and has a reputation for great ice cream cones. Rankin Smith has owned the resort for more than 15 years. It is a busy, cheery place, accessible by boat, plane and car.

It's about a five minute row from the public wharf over to the marina, but it is at least a mile walk over dusty hilly roads, believe it or not.

Isolated winds reputedly blow through the bay when it's calm outside. But we found that the winds blowing through were also blowing gales outside.

This may be a radio hole—we had trouble reaching out on VHF—and so did others.

Leaving Cortes Bay there is a cove with a pebbled beach and some summer homes on shore around the headland to the southwest. This cove is just across a narrow neck of land from the Marina in Cortes Bay.

Quai's Bay is not noted on the charts as it is a local name. It is the deep tideland inlet south of Cortes Bay which is fronted by a small island. This island extends back almost to the tideflat on shore, so there would be very little room behind it for moorage. The rock off the center of Quai's Bay is about 500 feet from the island. There is a small niche just before you get to Quai's Bay. We saw a sailboat stern-tied in it. There is a big house above it.

Just beyond Quai's Bay is **Hank's Beach.** We never found out just who 'Hank' was. It is apparently a favorite camping ground. You will probably see some vans and tents on the beach as you cruise past.

Heading toward the narrow cut between Hanks Beach and the corner of Twin Islands, the Cortes Island shore is littered with driftwood and there are two little pockets (one we have noted before across a narrow isthmus from the marina) and one farther south. Both have nice beaches.

At this point, it would be well to find page 5 of Chart #3311, or you can stick with #3538 if you have it. They have the best coverage from Cortes Bay to Mansons Landing on the western shore of southern Cortes.

Twin Islands

They are called the 'Hapsburg's Islands' because they were—or are—owned by a descendant of the royal house. There is a small forested island off the northwest corner. This island, like the rest of the island area, has a sign marked 'No Trespassing.'

The little pocket between this island and the bigger islands is attractive and would make an excellent anchorage except it is open to winds from the southwest. (I wouldn't expect their Royal Highnesses to invite you to tea, though.) Queen Elizabeth, the Duke, and Princess Anne were there in the early 1970s.

The northwest corner of Twin Island has a rocky peninsula which points a finger at **Little Rock**. This peninsula has a little rocky driftwood beach behind it.

As you approach the waist that divides the two sections of Twin Islands, you will want to eyeball the rock that sits in the entrance to the area. It is on a line from the above-mentioned peninsula to the general shore contour of the southwest side of the south island. It is on a reef that is 2.3 m. above low tide. We personally hate those rocks marked ' + '. As far as we're concerned, they're very negative!

The mansion or manor house or whatever it is, can be seen in the narrow neck between the islands. A friend on Cortes said there are 15 bedrooms in the big house. (*Boy, they must shop the August White Sales!)* You can see the causeway that has been built behind it. There is a dock and a boat house in the shallow bight on the south island near the divide.

The view from here is quite rewarding. You can see Mitlenatch Island in the distance, with a number of boats fishing around it. You see Hernando Island off to the left. Mitlenatch is a wildlife preserve and you're supposed to contact the ranger before you go there, we're told.

There are several little indents as you approach the southwest corner of Twin Islands. We saw some eagles, posted like sentinels up in some dead snags. They may have been commissioned by the aristocrats.

Across Baker Passage, the end of Hernando Island has some beautiful white beaches out near Spilsbury Point at the end of Stag Bay. They are reputed to be the most inviting of all the beaches in B.C. If the weather is gentle, you might want to go over there and make a lunchhook stop. It would give you a chance to row ashore and beachcomb and swim. You can see how Hernando Island could be picked up like a piece of a jigsaw puzzle and inserted in the bay between Twin Islands and the Cortes beach area.

From **Echo Bay** you can see smoke rising in the west from Campbell River. This bay is shallow-profiled and the water is deep up to the shoreline. The beaches are pebbled and rocky. It would be wide open to southerly winds. There is a tiny hook on the left side which might provide minimal protection.

From the southeast corner of Twin Islands there is an absolutely spectacular view of the mountains of Desolation Sound and the Redonda Islands. It is a panorama, all misty and mirage-like.

Iron Point is aptly named. You can see great streaks of rust colored rock which make vertical bands from the water up to the tops of the rock faces. This is truly a beautiful island!

Going along the east side toward the narrow junction between the islands, we saw the remains of a boat hull up on shore. Beyond that are number of outbuildings. The reef and rocks on the curving shore of the northeast side of the island are pinnacles which reach up from 30 m. depths.

Central Rock bares at 2.7 m. and is not easy to find. We saw only a couple of inches of rock at mid-tide.

Forward, Around Cortes!

We have now circumnavigated Twin Islands and we're heading south again along Cortes Island.

Just off the curving beach below Quai's Bay is a compound dedicated to the pursuit of mental health. *(We love Wolferstan's tongue-in-cheek reference to this place!)* The lodge at the 'Hollyhock' establishment is nicely hidden in the trees and you can only see the two white chimneys from the water. There is a flight of wooden stairs leading down to the beach at this point. You will see a mooring buoy a hundred yards or so offshore. There are quite a few other buildings that seem to be associated with the institution. One cabin is right down on the beach.

From there to Sutil Point you will see homes all along the shore. This is a combination of summer homes and retired residents. There is a cluster of gray houses at one point. Unlike much of the area, along here there are shallow beaches and you need to stay offshore a bit.

Sutil Point has rocks studding the water out from the point. Up until 1945 this dangerous, mile-long reef was called 'Reef Point'.

At this juncture, you start looking for the red marker at the end of the shoals off Sutil Point. When you finally spot it, it will come as something of a surprise. You'll say, "It must have been there all along!" as it jumps into view. You will see a string of rocks sticking up like dragon's teeth in a straight line from the point to the buoy. Notice that you swing well south of the buoy before passing it.

The wind usually blows in this area, even if it is quiet elsewhere. This is the junction of several straits, including the north end of the Strait of Georgia. A local sailor told us that if the wind is making up in the Strait, the south end of Cortes is 'bad news'. He said he always heads up Lewis Channel and goes up and around Cortes—just to be safe.

Smelt Bay Provincial Park is a beautiful and popular camp site today. It was originally the home of Coast Salish and Klahoose Salish Indians. The local natives were constantly fighting intruders, like the frightening Haidas and Euclataws from up north. The rolling small hillocks at Smelt Bay were fortifications against attack from these vicious aggressors. Our friend who lives just north of the park said she has found many artifacts above the beach line, including harpoon points, arrowheads and a perfect pestle.

As you near the park, you will see a house with a very elaborate log fence and breakwater. The park area also has a fence and a nice pebbly beach. You will probably see cars parked in the lot.

Smelt Bay is also a popular summer home area. The population in 1981, according to the *Coast Pilot,* was 92. It must have doubled by now.

The charts indicate an Indian Reserve on the bulge of the shoreline north of Smelt Bay, the old Indian village of 'Paukeanum'. Along the beach just north of this is the famous petroglyph carved into a huge granite boulder. The pecked outline of a fish faces toward Marina Island, and can be seen only at low tide. The carving is about nine feet long. The legend we heard was that this fish was welcoming other fish so the Indians could catch them.

Our rock art expert, Doris Lundy, says this petroglyph may be a representation of a whale, or a seal or even a sea lion. It could also be a mythical creature with the attributes of all of these creatures.

While you can see the rock from your boat, it's hard to distinguish the carving from that far out. You can see the rock by looking northward along the shore from the sandy beaches to where they become rocky and there are two prominent large rocks. The one out near the water is too rounded to provide a space for drawing. The rock which is near the high-tide line is flat on the face looking toward the water. It is also remarkably light. You may see the petro on its seaward side with good binoculars. The best way to see the rock is the way we did—walk along the beach from Mansons Landing. We even swam out from it and saw it from sea level.

Mansons Landing Petroglyph

A Sliammon story says that it was carved by a man named Tl'umnachm. That name means 'only room for himself.' He got that name because he had a special relationship with fish and seal and deer and they would come to him to be killed and put in his canoe. He filled his boat with so many porpoises one time that he could hardly get in it to paddle home. He decided to tell the world that the greatest porpoise-killer of the land lived here, so he carved a picture of it on the rock.

The Mansons Landing Public Dock.

Nearing the boundary of the Mansons Landing Marine Park you will see a giant black snag extending up.

Mansons Landing Marine Park

The two islets in the entrance to **Manson Bay** are called **Cat Islet** and **Sheep Islet.** We know, because they are mentioned in several books on cruising the Desolation Sound area. There is just one big problem. The two islands are not labelled on the charts. So—which is Cat and which is Sheep?

The one nearest the public wharf, Cat/Sheep, has a nice house facing the landing. This island (whatever its name) is separated from its companion by a small cut. We saw a boat anchored in the passage behind Cat & Sheep Islets.

The public dock has 110 m. of moorage, a derrick and a seaplane float. Just above the public wharf is the Mansons Landing store, which carries some fresh produce, baked goods, canned and frozen things, fishing gear and licences, ice, video rentals, fuel and petroleum products and a pay phone. There is no fuel dock here.

The beach here is lovely and sandy. There is a large saltwater lagoon at Mansons Landing which is a Wildlife preserve, although clams and oysters are harvested in there. It goes completely dry at low tide. You can walk a trail along the southwest shore which will take you along the lagoon, through the woods and across a road to the gorgeous freshwater sandy beach at Hague Lake. It's all part of the Marine Park. You can swim in the warm water, but since this is also a reservoir, you are not allowed to use soap or shampoo in the lake. To the north of the main beach area, we discovered there is a sun-bathing rock and skinny-dipping beach.

To some visitors, they're all 'skinny-dipping' beaches.

Good Old Mike Manson

Doris Anderson, in her rich and charming book **Evergreen Islands,** tells the story of one of the true pioneers, Mike Manson.

He came from the Shetland Islands to Canada in the mid 1800s. His first stop was at Nanaimo, where he went into storekeeping with a partner, named Mr. Renwick. Renwick's daughter was apparently a beautiful young lady named Jane. Her father seems to have been something of a tyrant. So Mike borrowed a dugout canoe from an Indian friend and eloped with Jane to Victoria where they were married. They eventually had 13 children.

He came to Cortes Island in 1886 and pre-empted some land, which was then called 'Clytosin'. After he got a Crown grant in 1913, the place became known as Mansons Landing.

There is a great story about Manson and the Indians, on pages 90 and 91 of her book. Read it, you'll love it!

More About Mansons Landing

A sign at Mansons Landing gives us a better look at the history of the place from the late 1700s.

Thigh-too-thein or **'facing inward at the mouth'** was the name given to the entrance of Mansons Lagoon by the native inhabitants. The only remnants of the village are clamshell middens, indicating the abundance of food resources.

Approximately one hundred years after Captain Vancouver's expedition, in the late 1800s, two young Scotsmen, Mike and John Manson, established a trading post near the abandoned Indian village. Both natives and settlers traded logs, deer hides, furs and dogfish oil for firearms, food, staples and convenience items.

As more settlers were attracted to the logging and fishing resources, larger trading posts were established in Vancouver. The Union Steamships began transferring supplies to villages and logging camps and the Manson Brothers, unable to compete, closed their trading post.

In 1974, Mansons Landing Provincial Park and Recreation area was established. Accessible by boat or vehicle, the park provides a unique combination of lake and seashore environment. Enjoy your visit.

Now that you've had a rest and a swim, it's time to press on.

Just northwest of Manson Bay is a deep cove. It has no shelter from the southwest winds and there is a rock at datum level in the middle of the area.

Deadman Island is domed and high with trees. There is a house on its E corner. It was supposedly an Indian burial ground. Note that the Indians did not inter their dead, they stuck them up in trees and let nature and the scavengers do their work. There is no passage behind Deadman Island.

Guide Islets, just outside the entrance to Gorge Harbour, are fairly barren and topped with grasses. There must be good fishing around them, we have seen a number of kicker boats drifting around them.

Just south of the entrance to Gorge there is a big, complex white house built on several different levels.

The cliff line on the western side of the entrance is beautiful. It is on the western cliff that you will find the well-known pictographs. On that side you will find that there are two separate cliffs, with a deep ravine between. The picto is on the outermost of the two faces. It is about 20 feet above the water, on rocks which are smooth and face the same direction—out of the Gorge. The two sets of pictures look like smudges at first. The pictures seem to be those of fish—mostly vertical lines. As pictographs go, frankly, they are not very impressive. There are ledges on which the artist could have stood. Below the innermost set, you will see that the ledge has red splotches—maybe spilled paint?

It seems very likely that these pictures are a kind of billboard or 'city-limit' sign.

Short courtesy tie-ups and a welcome fuel dock at Gorge Harbour.

They are usually in places that can be seen by approaching boats. They may have been an announcement to visitors, both friendly and hostile, that the area is the territory of a specific band.

On the same shore, south of the pictographs, you will find some graffiti in white—the name of a boat, apparently: Aragon?

Sliammon history says that Gorge Harbour used to be called *'ip'iikwu'* which means 'to break ice'. In olden days, the entrance would freeze over in the winter and the Indians had to break the ice to get into the harbour in their canoes.

Gorge Harbour

Tide Islet. Off to the right as you enter past Tide Islet you will see a big home on floats. Aquaculture extends over to the islet—oyster strings.

In Gorge Harbour we anchored off to the left (west), past the marina, in a bight beyond the charted rock. We hunted for it and never located it. We went to bed half expecting to hear the keel crunch on it at low tide, but it didn't. Darn those ' + ' rocks! We found the water was warm enough for swimming, about 70 degrees.

The next morning we went to the Gorge Harbour Marina and tied up to go shopping. There was a sign saying that there is courtesy moorage for an half-hour and then it is $1 per hour after that. On the other hand, it's 30 cents a foot for the night. The bull rails are painted off in one-foot increments. Handy, eh? There is a fuel dock, water and power, a dinghy float, and a launching ramp.

If you take a short path up a hill you come to a restaurant which featured an 'all-

Gilean Douglas

We visited by telephone with a wonderful writer on Cortes Island, Gilean Douglas. She has written a lovely series of essays about her life on the island, **The Protected Place,** a truly beautiful book. She also has written several poetry books. All her works are sold on the island, and well worth purchasing.

you-can-eat' Sunday brunch for a very modest price. It was one of the bits of information exchanged by boaters in the various anchorages in Desolation Sound. We weren't there on Sunday, unfortunately. There is also a marina store and office. The store offered groceries, ice, ice cream, fresh produce, fishing supplies and lots of fishing supplies. There were also showers and a laundromat.

Gorge Harbour Government Dock, just to the east, offers 41 m. of moorage *and that is all!*

There are several clusters of islets in the Harbour. Along the shore, eastward, you will find **Stove Islets** and **Pill Islets**. They are surrounded by drying and submerged rocks, and make anchoring in the area tricky. The eastern head has a cove that is good for stern-tying. There is very little opportunity for anchorage in the area of **Neck Islets**. We saw boats on hooks around **Ring Island** and the south side of **Tan Island. Bee Islets** are visible at most tides and stand in the course from the Marina to the entrance.

Whaletown/Gorge Harbour Walk

Cortes Island does have lots of walks. This is one that is not deep in the woods, but on a road with cars and all that sort of modern thing. In a little over a mile you can go from Gorge Harbour Marina to Whaletown. You walk to Gorge Harbour Park, near the resort, where there are trails and picnic tables. Then you can walk on to Whaletown. Along the way you'll see a huge fir tree, purportedly nine feet in diameter. It was just a baby some 2,000 years ago—maybe about the same time the Indians were painting pictographs in the Gorge, or perhaps rolling rocks from the cliffs onto the canoes of attacking Indians.

Continuing north from Gorge Harbour, we will work our way up to famous Von Donop Inlet, making some stops along the way.

Let's get a fresh start, however.

Meet the newest member of the Sea Witch crew—Al B. Tross.

The S/V 'Sea Witch Gets A Mascot'

It's getting to be a status symbol, this business of rowing some piddle-prone pooch to shore every few hours. No matter where we stay, we see the steady stream of dinghies heading for shore with pent-up poodles in the prow. What a happy symbiosis of man and mutt this must be! We often think about taking on a four-legged crew member so we can be part of the parade.

However, the sloop is too small for Zo's favorite species of canine—a black Lab. We decided on our trip to Desolation Sound that we would consider some other pet. Maybe a sea-cucumber?

Well, in Mansons Lagoon we found exactly the right mascot. It was a bird, a long-legged bird. It didn't need a cage. It didn't have to be fed. It would never be as indiscreet as a sea-gull. And, best of all, it would never utter a peep or chirp.

It is now carried, proudly, with us. It perches on the mast, facing the wind.

Its name is Al B. Tross.

It used to work as a pink lawn flamingo, until we found it, badly wounded, on the shores of the Manson Lagoon.

You have to look close to see the stick figure man.

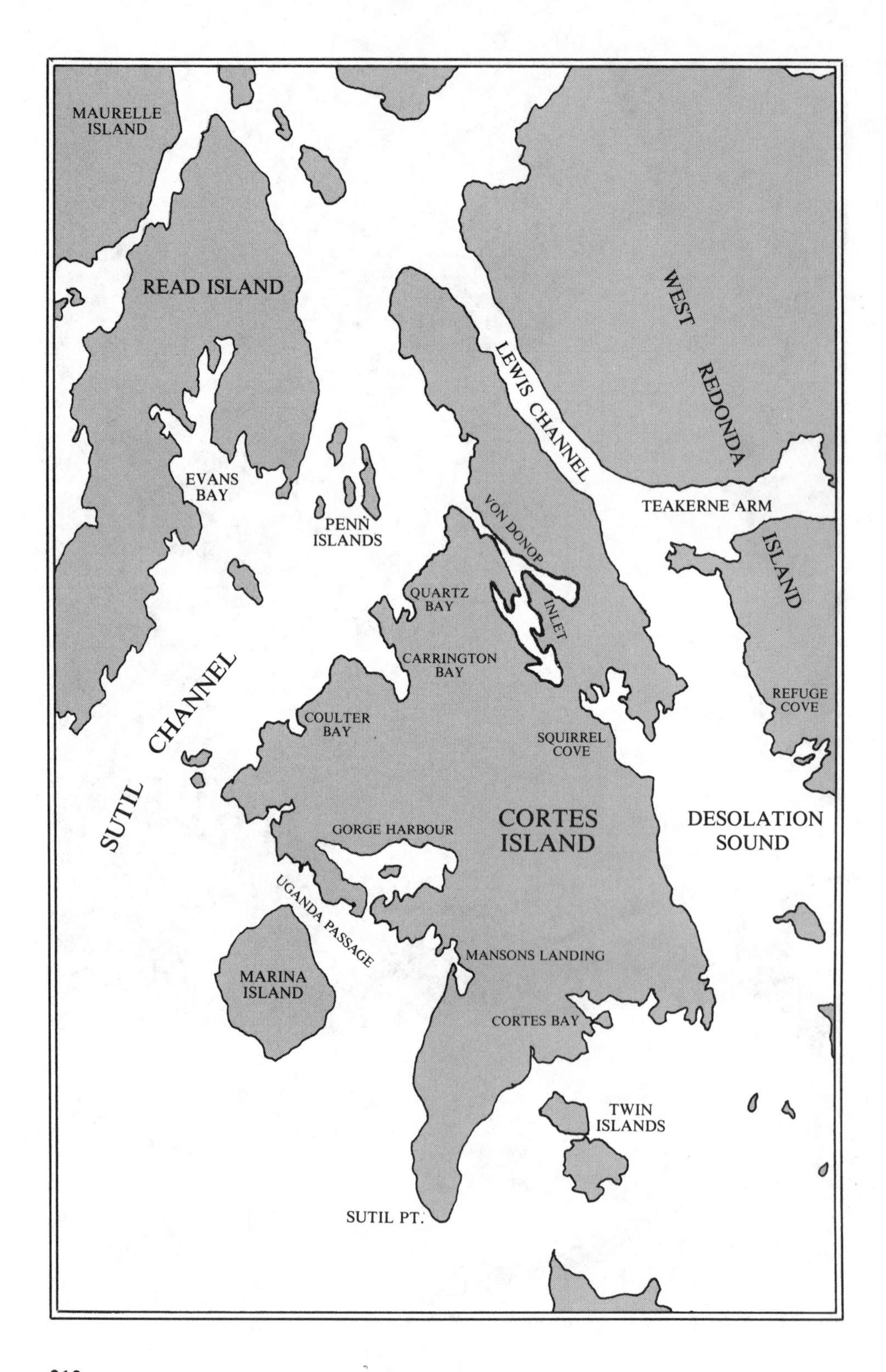
MAURELLE ISLAND
READ ISLAND
WEST REDONDA
LEWIS CHANNEL
EVANS BAY
PENN ISLANDS
TEAKERNE ARM
VON DONOP
INLET
ISLAND
QUARTZ BAY
CARRINGTON BAY
SUTIL CHANNEL
COULTER BAY
REFUGE COVE
SQUIRREL COVE
CORTES ISLAND
DESOLATION SOUND
GORGE HARBOUR
UGANDA PASSAGE
MANSONS LANDING
MARINA ISLAND
CORTES BAY
TWIN ISLANDS
SUTIL PT.

Chapter 16

Through 'Uganda'—*Uganda??*

We're going to be headed toward Uganda in a bit. But before you start looking for your pith helmet and trusty Watusi guide, we should point out that it's Uganda in British Columbia, not Uganda in Africa. (It *is* in Africa somewhere, isn't it? World geography is not our strong suit.) By the way, you can now get off the strip chart and onto page 19 of Chart #3312 or stick with good old #3538.

Exiting Gorge Harbour heading toward Uganda, you will run along the rocky south shore of Cortes Island. As you head toward the **Heather Islets,** there is a cove to the right. It has no value as a stop—too deep and too exposed to southerlies up the channel.

It also looks like you could pass between the finger extending from Cortes shore and the Heather Islets. There may be passage at high tides with very careful maneuvering. It doesn't seem worth the effort, though.

There is a beautiful big home on the spit reaching toward Heather Islets. It's back in a little crease. The charts shows that there is aquaculture in that unnamed cove, but we didn't spot it. It doesn't offer much in the way of shelter, anyhow.

North and South Heather Islets are almost identical in size. They have some trees, especially the outermost island facing the passage to the south. There's another house in a little nook behind the peninsula that is north of the Heathers. It has a long curving ramp leading down to a dock—and there is another house back in the woods.

The **Marina Island** shore along here is a beautiful curving sandy beach which terminates at **Shark Spit.** It is great for beachcombing if you want to take the time and drop the hook and row over on a calm day. The beaches are spectacular and usually pretty deserted. A good place for the kids to run if they've been getting bored. There is even a grassy camp site atop an old Indian midden. The island was homesteaded during the last century and foxes were once raised there.

You're now in **Uganda Passage.** A friend of ours says it can be "meaner than Idi Amin".

Remember the 'red-right-returning' rule? You will want to keep **left** of the red buoys and right of the green ones; as if you're going 'back home to Whaletown'. You will see a red conical buoy first—marked 'Q14'. It is associated with a small un-

Hernando Cortez's Mexican Mistress

We think it's interesting—the fact that Marina Island was named after a beautiful slave and mistress of the Cortez who invaded Mexico. Remember, she was the one who finked on her kinfolks and helped her old man defeat them? Well, in 1849 the cartographers decided Marina was not a nice enough lady to have an island named after her, so they changed it to 'Mary Island.' In 1906, less blue-nosed mapmakers gave her back her island.

Uganda Pass is narrow and twisty—but well-marked.

named islet which is dry at all tides. As you pass it, look for the next marker which is green and marked 'Q13.' It is a spar— not as easily seen as the conical red buoy. You are going to want to make a sharp left turn and pass left of the red-light tower. It is quick-flashing red at night and about 20 feet high. Give the green buoy a sort of wide berth. There is a rock, close by to the south which can go dry at about 1 m. As you approach from the southeast you may get the impression that they are right beside each other. When you get to the spot, you will see plenty of room between them. Your fathometer can read 8 m. in here. Keep the next green buoy, marked 'Q11', on your left.

If you check, you can see a little house on a knob behind the red concrete standard. There is also a range marker on shore. It consists of two rocks with red paint splotches. You could probably line up in the channel by arranging them—one on top of the other. They may have been put there before the buoys were installed.

Shark Spit extends way out and it's almost a dream beach. The beach on the northwest side of the spit is sandy with large rocks that are sprinkled all along it. Several of them are very visible. They are charted, incidentally.

Whaletown Bay

Nearing Whaletown Bay, you can see the ferry landing, of course. Keep the green light tower at the entrance to port. You can pass either side of the red buoy outside if

Your Basic Hermit Story

There's a rather charming story about Cortes Island that we heard. It seems that there was an old hermit who lived on the northeast shore of Marina Island. He had a friend who was also a hermit; this man lived near the entrance to Gorge Harbour. The tale is that they argued over something and stopped being friends. They didn't speak to each other for years. But out of habit, they would look across the channel to see if the other man's light was on at night.

Well, the Gorge Harbour man didn't see his ex-friend's light for a couple of nights, so he rowed over to check on him. He found the man bedridden and very sick. He loaded the guy in his rowboat and put him aboard a steamer to Vancouver. The old hermit lived for a while in the hospital, but eventually died. The story doesn't say whether the Gorge Harbour man ever came to visit him. It also doesn't say whether he spoke to his sick old chum while he was trying to save him.

If you want to retell the story, you are free to add your own imagination—that's the way great legends are born.

You could say that the rescuer never said a word to the sick guy. He just bundled him up and carried him down to the beached canoe like a sack of potatoes. Then, when the Gorge Harbour man started to row, the Marina Island man said,

"Well...she did!"

And the Gorge Harbour hermit said, "She did not!"

And the argument ended there.

you watch your chart. This buoy, 'Q10,' indicates a reef with a troublesome rock which is awash at 0.3 m. Fishing is said to be good off this buoy, which has kelp around it. We didn't catch anything there, but that doesn't mean anything!

Coming into Whaletown, you will see a black daybeacon. You can pass on either side, but the right channel is the deeper if you're headed for the dock. The inner green light mentioned on the chart is the light on the ferry dock off to your left. This is the ferry that connects Cortes to Quadra and to Campbell River.

Gotcha!

Long before the white men were using Whaletown as the last stopping place for many of the marine mammals, the Haidas would descend on Cortes Island to raid the Indian villages for slaves. A Sliammon Indian saw some Haidas hiding in Whaletown and warned his people of the attack and saved the day. Since then Whaletown has been known as **T'ik'tn**-'The place where you get discovered.'

This is a very small cove and is surrounded by houses. Whaletown is not a genuine town—more a community or village with some of the amenities. This area is said to be very much protected from winds, according to a resident, although there is a swell. He said that winds from both north and south tend to skirt around the bay. The room for anchorage is minimal.

There is 118 m. of berthage at the public dock, and you may have to raft up to a fish boat. The dock does have water, garbage disposal and a derrick. The chart of facilities put out by the Canadian Hydrographic Service didn't show these utilities. They may have been added recently. It does not have power. Incidentally, there is no fuel available in Whaletown.

The town was established in 1867 for the purposes of chopping up whales that were caught in the Strait of Georgia by the Dawson Whaling Co. There are precious few whales in the Strait now—and if you did manage to catch one and *they* caught you—you'd be in deep doo-doo!

Leaving Whaletown and heading north through **Plunger Passage**, you approach the **Subtle Islands**. You will see that the south one is relatively circular and the north island is kidney-bean shaped. Both are the same height. The south end of the south island has a lot of driftwood piled up on the beach, since it faces the Strait. In the waist between the two islands there is a low spit which is a favorite camp ground for

Whaletown

Whaletown is a community of about 140 persons living in the general area of the bay. A whaling station operated there from 1869 to 1870.

The community includes the Whaletown Store, at the head of the government wharf, owned by Hazel and George Frost who bought it in 1988. It is a general store carrying fishing gear and licences, propane, hardware, ice, video rental, wonderful ice cream cones, lavishly served. On Fridays they get deliveries of homemade breads and baked goods, made on the island, fresh meats and vegetables. There is even an outdoor picnic table where you can eat your ice cream, or just sit and visit.

Whaletown boasts a general store, a church and a library—all picturesque.

Across the road from the store is the post office. It is opened on Monday, Wednesday and Friday from 8:30 to 9 a.m., and from 1 to 4 p.m. A hop, skip and a jump away is the tiny Louisa Tooker Library, open on Fridays from 2 to 3:30 p.m. Whether open or not, you can step into the tiny foyer of the Post Office and read all the wonderful notices of island happenings, including the fact that Linnae Farms (which is also a hostel) had market days on Friday during July and August. Biggest problem is that Linnae Farms is inland on Gunflint Lake and not easily accessible to boaters.

They have a philosophy of stewardship and not ownership, with the motto: 'We live on a Parent—not a Planet.'

And of course Whaletown Bay is the site of the island's link to civilization: the Whaletown Ferry Terminal. The ferry leaves daily every two hours from 7:50 a.m. to 5:50 p.m. running to Quadra Island which has another ferry over to Campbell River. In other words, if you choose to live on Cortes Island, you do so knowing that leaving is not always easy!

And a few steps past the library is the white Mission Church, St. John the Baptist.

locals. Both islands are posted no trespassing. The tideland, is of course, public. There is a nice little meadow on the north side of the neck on the north island.

On the Cortes Island side of Plunger Passage there is a point that comes out with one tree and some grasses. Look for an islet just off it that is exposed at all waters. There is a reef just north of that, so favor the Subtle Islands shore.

You may have flashed on the fact that the Subtle Islands are in **Sutil Channel**. The Spaniards somehow got the notion that the passage was 'subtle'— maybe in the sense of being 'sneaky.' The English thought they were obliged to make the translation.

The cove in the Cortes Island shore just northeast of the Subtles in Plunger Pass has an island and two rocks which are 3 m. above datum. There is a lot of kelp around the rock off the islet in here. Passage would be possible on either side of this rocky islet which has several trees. We saw several boats in there, but we couldn't tell if they belonged to residents. At the end of this cove is a drying beach.

On the top of the bluff of this unnamed bay you'll see a beautiful house with what must be a commanding view.

Centre Islet, off the northwest side of the Subtles is a loaf shaped rock with drying grasses.

Hill Island in the distance is an almost perfect mound with shoulders to the east and west.

Entering Coulter Bay from the south, it'll be necessary to go out and around **Coulter Island.** This is a big island. It looks like a jigsaw puzzle piece which has been lifted out of Coulter Bay. An islet and a reef connect it to the Cortes Island shore.

Coulter Bay

This bay is unique because of the several beautiful buildings near its south end. One of them, three stories high, is visible as you round the island from the south. At the entrance you will see several rock fingers pointing out into the channel. There is also a reef which you can see. Once past it, you can look down into the entrance to the bay. It narrows considerably before it opens at the head.

In this channel there is a big boathouse and cabin, and a ramp leading down to a dock. A sign on an outbuilding says 'STAFF PARKING ONLY.' A sign on the shore indicates that there is a water line along the bottom between the island and the shore.

A home is at the end of the island. It has a satellite dish and a long ramp down to a boat house with a roof. One of the homes has a big greenhouse attached to it.

At this point our sounder read 4.5 m.

Coulter Bay looks like an ideal gunkhole. It has all of the protection in the world and tolerable depths. To be sure, there are a few houses around but it is still scenic. There is a reef just in front of the shoal at the head.

As you come out of the bay, looking up the Sutil Channel, you will find another scene of real grandeur. You will see the mountains and glaciers of the **Downie Range** farther north.

Carrington Bay

The south entrance to Carrington Bay is marked by a long string of rocks extending out from shore. It is shown on the chart as a curving reef, but we thought the

The entrance to Carrington Lagoon is piled high with drift.

rocks were farther out than indicated. The shore is marked 'OYSTER LEASE.' A little niche just outside the north entrance to Carrington has an imposing rock face which extends out over the water.

The bay was named for R.C. Carrington, a draughtsman with the Hydrographic Office.

As we entered the bay, we remembered the little creek which ran from **Carrington Lagoon** and was an ideal swimming hole about 20 years ago. When the tide was running out we would 'body-surf' into the bay. When it started running in, we body-surfed the other direction. In fact, we found Carrington such a delightful spot back then that we named a favorite crew kitten 'Carrington'.

This time we dropped the hook near the shore in the head of the bay. We found that storms over the last few years have heaped drift logs up over the creek. The logs were so tightly packed that we had to peer down between the crevices to see the clear stream running below them. The lagoon was not very inviting any more. It had a lot of algae-covered sunken logs and rocks. Portaging even our fairly light kayak over the logs to the lagoon seemed like a lot of work and wouldn't be very rewarding.

There still was quite a lot to see in the area, though. Lodged into the drift-logs was a big old float made up of very heavy timbers. On the west side of the creek, there was the remains of an old farm house. A shaky float was on the shore of the lagoon. A path led up a small rise from the creek. There was an old boat house on the shore of the bay. In it was an old hulk that somebody had tried to rebuild at one time. There was one piece of deadwood with some fancy carving still visible. In a shelter nearby we found the remains of old engines and transmissions.

There is not much in the way of anchorage along the south shore of the bay. There is only minimal anchorage on the opposite shore. The best spots would be behind two islets in the bay. One is small and unnamed, about three-fourths of the way down the north shore. It stands off a small niche which has a house on shore. Some anchorage could be found behind **Jane Islet**. There are several rocks and reefs off the south shore of the islet in the shallows. Depths close to the islet are in the order of 17 m. in its lee.

Quartz Bay

Around the corner from Carrington is another bay with somewhat better places to anchor. The hill behind **Quartz Bay** is about 700 feet high. The northern shores of the entrance has steep faces. There is a cabin just inside the entrance on the north side which is up on stilts. There is a big boathouse down toward the left fork of the bay. It seems to be part of an aquaculture installation. The passage between the island in the bay and the Cortes Shore has oyster strings across it.

There are still some sheltered places in the southeast head of the bay. It was named Quartz Bay because some geologists found some veins of the rock nearby. It was never quarried, however.

Just beyond Quartz Bay, about one-and-a-half miles, is the entrance to one of the choicest harbours in Desolation Sound.

Von Donop Inlet

It is not easy to spot the entrance to Von Donop from the south. In the distance, you will see a little nook which looks like it might be the entrance, but it is the cove beneath **Robertson Lake.** The entrance to Von Donop is just over a half-mile south of there. Another way to spot the entrance is to watch for other boats going in or out. That's a problem with Von Donop—it's not a secret.

Before entering, we have a new view of Sutil Channel up toward the **Penn Islands.** It is yet another marvelous panorama. This is indeed awesome country.

There is nothing remarkable about the shore line south of the entrance to Von Donop until you are almost to the cleft. As you near the entrance, you will notice that the skimpy beaches along shore disappear and a bluff rises to the point of entrance on the south side. The shoreline suddenly breaks and some reefs emerge and

Von Donop

The Klahoose Indian name for a shallow lagoon off Von Donop is **'Tl'itl'aamin—a small place that you head toward'.** This lagoon was the place where young Klahoose men would 'prove their manhood' by wrestling with porpoises. Young Indian maidens would scare porpoises from deep water into the shallows of the lagoon by shaking clam rattles. The men would be waiting for the porpoises and then wrestle them onto the beach to impress the ladies.

you can see water leading behind the low bluff. The entrance is like a long funnel.

There are shellfish contamination warnings on both sides of the entrance. We think they are there permanently—the theory of the management people being that it is better to err on the side of 'chicken,' because they can't keep checking the water continually.

This inlet was originally named Von Donop Creek for Victor Edward John Brenton Von Donop, a midshipman aboard *H.M.S. Charybdis,* by Capt. Pender in 1863.

The entrance continues at fairly parallel lines until it reaches a small niche on the right. Just beyond that it narrows considerably. Here is a little drying shore. A few hundred feet beyond this is another small hook. It looks like the ground between them is a potential islet.

Now the passage begins to narrow. The water remains deep until you enter the close quarters—18 m. At a 2-½ m. tide, we had about 4 m. under the keel at the shallowest point.

There is a rock in the middle of the narrowest point which is a hazard, according to all of the information. We have never seen it. It is supposed to be covered with kelp, but in some years the kelp tends to disappear so it is not a good indicator. It sometimes even disappears at low tide. One of the reasons for this might be that smaller, fast boats which plow down the center of the channel, missing the deeper water to the right, chop up the tops of the kelp. The second reason for missing the kelp is that, when the current is running, the tops are below the water line.

Scuttlebutt has it that the rock is pointed to by a tree on the southwest shore that elbows out over the passage.

We went back and scouted the area in the kayak at low tide but could not find the reef that is in the center of the passage at that point.

Beyond it, the inlet now widens out and the depth goes to 10.5 m. You will see, off to the left, the inlet to a cove which leads to the creek coming down the lagoon.

'Easy does it,' entering Von Donop.

Still usable! What a waste!

Boats often stern-tie in this area. There is an old logging road above this cove which makes a nice walk past old logging machinery and into the forest.

The water narrows again after the first basin and we come right to another lobe which is elongated all the way to the head. Off to the right, you will see a peninsula and behind it is a tideflat which ends in a mud beach. Off to the left is a shallow bay which is a good anchorage providing there aren't going to be any really low tides. It is private and protected.

The head of the inlet is arrowhead shaped. There is another drying flat off to the right which is fed by a stream. Log booms occasionally tie off on the east side of that spit.

A choice anchorage area is the north hook of the arrowhead. It is sheltered from most winds and has excellent depths for anchoring.

Beachcombing can be interesting, as can seeing the entire inlet by small boat. In the marshy hook of the arrowhead, you will find a logging road and evidences of some recent cutting. There is a picturesque old rusty winch unit back in the grass. The water in this tideflat is the warmest of any place in Desolation Sound, we think. We did a lot of swimming there.

Another good place to swim is in the narrow inlet that hooks back north into a marshy area. On shore is the portage trail to Squirrel Cove marked by a small sign: 'Squirrel Cove Nature Trail'.

Von Donop To Squirrel Cove Hike or Vice Versa

When you're looking for a good hike on Cortes Island, we can give you a great one from Von Donop to Squirrel Cove and back. You can make it either a long walk or a short, depending on your 'druthers.'

Take a look at the chart of Von Donop. Far down in the southern tip there is a tiny islet. On the chart, just to the left of it there is a little nook. Right there is a trail which will lead up a hill and end up at a logging road. Follow the logging road, veering somewhat left, and after a long, hot time, you'll reach the Whaletown Road. It's paved and will take you eventually to Squirrel Cove Store.

From there, after you get a can of cold pop or an ice cream cone, you can return the same way. Or else, if you're really masochistic, you can pick up a Cortes Island map and see how you can go from the store back along Whaletown Road and then turn right on Tork Road to the Squirrel Cove Indian Village. From there you head through the village, on a trail past the cemetery and through the woods where you come out in a little tideflat cove at the southern end of Squirrel Cove. Follow along the muddy rocky beach (we found swimming that part easier) until you eventually find a sign on the left and a nice wide SHORT trail through the woods back to Von Donop. Easy as pie. Hah!

Or, you can just take the short trail either direction to see what it's like on the other side. We did it the long, hard, hot way, just so we could tell you about it.

Just ask Joan Lawrence if the path gets muddy!

'And, so, we leave the friendly shores and dusky maidens of....blah, blah blah...' Remember that dork who used to do the cornball travelogues? Well, we feel something like him, right now. We are about to throw off our tow-line and set you free to explore on your own.

But first we have to, for neatness sake, take you around the top of Cortes Island.

Proceeding north on the Cortes Island shore toward **Bullock Bluff,** we pass a cove about a quarter-mile north of the Von Donop entrance. It is the exit of a creek from Robertson Lake. We will call it **Robertson Cove.** There are two low cedar buildings in its head and between them are fish pens. Scratch one more potential anchorage.

Looking up Calm Channel in this area, you will see a series of V-shaped divides which looks like a giant river coursed down between them. They may have been created by massive earth-moving glaciers. The scene is worth a photo.

Bullock Bluff. As you round it heading toward Lewis Channel you see a totally denuded mountain face. It looks as though every living thing has been stripped away in the logging process. The scar must cover hundreds of acres. It extends up to a small belt of evergreens near the summit. The only thing interesting in this area is a switchback logging road.

And that's it, mates. We've done 'The Princess' and 'Desolation.' We're bugging out here so you can find your own hidey-holes.

Maybe we'll see you again in a year or two and we'll all go together 'Gunkholing the Upper Yangtse River.'

Desolation Sound has many popular rendezvous spots.

BIBLIOGRAPHY

Books

Andersen, Doris. *Evergreen Islands.* Whitecap Books, Ltd., North Vancouver, B.C., 1985.

Ashwell, Reg. *Coast Salish, Their Art, Culture and Legends.* Hancock House Publishers Ltd., Surrey, B.C., 1978.

Bingham, Bruce. *The Sailors' Sketchbook,* Seven Seas Press Inc., Newport, R.I., 1983.

Blanchet, M. Wylie. *The Curve of Time.* Gray's Publishing Ltd., Sidney, B.C., and Whitecap Books, Ltd., North Vancouver, B.C., 1968.

Bradley, R. Ken. *Historic Railways of the Powell River Area.* B.C. Railway Historical Association, Victoria, B.C., 1982.

Calhoun, Bruce. *Mac and the Princess: The Story of Princess Louisa Inlet.* Ricwalt Publishing Company, 1976.

Chapman, Charles F. *Piloting, Seamanship and Small Boat Handling.* Hearst Corporation, New York, N.Y., 1975.

Chettleburgh, Peter. *Marine Parks of British Columbia.* MacLean Hunter Publication, Vancouver, B.C., 1985.

Cluff, Alice. *Powell River and District Schools, 1898-1983.* Powell River Phoenix Printers, Powell River, B.C., 1983.

Douglas, Gilean. *The Protected Place.* Gray's Publishing Ltd., Sidney, B.C., 1979.

Hill, Beth. *Upcoast Summers.* Horsdal & Schubart Publishers Ltd., Ganges, B.C., 1985.

Kennedy, Dorothy and Bouchard, Randy. *Sliammon Life, Sliammon Lands.* Talonbooks, Vancouver, B.C., 1983.

Maud, Ralph (Editor). *The Salish People, Volume IV: The Sechelt and the South-Eastern Tribes of Vancouver Island.* Talonbooks, Vancouver, B.C., 1978.

Meany, Edmond S. *Vancouver's Discovery of Puget Sound.* Binfords & Mort, Portland, Oregon, 1957.

Newcombe, C.F. (Editor). *Menzies' Journal of Vancouver's Voyage, April to October, 1792.* Kings Printer, Victoria, B.C., 1923.

Southern, Karen. *The Nelson Island Story.* Hancock House Publishers, Ltd., Surrey, B.C., 1987.

Walbran, Captain John T. *British Columbia Coast Names, 1592-1906.* J.J. Douglas Ltd., Vancouver, B.C., 1971.

White, Howard (Editor). *Raincoast Chronicles—Forgotten Villages of the B.C. Coast.* Harbour Publishing, Madeira Park, B.C., 1987.

White, Howard (Editor). *Raincoast Chronicles First Five—Stories and History of the B.C. Coast.* Harbour Publishing, Madeira Park, B.C., 1976.

Wolferstan, Bill. *Pacific Yachting's Cruising Guide to British Columbia Vol. II, Desolation Sound and the Discovery Islands.* MacLean-Hunter Ltd., Vancouver, B.C., 1980.

Periodicals

British Columbia Coast (South Portion) Sailing Directions, Volume 1, 13th Edition, Department of Fisheries and Oceans, Institute of Ocean Sciences, Patricia Bay, Sidney, B.C., 1984.

Canada Chart No. 1—Symbols and Abbreviations used on Canadian Nautical Charts. Canadian Hydrographic Service, 1988.

Canadian Tide and Current Tables, Volume 5. Fisheries and Oceans, 1988.

Diver (magazine). Hulks. Willoughby, Jim. Jan/Feb 1980.

Drop Anchor on the Sunshine Coast, Spring/Summer 1988, Supplement to *The Press,* Richard Proctor, Publisher, Sechelt, B.C.

Jervis Inlet & Desolation Sound and Adjacent Waterways. Canadian Hydrographic Service, 1986.

List of Lights, Buoys and Fog Signals—Pacific Coast including Rivers and Lakes of British Columbia. Canadian Coast Guard, 1985.

Northwest Boat Travel, Volume II, Number 2, Anderson Publishing Company, Inc., Anacortes, Wash., 1988.

Savary Survival Sheet, Savary Island News, 1987.

Small Craft Guide—British Columbia, Boundary Bay to Cortes Island, Volume II, Seventh Edition, Fisheries and Oceans, 1988.

Whaletown National Enquirer, Volume II, Number 6. Cortes Island, July, 1988.

TO FIND YOUR WAY FROM NANAIMO TO DESOLATION SOUND AND PRINCESS LOUISA YOU'LL USE THESE CHARTS:

#3310 — "GULF ISLANDS—VICTORIA HARBOUR TO NANAIMO HARBOUR." Four strip charts, 1:40,000.

#3311 — "SUNSHINE COAST—VANCOUVER HARBOUR TO DESOLATION SOUND." Five strip charts, 1:40,000.

#3312 — "JERVIS INLET AND DESOLATION SOUND." Small craft navigation atlas with 29 chartlets at various scales and other information.

L/C**#3512 — "STRAIT OF GEORGIA, CENTRAL PORTION."** 1:80,000.

#3514 — "JERVIS INLET," 1:50,000; **"MALIBU RAPIDS,"** 1:12,000; **"AND SECHELT RAPIDS."** 1:20,000.

#3538 — "DESOLATION SOUND AND SUTIL CHANNEL." 1:40,000.

#3541 — "APPROACHES TO TOBA INLET." 1:40,000.

#3555 — "PLANS—VICINITY OF REDONDA ISLANDS AND LOUGHBOROUGH INLET: REFUGE COVE," 1:12,000; **"SQUIRREL COVE,"** 1:12,000; **"REDONDA BAY,"** 1:12,000; **"BEAVER INLET,"** 1:18,000, and **"PRIDEAUX HAVEN,"** 1:6,000.

#3559 — "MALASPINA INLET, OKEOVER INLET AND LANCELOT INLET." 1:12,000.

#3594 — "DISCOVERY PASSAGE, TOBA INLET AND CONNECTING CHANNELS." 1:75,000. This chart is out of print—hang onto it if you have it, or beg, borrow or steal it!

In addition, valuable information for getting to Princess Louisa and Desolation Sound is contained in Walt Woodward's valuable book *How to Cruise to Alaska—Without Rocking The Boat Too Much*—also published by Nor'westing, which contains, among other things, a list of the charts needed to cruise anywhere between Olympia and Juneau, Alaska.

INDEX OF GEOGRAPHIC FEATURES

T

U